DESIGNING EARLY LITERACY PROGRAMS

Also from Lea M. McGee

Teaching Literacy in Kindergarten
Lea M. McGee and Lesley Mandel Morrow

Designing Early Literacy Programs

SECOND EDITION

*Differentiated Instruction
in Preschool and Kindergarten*

**Lea M. McGee
Donald J. Richgels**

THE GUILFORD PRESS
New York   London

© 2014 The Guilford Press
A Division of Guilford Publications, Inc.
72 Spring Street, New York, NY 10012
www.guilford.com

Printed in the United States of America

This book is printed on acid-free paper.

Last digit is print number: 9   8   7   6   5   4   3   2   1

Library of Congress Cataloging-in-Publication Data

McGee, Lea M.
    Designing early literacy programs : differentiated instruction in preschool and
kindergarten / Lea M. McGee, Donald J. Richgels. — Second edition.
        pages cm
    Includes bibliographical references and index.
    ISBN 978-1-4625-1412-0 (paperback) — ISBN 978-1-4625-1424-3 (hardcover)
    1. Language arts (Preschool)—United States—Case studies.   2. Children with
disabilities—Education (Preschool)—United States—Case studies.   3. Literacy
programs—United States—Case studies.   4. Individualized instruction.   I. Richgels,
Donald J., 1949–   II. Title.
    LB1140.5.L3M36 2014
    372.6—dc23
                                                                        2014001296

About the Authors

Lea M. McGee, EdD, is the Marie M. Clay Chair of Reading Recovery and Early Literacy at The Ohio State University. She studies the effects of preschool classroom interventions on preschool and kindergarten literacy achievement, the impact of kindergartners' "fingerpoint reading" on their first-grade text reading, young children's responses to literature, and the effects of a systematic approach to drama and retelling on kindergartners' comprehension and vocabulary development.

Donald J. Richgels, PhD, is Distinguished Research Professor Emeritus in Literacy Education at Northern Illinois University. His research interests are preschool and kindergarten classroom practice and the relationship between spoken language acquisition and literacy development.

Preface

As we wrote the second edition of this book, we were even more keenly aware than at the writing of the first edition of the unprecedented attention given to early literacy instruction in preschool and kindergarten. Historically, beginning reading instruction—not early literacy instruction—has been the major focus of concern. That is, the instruction provided to most 6- and 7-year-olds during first grade in the United States was considered to be the most critical contributor to their literacy development. However, recent legislation (Early First Steps within the No Child Left Behind Act of 2002) acknowledged that literacy experiences in the preschool and kindergarten years provided a foundation for later successful beginning reading and writing. This legislation drew heavily on the research reviewed and policies recommended by the National Research Council in *Preventing Reading Difficulties in Young Children* (Snow, Burns, & Griffin, 1998). Two outcomes were clear from this report: literacy development before and during kindergarten does matter, and some children are behind in literacy development even before they enter kindergarten. More recent attention to the critical role of instruction and learning during the early period of birth through age 5 was the focus of the *Report of the National Early Literacy Panel* (National Early Literacy Panel, 2008).

Rather than being a frill, certain literacy knowledge acquired prior to the initiation of beginning reading instruction is necessary for early reading success. Increasingly, researchers have found that high levels of knowledge in foundational areas of literacy development are critical for later successful reading and writing. Unfortunately, children from low-income families who are likely to attend schools with low reading performance are less likely to have acquired such knowledge. According to *Preventing Reading Difficulties in Young Children*, "reducing the number of children who enter school with inadequate literacy-related knowledge and skill is an important primary step toward preventing reading difficulties" (Snow et al., 1998, p. 5). The purpose of this book is to help educators and caregivers in kindergartens, preschools, nursery schools, and child-care centers reach the goal of providing every young child the language and literacy foundation necessary to become a successful reader and writer.

We believe that the good news about the current attention to early literacy instruction is that more children—especially those children who most need early literacy experiences—may have access to high-quality early literacy programs. Nonetheless, we have grave concerns about the nature of literacy experiences and activities that will be the outcome of such unprecedented attention to literacy instruction in preschools and kindergartens. Like many others, we have long advocated for early literacy programs and instruction that balance child-initiated experiences with teacher-planned activities and instruction. We have argued that the best early literacy programs are based on attention to children's literacy development and respect for their intellectual capacity. We have written this book to provide the best possible advice for designing effective early literacy programs. Toward that end, we have carefully reviewed case studies of young children's literacy development and critically examined research on the effectiveness of early literacy intervention programs. We have drawn together insights from high-quality research and from our collective 70-plus years of experience working with young children and their teachers. We make recommendations about the nature of instruction best suited to allow all young children to have a strong and successful start in reading and writing. *Designing Early Literacy Programs* is intended to provide guidance for literacy supervisors, principals, teachers, and other early childhood caregivers as they implement early literacy programs for young children at risk for reading difficulties.

What is new in this edition of the book is the attention given to how children are identified as at risk even at these young ages and the nature of intervention programs provided to children so identified. Increasingly, school systems, Head Start programs, and other educational programs are assessing children immediately upon entry, using commercial, standardized assessments with benchmarks that identify children who are not on target for success. Intervention for children at risk is often mandated, and intervention programs are increasingly aligned with strategies used with children identified as having special needs, including the use of frequent monitoring assessment of conventional skills. Thus, the need for careful consideration of individual children's development and for accelerated learning is even more critical today than when we first wrote this book. We address these concerns by maintaining our original focus on the balance between child discovery and exploration and teacher-directed instruction.

We would like to acknowledge several teachers and other supervisors who have welcomed us into their classrooms and shared with us insights about their teaching craft. We would especially like to thank Mrs. Karla Poremba, kindergarten teacher extraordinaire, who has taught us how to listen better to children. Thanks also to Dr. Judy Walis, formerly language arts supervisor of the Alief Public School systems, and to all the prekindergarten and kindergarten teachers in that system. We thank especially Ms. Michelle Bellamy and Ms. Suzanne Ballard of Heflin Elementary School for sharing samples of their children's writing. We also acknowledge Dr. Vicki Dick, Curriculum Coordinator of Talledaga Public Schools, and all the prekindergarten and kindergarten teachers in Illinois, Massachusetts, Texas, and Alabama who willingly opened their classroom doors to us. We would also like to thank the teachers in two Early Reading First projects in Alabama and Mississippi, along with the dozens of teachers in other Early Reading First projects in Ohio, Louisiana, Arizona, California, Florida, Georgia, and Washington, DC, who opened their classrooms to us and provided the very best feedback to our instructional advice.

Contents

DESIGNING EARLY LITERACY PROGRAMS

CHAPTER 1

Who Is at Risk for Reading Difficulties?

Implications for Prevention and Intervention Programs in Early Literacy

We know that children's literacy experiences prior to first grade are especially critical for their success in learning to read and write. Unfortunately, we also know that a growing number of children, because of their families' social and economic circumstances, are at high risk of failure even before reaching first grade (Wertheimer, Moore, Hair, & Croan, 2003). Children who are most vulnerable are growing up in poverty, although other factors contribute to risk, such as limited English proficiency. Regardless of the risk factors, research syntheses suggest that early prevention and intervention programs in preschool and kindergarten can produce important and lasting gains for high-risk children (Neuman, 2009). Prevention programs provide high-quality educational experiences with well-trained classroom teachers who can accelerate children's learning to reach outcomes expected of all children. High-quality prevention programs are based on thorough understanding of the foundations of language and literacy, assessments that provide information for teaching, and differentiated instruction that can meet the various needs of the diverse children found in today's preschools and kindergartens. Interventions are supplementary programs, provided in addition to regular classroom differentiated instruction, that are designed to bring targeted instruction to children most at risk. The purpose of this book is to describe the characteristics of and instructional approaches used in high-quality prevention and intervention early literacy programs that serve the needs of our most disadvantaged at-risk children.

LITERACY FOR ALL: READING ON GRADE LEVEL BY THIRD GRADE

At no time in history has learning to read and write at high levels of proficiency and with great insight been both more valued and more hotly debated in our society. Our children's futures—and the economic future and national security of our nation—depend in part on how well children learn to read and write, especially during the early primary grades. Educators must prepare children for a future that will demand ever higher levels of literacy. In order to meet the ever-increasing demands for high levels of literacy accomplishment, many states are adopting legislation related to what is often referred to as the "third-grade guarantee" whereby third graders who cannot read on grade level are held in grade. Legislators hope this mandate will spur schools to provide the necessary levels of intervention support early so that all children can reach these demanding levels of performance.

Literacy Matters, but Who Receives Instruction?

Aside from the connection between high levels of literacy and our nation's well-being and economic security, statistics demonstrate that failure to achieve high levels of success in reading and writing adversely affects children's futures as adults. The U.S. Department of Education's National Adult Literacy Survey (National Center for Educational Statistics, 1999) used a 4-point scale: below basic, basic, intermediate, and proficient. The results revealed that adults living in poverty were more likely to have lower literacy scores than adults not living in poverty, that 50% of adults without a high school diploma had below basic literacy scores, and that incarcerated adults scored lower on literacy than adults not incarcerated.

For many children, especially children living in poverty, the future is bleak. We know that there is a high correlation between living in poverty and low reading achievement. And yet few children receive educational services during their early childhood years that could ameliorate much of the impact of growing up in families of low socioeconomic status (SES). Statistics show that:

- Five and a half million children (23%) in the United States are living in poverty (National Center for Children in Poverty, 1998). The percentage for African American and Hispanic children is even higher.
- Only 40% of the eligible 3- and 4-year-olds are enrolled in Head Start programs.
- Five million children in the United States attend child-care centers daily, but only one in seven child-care centers provides adequate language and learning experiences (Helburn, 1995).

Children who are denied high-quality early childhood services achieve poorly in elementary school. Data from the National Assessment of Educational Progress (NAEP) revealed that 40% of fourth graders failed to comprehend well because they did not make inferences or connections between the text and their experiences; the failure rate is even higher for children from low-income families (National Center for Educational Statistics, 1996). However, research on early literacy intervention programs has demonstrated that children struggling to learn to read and write can make significant progress with the appropriate instructional support (Hiebert & Taylor, 2000; Neuman, 2009).

Shifts in Beliefs: Ability versus Opportunity to Learn

Historically, the goal for all children was to read and write on grade level; however, in reality few educators believed this goal was possible (Allington, 1995). Even logical thinking suggests this goal is ludicrous. For example, it is statistically impossible for all children to score at the average level on any normed assessment of reading because the tests *are designed* so that scores range above and below the average. This artifact of normed standardized tests even affects children's grade-equivalent score. The grade-equivalent score, like the raw score, also ranges above and below grade level. However, if the term "on grade level" is interpreted not as an average on a norm referenced test nor as a grade-equivalent score, but rather as children's ability to read with comprehension and fluency "texts generally considered appropriate for children's age or grade, . . . then the notion of *almost all children reading on grade level* may not be dismissed on purely logical grounds" (Klenk & Kibby, 2000, p. 684, emphasis in original).

There is a second reason that historically we have, at least intuitively, rejected the notion that all children would learn to read and write at the same time as their peers. Reading achievement was long believed to be related to ability. That is, we assumed that some children could read better than other children because they had better reading ability. Ability was conceived of as an inherent trait—one endowed at birth but certainly enhanced by particular experiences or made to atrophy by the lack of those experiences.

Ability was a critical determinant of reading instruction. The type of instruction and its pace were determined by the reading group in which children were placed. Reading groups were assigned by a teacher's determination of ability. Scoring well on a reading-readiness test in kindergarten was interpreted to mean that the child had high ability. Scoring low on the reading-readiness test was interpreted to mean that the child had low ability. Children in the "high"-ability group were provided reading instruction, and the pace of instruction was fast. Children in the "middle"-ability group were provided some reading-readiness activities before reading instruction was initiated (to catch up on the skills the readiness test indicated they had not acquired). Instruction then proceeded at a moderate pace. Children in the "low"-ability group received a great amount of reading-readiness training, and instruction in conventional reading was considerably delayed. Once it began it moved at a slow pace. It was not surprising that, over the elementary school years, children who started in the "low" group rarely left it and made significantly fewer gains in reading than children who started in the "middle" or "high" reading groups. In defense of this practice, it is true that many children did need additional opportunity to learn the foundational literacy skills critical for beginning conventional reading.

Only slowly did the realization come that what many children in the "middle" and "low" groups lacked was not ability but *opportunity to learn*. Nonetheless, our thinking about reading ability has shifted drastically. In addition to assessing children's foundational reading abilities, we ask questions about their prior experiences or opportunities to learn in literacy events at home, in preschool, and in kindergarten. Compared to children who have had relatively few literacy experiences, most of those who have had intensive early literacy experiences score better on reading and writing achievement measures at school entry. Thus, this difference is not related to different levels of inherited reading ability, but to different opportunities to learn. Middle-class children are more likely to have attended a high-quality preschool with frequent informal literacy experiences (Cochran-Smith, 1984; Rowe, 1998). They are also more likely to have parents who encouraged, supported, and provided direction for early writing experiences (Baghban, 1984; Bissex, 1980; Schickedanz, 1998). However, the advantage of early and intensive experiences with literacy is not limited to middle-class children. Children from low-income families and from diverse cultural backgrounds who have had high levels of literacy support in the home or in preschool also display high levels of reading and writing knowledge at school entry (Barone, 1999; Taylor & Dorsey-Gaines, 1988).

Providing the Support Needed for Reading Success

Today most educators acknowledge that the goal of having nearly all children reading on "grade level" by the end of third grade is achievable. It is not the impossible ideal of politicians seeking votes. However, we recognize that "ensuring success in reading requires different levels of effort for different segments of the population" (Snow et al., 1998, p. 16). The Committee on the Prevention of Reading Difficulties in Young Children (Snow et al., 1998) differentiated among three levels of prevention and intervention needed to support the reading achievement of all children. Good classroom instruction is at the first level of support for literacy success. All children need coherent and effective reading and writing instruction delivered by a well-qualified, caring teacher. At the second level of support, children who are in groups that have been identified as having higher incidences of reading failure need prevention programs that deliver enriched, enhanced, focused, and highly effective instruction. Ideally, this instruction occurs during preschool and kindergarten, prior to the onset of reading difficulties. Finally, children who are identified as already having reading difficulties need intensive, individualized instruction from highly trained reading specialists. Intervention instruction can begin as early as the beginning of kindergarten and, as long as children continue to need such support, must extend through the primary years.

The three levels of increasing support for children's learning are a significant part of the 2004 Individuals with Disabilities Education Improvement Act (IDEA, 2004), in which response to intervention (RTI) was introduced. RTI is a three-tiered method of identifying children with learning disabilities by providing them with early intervention and assessing their ability to benefit from it. Normal classroom instruction is Tier 1. All children receive screening assessments of their foundational literacy skills. Children with screening scores that put them in the lowest 20–25% of students are selected for intervention instruction in the area of risk. They may have demonstrated less knowledge than most children at the beginning of the year or inability at other times in the year to benefit from Tier 1 instruction. Thus, they are provided with more intensive Tier 2 instruction in smaller groups. This instruction might be provided in the classroom by the teacher to a small group of children or by a specialist. After some weeks of targeted instruction, teachers use progress monitoring (assessment of the target area of instruction) to determine whether children have made sufficient progress to return to only Tier 1 instruction or to continue with Tier 2 instruction. Children who receive several months of Tier 2 instruction without making adequate progress are provided with even more intense Tier 2 instruction (perhaps delivered in one-on-one tutoring by a specialist) before being recommended for Tier 3 instruction, which leads to special education identification. Thus, children who are not responsive to either classroom instruction or extensive, intensive small-group instruction in a targeted area of need may be identified as having learning disabilities and provided with special education services (Fuchs & Fuchs, 2005).

The purpose of this book is to describe approaches to prevention and intervention programs for young children prior to first grade. The Committee on the Prevention of Reading Difficulties in Young Children noted that preschool and kindergarten programs can be highly effective in preparing children for success in beginning reading. Many states are considering mandated preschool programs for 4-year-old children in an attempt to reduce the number of children who fail at reading and to increase the percentages of upper-grade children who can read at high levels of proficiency. In years to come, we anticipate that more efforts will be directed toward providing early education for preschool children and redesigning kindergarten curricula to better meet the needs of children who are at risk for reading difficulties.

Ironically, the Committee on the Prevention of Reading Difficulties in Young Children noted that we cannot predict with much accuracy which particular young children will have difficulty in learning, especially in preschool. All children may enter with very little conventional knowledge. Instead, the committee recommended that *prevention efforts be available for all young children.* Further, they cautioned that prevention efforts should "not, as a rule, require qualitatively different instruction from [that provided to] children who are 'getting it' " (Snow et al., 1998, p. 12). Therefore, one purpose of this book is to describe elements of effective prevention programs for all 3-, 4-, and 5-year-olds, including those who are in groups that have been identified as having higher incidences of reading failure.

Ideally, early language and literacy experiences will be available to all children both in their homes and in high-quality preschool and kindergarten programs. School systems would provide quality preschool programs for all preschool children in the district and support high-quality parent-involvement programs. However, even when this is the case, we need to know which children are most at risk for reading failure. That is, even when all children participate in prevention programs, we would like to identify those who need special consideration. We have some ideas about how to identify such children. But, unfortunately, our knowledge of risk factors is not complete.

RISK FACTORS: THE CHILD

The best use of limited educational funds would be to target particular children who are most in need of literacy prevention or intervention instruction. In other words, money would best be spent when we could predict with 100% accuracy that a particular child would struggle in learning to read without prevention or intervention. While we cannot make such predictions with 100% accuracy, consideration of children's language development and literacy experiences offers some promise of identifying individual children's levels of risk.

Language Development

During the preschool years the onset and pathway of language development vary widely from child to child. Nonetheless, children are expected to achieve certain milestones of language development within that wide normal range. In particular, three language abilities are moderately correlated with reading achievement in the early grades: mean length of utterance (the average number of morphemes—that is, meaning units such as root words and prefixes and suffixes—in a speaking turn), syntactic complexity of utterance, and number of different vocabulary words (Scarborough, 1991; Walker, Greenwood, Hart, & Carta, 1994). Language ability at kindergarten entrance—including the abilities to repeat sentences or recall stories and to name objects in pictures (expressive vocabulary)—continues to be related to success in reading achievement during the early primary grades (Snow et al., 1998). Therefore, children with delayed spoken language development are far more likely to experience reading difficulties than children with well-developed spoken language abilities.

Another language factor—children's ability to produce extended *decontextualized* accounts, explanations, and narratives—is also related to later reading achievement (Dickinson & Smith, 1994). An example of decontextualized language is when children describe a past event (or an event only in the imagination) without the support provided by another speaker within a conversation. For example, with decontextualized language, children would describe how they helped their grandmother wash dishes over the weekend. They might talk about how they played with the soap bubbles, the stool they needed to stand on, and the dollar reward they received for their work. In contrast, most everyday conversations are about activities occurring in the here and now—about washing dishes as they actually do the task rather than a day or two later. Children who are able to produce decontextualized accounts of past events are more likely to succeed in reading than children who are not able to produce this kind of talk.

Phonemic awareness is another language factor that has been shown to be highly related to reading success. Phonemic awareness is necessary for reading development because of the alphabetic nature of our system of written language. The alphabet letters in written English words are related to *phonemes* (roughly, sounds) in spoken words. Beginning readers must grasp the notion that the letters they see in written words are related to the phonemes they speak and hear in spoken words. They must be able to attend to these individual sounds or phonemes and use them during reading and spelling. Eventually, they will be taught *sound–letter relationships* as part of *phonics* instruction.

While research has shown that phonemic awareness is related to later reading achievement, this does not necessarily mean that lack of phonemic awareness at kindergarten entrance dooms a child to reading failure (Adams, 1990; Snow et al., 1998). Children who have strong understandings about the phonemic structure of spoken language (that spoken words are comprised of phonemes that can be segmented) are very likely to become good readers. On the other hand, it is possible for children who begin kindergarten with little phonemic awareness to develop it in kindergarten and learn to read without difficulty.

Early Literacy Experiences and Knowledge

Children who have many high-quality literacy experiences at home and in preschool are also more likely to become proficient readers and writers. Early literacy experiences include occasions when children observe family members reading and writing for purposes critical to their daily lives, when children interact with parents or others in activities that include emergent reading and writing, or when children engage in literacy activities on their own (Purcell-Gates, 1996). Clearly, such experiences provide children with many opportunities to learn. Children who have had these opportunities acquire stronger early literacy concepts and, therefore, learn to read and write more successfully than children who lack these opportunities (Purcell-Gates & Dahl, 1991). The effect of literacy experiences on children's literacy knowledge holds regardless of family SES level, ethnicity or race, culture, home language, and physiological factors, such as exposure to crack or cocaine (Barone, 1999; Lesman & deJong, 1998; Purcell-Gates, 1996).

Thus, an effective approach to identifying children who are and are not at risk for reading failure is to assess their early literacy concepts. Research has helped to identify some concepts that are related to later reading achievement (National Early Literacy Panel, 2008). These concepts include children's ability to identify and write their names, identify and write alphabet letters, demonstrate an understanding of concepts about print, demonstrate phonemic awareness, use knowledge of letter–sound relationships to decode and spell words, learn some known words in reading and writing, and understand highly complex texts that are read aloud. Despite the cost in time and dollars, high-quality prevention programs conduct screening assessments of all children's literacy concepts (based on developmental levels of the children and their prior instructional experiences), monitor their progress in the classroom and in interventions, and delineate expected learning outcomes for use in planning differentiating instruction and interventions.

Learning to "Do" School

A risk factor that we are just beginning to understand relates to children's ability to move successfully from home to school. Schools are social settings with special rules, both stated and unstated, about how to enter and be accepted in the peer culture, how to interact with the teacher and with the content of instruction, and ultimately how to be seen as a capable learner. Children bring with them their characteristic ways of interacting with the world, including their dispositions toward certain kinds of children, activities, and interactions with adults.

Many children come to school with dispositions, behaviors, and ways of interacting with others that are congruent with most teachers' expectations. "Some children may appear 'ready' for school because they come with a selective repertoire of social and communicative practices upon which school literacy learning is contingent. In contrast, other children may appear 'unready' for school literacy learning because their participative repertoires are different from those required for literacy lessons" (Comber, 2000, p. 40). That is, some children, including some from middle-class backgrounds, have behaviors, dispositions, and ways of interacting with others different from those that are expected in school. Their difficulty in "fitting in" the classroom culture may actually impede learning. Even when they do possess moderate or even high levels of literacy knowledge at school entry, they are at risk for being identified as "immature," having "behavior problems," or "lacking literacy knowledge" (McMillon & Edwards, 2000). Children from diverse backgrounds are particularly at risk for being identified as having low levels of literacy knowledge because of their difficulties in "doing school" rather than because of actual low levels of knowledge.

RISK FACTORS: FAMILY AND COMMUNITY

Although we have described a number of risk factors that can be related to particular children, wholesale individual assessment may not be practical or even highly effective when identifying preschool children for admission to prevention programs. With the exception of obvious language delays (or specific language impairments), hearing impairment, or visual impairment, individual risk factors rarely emerge with high levels of predictability until children have already begun instruction in literacy. Therefore, the Committee on the Prevention of Reading Difficulties in Young Children suggests that early identification of young children might "proceed better by considering target groups rather than by assessing individuals" (Snow et al., 1998, p. 119). Group factors include minority status, SES, and limited English proficiency. These factors are usually overlapping and interactive.

Minority and Socioeconomic Status

In general, nonwhite children's reading achievement, despite gains in recent decades, continues to lag behind that of their white peers (National Center for Education Statistics, 1996). This factor is compounded by SES since significant numbers of minority children are also in low-SES families. SES is usually identified through level of household income and level of parents' education and occupation. The socioeconomic level of a school is usually estimated by the percentage of children who receive free or reduced lunch.

Regardless of how SES is determined, there are significant differences in reading achievement among children who vary by SES. Children from middle- and high-SES families enjoy greater reading and writing success than children from low-SES families even before entering school (Lonigan, Burgess, Anthony, & Baker, 1998). For example, in one study 86% of entering kindergartners with college-educated mothers knew the alphabet letters and 50% could identify the beginning sounds in words, while 38% of children whose mothers did not graduate from high school knew letters and only 9% could identify beginning sounds (National Center for Education Statistics, 2000). However, the SES of the family and of the school interact. Regardless of the family's SES, children who attend school in affluent suburban neighborhoods score significantly above children who attend school in poor urban or rural schools. Therefore, family SES alone is not a strong risk predictor. That is, children who come from low-SES families but attend school with high percentages of middle- and high-SES children tend to have higher achievement scores than other low-SES children.

School SES data can predict children's reading and writing achievement. In general, children who live in poor neighborhoods attend school with other children living in poverty. These schools have chronically low achievement scores compared to schools where more children come from low- to middle-income families. Unfortunately, school systems may support the cycle of low achievement. In general, schools in poor neighborhoods have lower-quality libraries and fewer books in the classrooms (Duke, 2000). Children there have school experiences with literacy that involve less focus on extended texts (such as fewer discussions of the meanings of texts they read and hear read aloud) and more time completing worksheets. Therefore, SES seems to have a cumulative effect. Children from low-SES families who attend schools with high percentages of low-SES children tend to have the lowest achievement scores. Children who live in low-SES families and attend low-SES schools are most at risk for reading difficulties.

SES is related to still another risk factor: the number and quality of print materials found in the neighborhood environment and in public institutions such as libraries (Neuman, 2009). Most low-SES parents have the same desire for their children's future academic success as most middle- and high-SES families. However, limited literacy resources in low-SES extended neighborhoods and communities can shape the nature of literacy experiences that are given young children within that environment. In other words, we know that, in general, children in low-SES families have fewer book-reading experiences than children in middle-SES families, although there is a great variation in the frequency of literacy events in low-SES families, with some engaging frequently in literacy events and others rarely doing so (Purcell-Gates, 1996). Most explanations focus on the resources of the family as an explanation for low-SES children's fewer experiences with books. Yet research has shown inequity in

> the number of [literacy] resources, choice and quality of materials available, public spaces and places for reading, amount and quality of literacy materials in child-care center resources—even in the public institutions, the schools, and local public libraries in the community. Long before formal schooling begins, considerable variations in patterns of early literacy development are likely to be evident based on the ways in which print is organized in communities. (Neuman & Celano, 2001, p. 24)

Limited Proficiency in English

Having limited proficiency in English is a strong risk factor. Despite recent gains in achievement, Hispanics, the largest group of English language learners (ELLs), score lower on reading achievement tests than whites (National Center for Education Statistics, 1996). This issue is of special concern in that approximately 8% of all kindergartners are ELLs (August & Hakuta, 1997).

The difference in achievement between non-English-speaking and English-speaking children is due to more than the simple difference in language of instruction and assessment. Even when Hispanic children are instructed and tested in Spanish, they exhibit low reading achievement (Goldenberg & Gallimore, 1991). It is also too simple to infer that children from non-English-speaking families have lower achievement because their parents have different beliefs about the importance of reading achievement and the role of parents in reading development or have low educational aspirations for their children. Some researchers have found high motivation for educational achievement in bilingual communities (Goldenberg & Gallimore, 1995) as well as parents who are willing and able to help their children improve reading abilities.

Low SES, minority status, and limited English proficiency interact. Higher percentages of children who are nonwhite and non-English-speaking are living in poverty. These three factors, alone and in combination, are the best predictors of groups of children who will fail to learn to read and write well.

The Need to Look beyond Risk Factors

When school systems cannot provide prekindergarten programs for all 4-year-olds in the district, then the best and most efficient predictors we currently have for identifying target preschool children are that they (1) will attend a school with low achievement levels, (2) reside in a low-income family and neighborhood, and/or (3) have limited proficiency in spoken English (Snow et al., 1998). Unfortunately, these predictors overlook many children who are middle-class and English-speaking but who will later develop difficulties in learning to read and write. At kindergarten entry, children can be screened for levels of language and literacy knowledge, including letter naming, concepts about print, phonological awareness, story recall, vocabulary, and knowledge of letter–sound correspondences as additional indicators of risk factors.

Unfortunately, the way we currently understand these risk factors emphasizes the negative consequences of being poor and/or non-English-speaking rather than the positives associated with working with children from diverse backgrounds with rich cultural capital. Children who are poor and/or non-English-speaking are active learners as they engage in problem solving in their environment. They bring specialized funds of knowledge to early childhood settings (Neuman & Celano, 2001). However, current conceptions about early literacy clearly privilege certain kinds of decontextualized and school-like literacy behaviors and knowledge over the more contextualized and functional knowledge about literacy that all young children possess. Despite the often-heard refrain from teachers that "we meet all children where they are," actually capitalizing on all children's funds of knowledge can be a challenge. (See Ballenger, 1999, for a detailed description of a preschool teacher's thoughtful reflection on teaching bilingual children in a minority-neighborhood, inner-city preschool.)

Teaching other people's children, children who come from different cultural, socioeconomic, and racial backgrounds than most teachers, is perhaps the most critical element of the challenge of helping all children achieve high levels of success with reading and writing. Regardless of how children are selected for an early literacy program, it is critical that teachers resist seeing the children merely as "problem[s] to be solved and [their] literacy as an output to be measured" (Comber, 2000, p. 48). High-quality preschool and kindergarten literacy programs will be more than vehicles to get children "ready" to achieve high scores on later high-stakes tests of reading and writing. They will not focus narrowly on developing a few literacy skills that have been shown to be the best predictors of success. As we noted earlier in this chapter, preschool and kindergarten programs designed to prevent reading difficulties are not qualitatively different from programs offered to children who are obviously well along on their road to reading and writing. Embedded in the early literacy programs that we describe in this book are rich experiences that address a broad array of a child's development needs. They comprise a wide range of literacy activities, while recognizing, valuing, and extending children's diverse home literacies.

PREVENTION PROGRAMS CHANGE THE ODDS

In her groundbreaking book *Changing the Odds for Children at Risk: Seven Essential Principles*, Susan Neuman (2009), argues that we have sufficient research to show that prevention programs in preschool have lasting effects on children's lives. Programs such as the Abecedarian Project (Campbell, Ramey, Pungello, Sparling, & Miller-Johnson, 2002), the Perry Preschool Project (Schweinhart et al., 2005), Bright Beginnings (Smith, Pellin, & Arguso, 2003), and the University of Oklahoma PreK program (Gormley, Gayer, Phillips, & Dawson, 2005) make changes not only in children's achievement, but also in their social–emotional development, health, and contributions as adults to society. These programs have seven common characteristics: They target the neediest children, intervene early and when developmental timing is essential, coordinate services beyond educational programs, provide quality instruction on targeted goals, use highly trained professionals who have access to quality professional development, deliver instruction with intensity, and hold themselves accountable for actual results rather than merely serving clients or providing services.

Similarly, high-quality kindergarten instruction has been shown to have long-term effects. Economists from Harvard examined the lifelong effects experienced by nearly 12,000 kindergartners (Leonhardt, 2010). They found that by age 30, children who had a good kindergarten teacher and learned more in kindergarten were more likely to attend college, to earn more, and to save more than children who had less effective teachers and ended kindergarten with less knowledge. Although children were randomly assigned to teachers so that every classroom had a similar mix of low- and higher-SES children, some teachers were able to produce higher levels of learning in all the children. Thus, a press for higher achievement with high-quality instruction makes a difference for all children, including those from low-SES families.

Full-day kindergarten programs also have been shown to make a difference in children's cognitive development and achievement. For example children who attended all-day kindergarten were absent fewer days, less likely to be retained later in school, and had better standardized scores than children who attended half-day kindergartens (Entwisle, Alexander, & Olson, 1997). Further, children in kindergarten programs that targeted higher levels of literacy attainment had better reading outcomes even through high school (Durkin, 1974–1975; Hanson & Farrell, 1995). In one program aimed at inner-city schools with a majority of low-SES children, kindergarten teachers received 250 new books to read aloud to children and to use in content study. Half the teachers only received the books, while the other half also received 30 hours of high-quality professional development about kindergarten literacy development. Children whose teachers received both the books and the professional development made greater gains in understanding print concepts and being able to spell and read words. Even their vocabulary scores increased. Children whose teachers received only the books performed as well as students whose teachers received neither the books nor the professional development (McGill-Franzen, Allington, Yokoi, & Brooks, 1999). Thus, high-quality kindergarten prevention programs in typically low-performing schools can accelerate the learning of children at risk.

IMPLICATIONS FOR EARLY LITERACY PROGRAMS

The purpose of this book is to help teachers, supervisors, principals, and others develop high-quality prevention and intervention programs that primarily serve children at risk for reading failure. Much of what we describe in the book does not differ from the recommendations that we have made for the literacy development of all young children (McGee & Richgels, 2012). This is because high-quality instruction supports the learning of all children. However, when the program is designed specifically to meet the needs of children who are at risk, teachers need to keep in mind certain factors that may influence a variety of decisions about assessment, instruction, curriculum, and classroom environment.

One consideration is the nature of children to be served. The first step in planning an early literacy program for at-risk preschool children is identifying children who will be included in the program. We have argued that most selections for preventative early literacy preschool programs will be based on family income, home language, and minority status. For kindergarten programs, administrators will want to identify particular schools to target for prevention programs that will accelerate learning so that children can reach outcomes expected for all at the end of kindergarten. It is easy for teachers to overgeneralize that all the children in these programs will have low levels of literacy knowledge when they enter the program and, therefore, will require the same instruction. However, children who are provided only whole-class instruction are denied the opportunity to learn at the cutting edge of their knowledge. Instead, accelerating learning means that teachers should be aware of the level of knowledge of their children and frequently provide small-group, differentiated instruction. Instead of teaching one alphabet letter a week and having all the children study the letter *a* regardless of whether they already know the letter, teachers determine which children need to learn the letter *a*.

In order to be effective in bridging the gap between what at-risk children know and what they need to know in order to be successful early readers, teachers cannot provide same-size-fits-all instruction. We know that at age 4 (Smith & Dixon, 1995) and even by age 3 (Lonigan et al., 1998), many, but not all, children from low-SES families know fewer literacy concepts and have fewer words in their vocabularies (Hart & Risely, 1995) than their middle-class peers. We also know that differences in language and literacy knowledge usually persist from preschool to kindergarten and into first grade (Whitehurst & Lonigan, 2001). What this means is that many, although not all, children will enter preschool and kindergarten already lagging behind their middle-class peers. Without instruction that *accelerates* their language and literacy learning, they will remain behind.

Accelerating learning is difficult and requires much energy, flexibility, and commitment on the teacher's part. In order to accelerate learning, teachers must take the time to consider a child's strengths, how that child seems to learn best, and how to arrange the classroom schedule to provide time to meet that child's individual needs—while also individualizing instruction for as many as 18 other children. Whole-class instruction must be supplemented with daily differentiated small-group instruction. Teachers will need to draw upon the resources of the community and parents in order to accomplish their task well. This may mean that teachers will need to develop new skills in order to work effectively with parents and other volunteers.

Language and cultural differences may provide another challenge for teachers. Many teachers, especially those in high-need rural communities, find resources for ELLs to be unavailable. Other teachers, especially in large urban centers, can expect children to have a variety of home languages and represent several cultures. Reaching out to the community to provide information and guidance will be critical. One way teachers can extend their abilities to work well with diverse children and families is to read case studies of other teachers who have described how they faced these challenges (e.g., Ballenger, 1999; Meier, 2000). This book is designed to provide guidance to the teachers who willingly take on the many challenges of providing accelerated instruction for those children most in need of high-quality literacy experiences.

CHAPTER SUMMARY

We began this chapter by emphasizing the goal that all children can and should learn to read and write proficiently by the end of their primary-grade elementary school experiences. We argued that this goal is possible, but that children need a variety of support systems in place in order to achieve it. The purpose of this book is to describe preschool and kindergarten prevention and intervention programs that will provide all young children with the quantity and quality of experiences needed to support accelerated language and literacy growth. While the best approach is to provide all young children with extensive and high-quality early literacy experiences, including universal prekindergarten programs, most school systems will not find this approach practical. Therefore, school systems will need to identify target groups of preschool and kindergarten children most in need of prevention programs.

CHAPTER 2

Accelerating Children's Language and Literacy Learning in Exemplary Prevention Classrooms

Good classroom teachers are able to produce accelerated learning gains for all the children they teach, including those who enter with less knowledge than average. That is, effective teachers accelerate learning for the lowest performing children and not just for high-achieving children. In this chapter we describe the qualities of teaching that accelerate learning for our most vulnerable children in preschool and kindergarten. First, we consider different contexts in which children acquire literacy concepts and describe principles of learning that emerge from these contexts. Using these principles of learning, we make suggestions for enhancing the classroom environment, capitalizing on curriculum to produce high levels of learning gains, and using daily whole-class and small-group routines to boost children's interactions with language and literacy. We provide an example of how one preschool teacher changed her program to produce accelerated gains for her children.

HOW CHILDREN LEARN ABOUT LITERACY: PRINCIPLES FOR ACCELERATING LEARNING

We know that young children learn a great deal during the first few years of their lives. One context in which this learning occurs is the informal interactions between a parent and child as a natural part of living. This learning takes place as the child observes and participates with other family members in authentic activities—activities that occur during the ordinary routines of life (Neuman & Roskos, 1997), such as going to lunch at a fast-food restaurant (and seeing its printed menu and hearing it being read), stopping at the post office to buy stamps (and getting a receipt for the purchase), and calling grandmother on the telephone to discuss ingredients in a recipe for a dinner party (read aloud from a food magazine). As a part of such meaningful activities, children acquire concepts about the nature and purposes of language and literacy practices as they are embedded in everyday life. Such knowledge-in-practice is powerful in socializing young children toward the particular literacy practices of their communities (Collins, Brown, & Newman, 1989). Thus, an important context for accelerating children's learning in preschool and kindergarten is one in which children participate in life-like reading and writing activities, such as when teachers provide props and space to set up a classroom restaurant where children can pretend to be waiters, cooks, and customers. However, acceleration of learning is not achieved merely by providing materials and opportunities for children to dramatize real-life activities or to engage in language and literacy activities usually found in highly literate homes.

Highly literate home environments do have many literacy materials, such as large collections of books and other text materials. These include not just a wide variety of printed materials, but also computer games and apps. However, more important for children than having materials is having adults who model using literacy in a variety of ways and who invite children to participate in these activities. Adults play with children, offering ideas for play, modeling behavior and thinking, and extending children's engagement without taking over children's ideas about the directions of play. Adults help younger children, and less verbal or emotionally secure children, enter into ongoing play of other children and support them as they join into play. At least two reports, by the American Academy of Pediatrics and a consortia of child development experts, argue for the need for play not only in preschool but also in kindergarten (Milteer, Ginsburg, & Mulligan, 2012; Miller & Almon, 2009). Thus, the first principle of accelerated learning is that *play is a critical medium through which learning occurs with teachers' taking an active role in promoting and extending children's engagement during play*. Research has shown that in classrooms where children make greater academic gains, teachers regularly enter play by providing suggestions for sophisticated ways to use reading and writing during play (Casbergue, McGee, & Bedford, 2008).

The Critical Role of Play in Preschool and Kindergarten

The critical role of play in preschool and kindergarten cannot be overlooked in planning for accelerated learning by at-risk children. The first impulse when helping at-risk children close the gap between their achievement and the considerably advanced achievement of their middle-class peers is to increase the time spent teaching skills directly. In fact, several studies investigating how children spend their time in urban and suburban kindergartens have revealed that some kindergartners spend 3 hours or more per day in teacher-directed instructional activities in literacy and math (Miller & Almon, 2009). Many teachers report that they use scripted programs and that the amount of time spent in instruction as a result of using those programs has increased by 20%. While time spent in teacher-directed activities in kindergarten has increased, the amount of time children spend in free play has dropped by a quarter in home and other community settings (Wenner, 2009) and nearly disappeared altogether in kindergartens (Miller & Almon, 2009). In an article published by the American Academy of Pediatrics, Milteer and Ginsberg (2009) argue that because of the critical value of play, efforts to provide children with opportunities to reach their fullest potentials must include not only academic enrichment, but also free, unstructured play and other creative, physical activities. They argue that play in all its forms "needs to be considered as the ideal educational and developmental milieu for children" (p. 206).

Pretend, unstructured play is particularly important for developing social skills needed in the future lives of children. Studies of both children and animals (Wenner, 2009) have shown that free play encourages flexibility in thinking and problem solving, which later allows adults to be more resilient and confident, to manage unpredictable situations, and make connections with others. By encouraging empathy and the reduction of conflict, play also promotes better relationships with peers. It engages children in using symbolic thinking, such as when having a block stand for a cell phone (Lifter, Mason, & Barton, 2011). Studies have shown that unstructured play, whether on the playground or inside the classroom, lessens tension in children and actually reduces aggressive, nonproductive behaviors (Milteer & Ginsberg, 2009). That is, periods of free play interspersed with periods of teacher-directed activity may actually increase children's attention and the likelihood of their learning more during the resulting shorter periods of instruction.

However, unstructured play should not be confused with "anything goes." Instead, during unstructured play, teachers take an active role in preparing children for play and connecting the play materials with other ongoing curricula in the classroom: for example, teachers may set up a pretend veterinarian office at a zoo as part of a study of wild animals. Teachers must be clear how the pretend play areas they provide in their classrooms are connected to and supportive of other goals, such as specific oral language and concept targets. These may include providing children with opportunities to use new concepts and vocabulary.

Preparing play areas and connecting them to ongoing curricula are only the first step in capitalizing on the power of play. Bodrova and Leong (2005) recommend that teachers scaffold children's mature intentional play. Mature intentional play is pretend play in which children plan specific roles and actions they will take prior to actually playing. This type of play requires use of deliberate memory, negotiation with others, use of language to direct others and self, focused attention, and self-regulation of behaviors—all cognitive skills required for learning. Children who have achieved the level of mature intentional play have learned to focus attention and to use memory. Teachers play a critical role in helping children reach this level of play. First, they determine what level of play children have already attained. Teachers can observe young children playing in a pretend restaurant, for example. Children who manipulate the materials but take no obvious role (chef, waiter, etc.) and do not speak in role (saying what the chef or a waiter might say) are far from developing mature play (Lifter et al., 2011). Teachers can help these children by first talking about the roles with children during whole-class time, by reading books whose characters perform such roles, and by role playing what might be said. Before children go to a pretend play center, teachers can remind them that they will have to decide what role they want to play and plan it with the other children in the center. Teachers ask, "What role will you pretend today?" Teachers can also take on a role themselves and gently join in children's play, announcing first what their role will be and giving children options of roles they might take on.

Zone of Proximal Development and Intentional Teaching

Another context in which children learn literacy is during interactions in which parents (or teachers) are attempting to teach children more directly. The best of these learning interactions is set within a child's *zone of proximal development* (Vygotsky, 1978). In the zone of proximal development a child can successfully perform a task *only* with the support of another person. In the following example, a 3-year-old cannot write the letter *K* on her own. But with her mother's support, she gradually internalizes what her mother helps her do. This interaction began when Kristen decided she wanted to learn how to write the letter *K* herself. She had not previously written this alphabet letter herself, but had asked her mother to write it for her on numerous occasions.

Kristen Learns to Write *K*

Kristen's mother was writing at her desk, and Kristen was sitting on the floor drawing and writing with her markers. Kristen stood up and said, "I [with great emphasis] write *K*."

Her mother replied, "You write *K*? You want to write a *K*?" Kristen's mother picked up her pen and said as she wrote on a sheet of paper, "Line down [as she wrote a vertical line], now line in [as she wrote the diagonal line downward to meet the center point on the vertical line] and line out [as she wrote another diagonal line out and downward from the center point to complete the letter *K*]. Now you do it: first do down."

As Kristen wrote, her mother said, "OK, line down. Now do line in and line out." (Kristen's attempt at writing *K* is presented in Figure 2.1a.)

Kristen looked at the letter she had written and said, "No, no."

Her mother said, "Good job. I see a line down [she pointed at a line Kristen had written]. We need a line in and a line out [she said with emphasis as she pointed and drew imaginary lines with her finger]." (Notice that Kristen's attempt has a vertical line and a diagonal line; however, the diagonal line goes beyond the vertical line to make the letter look more like the letter *X* than the letter *K*.) "Try again. Line down. Now line in, line out [as she made these motions with her finger in the air]." (Kristen's second attempt at writing *K* is presented in Figure 2.1b.)

Kristen said in frustration, "No, that's an *H*!" (Notice that Kristen's attempt has two vertical lines that are prominent letter features of the letter *H*.)

Kristen's mother said, "Yes, it does look like an *H*. Try again with line *in* and *out* [with emphasis and finger motions]."

Kristen attempted to write the letter *K* two more times (as shown in Figures 2.1c and 2.1d), each time with her mother's repeating, "Line down, line in, line out." Finally Kristen wrote the letter in Figure 2.1e and said, "Hey, I wrote *K*. Look, look, I wrote *K* [with great excitement]!"

Her mother replied with the same excitement, "A *K*! A *K*! You did it. Can you do it again?"

Kristen immediately wrote the letters that appear in Figures 2.1f and 2.1g. She said, "*K*" in a very satisfied tone. Her mother replied, "Yes, *K*," in the same satisfied tone.

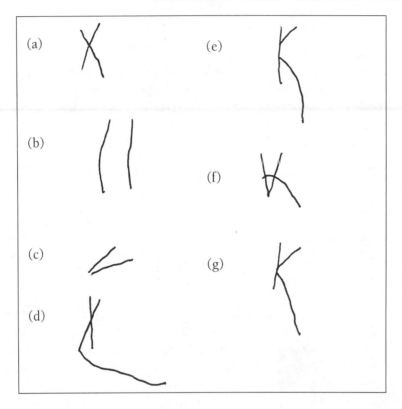

FIGURE 2.1. Kristen attempts to write the letter K.

Principles of Literacy Learning in Intentional Teaching

The example of Kristen's learning to write the letter K is one in which her mother provided support, but with the intention of teaching a specific outcome. Kristen's mother demonstrated that children's learning sometimes results from teachers' intentions to teach particular outcomes. From this kind of teaching we can see a second principle of accelerated learning: *Learning emerges from social interaction of the child and an adult during joint participation in hands-on tasks.* Kristen needed her mother's help to learn to do a task she wanted to do but could not do on her own—write the letter K. Both Kristen and her mother were involved in the task, with her mother demonstrating and Kristen attempting to follow the demonstrations. Learning in preschool and kindergarten rarely occurs through teachers' merely telling children what to do and how to do it. Rather, children need to be engaged in hands-on activities with teachers (Wright & Neuman, 2009).

Children learn through teachers' demonstrations and simultaneous directions with feedback on their attempts. So, a third principle of accelerated learning is: *Learning is accelerated through feedback on individual children's attempts.* Kristen's mother adjusted her directions and support to Kristen's attempts. She was responsive to what Kristen was doing and not doing. She realized that Kristen's problem seemed to be figuring out how to stop the first diagonal line at the center point on the vertical line and then changing directions to make the second diagonal line outward and downward from that center point. Kristen's mother provided feedback about what Kristen could do, "Yes, it does look like an *H* [in response to the two vertical lines Kristen had written]," and feedback on what needed to be adjusted, "Try again with line *in* and *out* [with emphasis and demonstrations with her finger]."

Kristen's mother was able to provide this feedback in a one-on-one teaching episode. If all classroom teaching occurs during whole-class lessons, individual children have very few opportunities to have personalized attention and feedback.

Teachers can make more frequent opportunities to interact with individual children throughout the day, but they also will be mindful of children's need for feedback as they provide many opportunities for children to learn in small groups.

Over the next year, Kristen demonstrated another principle of accelerated learning: *Learning is extended through independent practice of newly learned skills.* Once children have received instruction and mastered a new literacy concept or skill, such as learning to write the letter *K*, they need to engage in many activities that call for the use of the new skill in order to become fluent and independent. Research has shown that children make greater academic gains when teachers regularly give them free-choice opportunities to revisit materials they have experienced first in instruction or during whole-class book read-alouds (Casbergue et al., 2008). With such opportunities, children practice what was taught in small groups and become more proficient and flexible in their learning.

It is true that Kristen initiated this learning by her own request; nonetheless, skillful teachers know how to motivate children and get them engaged in the learning task at hand. Thus, a fifth principle of accelerated learning is that *learning emerges from tasks that are meaningful and motivating to learners.* It is important to keep in mind that Kristen was not born motivated to engage in literacy activities such as learning to write alphabet letters. Kristen *became* motivated to write because literacy interactions were playful and engaged her attention and participation, as when her mother said, "Look, I'll write *Kristen.* Do you want *Kristen* to be big [in an exaggerated deep tone] or little [in a squeaky high tone]?"

The sixth principle of accelerated learning during intentional teaching relates to knowledge Kristen already had when the learning activity began: *New learning is built from already known information and skills.* It just so happened that Kristen was prepared to learn how to write the letter *K* conventionally. The fact that she knew when her attempts did not look like that letter shows that she already knew how *K* looks. That she had some control over her motor movements in making and placing vertical and diagonal lines demonstrates that she already had developed many motor schemes for writing letters. She merely needed to learn to put all these skills together to write a conventional letter *K*. Excellent teachers will always consider what children already know and can do when planning lessons. Teaching that accelerates learning is always just at the cutting edge of what children already know, guiding them into the next step. If teachers determine that children lack needed prior knowledge (for example, knowing what "line down" means), they are sure to provide children with this knowledge early in the lesson.

Bodrova and Leong (2005) would add a final principle of accelerated learning: *Learning activities should help children self-regulate and make deliberate use of memory.* For example, children can be helped to wait to take a turn rather than impulsively reaching for materials, or to select activities for themselves and sustain attention for extended periods of time. In other words, teachers should be mindful not only of *what* specific literacy outcomes they want to teach, but also of *how* children will learn those outcomes, that is, of how they can demonstrate for children the profitable self-regulation of attention and behavior and the deliberate use of memory. Giving children choices about activities is a critical component of developing self-regulation (Bodrova & Leong, 2005). When teachers assign tasks to children and never provide them with choices, children always rely on the adult to guide their attention. Young children need practice in making choices and sticking to those choices. They need to focus their attention and keep that attention focused for extended periods of time if they are ever to become effective learners. Children who wander the classroom, picking up this activity or that and abandoning activities after only a few minutes, need teacher guidance to plan which activity would be of interest *before* going to that activity. They also need to state *what* they will do during the activity (for example, build a house with blocks, make a painting of the mouse in the story just read, or pretend to be a firefighter rescuing a cat in the dramatic play center) and then follow up on that plan.

Table 2.1 provides an overview of the seven principles of accelerated learning that should guide how teachers arrange space, develop daily routines, and use curricula.

The Playful Preschool and Kindergarten

As we have described principles of learning, we have advocated that children be included in teacher-directed, intentional teaching activities and have choices in selecting play-centered activities that include access to materials used during intentional teaching. Miller and Almon (2009) describe the *playful classroom* that is rich in child-initiated play supported by an active teacher who guides experiential activities with a focus on playful learning. Teachers are not passive as children play, but rather take extremely active roles in arranging materials and space, observing children, skillfully entering play to enrich children's role and activities, helping shy children enter play, and providing feedback to individual children. Teacher-directed activities are also playful, with teachers providing many hands-on materials for everyone in the group so that teachers

---

TABLE 2.1. Principles of Accelerated Learning in Playful Preschool and Kindergarten Classrooms

1. Play is a critical medium through which learning occurs with teachers taking an active role in promoting and extending children's engagement during play.

2. Learning emerges from social interaction of the child and an adult during joint participation in hands-on tasks.

3. Learning is accelerated through feedback on individual children's attempts.

4. Learning is extended through independent practice of newly learned skills.

5. Learning emerges from tasks that are meaningful and motivating to learners.

6. New learning is built from already known information and skills.

7. Learning activities should help children self-regulate and make deliberate use of memory.

and children can engage in a joint activity (Wright & Neuman, 2009). Teachers are aware of the developmental levels of individual children so that instruction can build from what they know and can do. They motivate individual children and provide feedback and support on their efforts.

In the playful classroom, there will be a balance of whole-class and small-group activities that are teacher directed with individual, hands-on activities selected by children. These hands-on activities might be provided in centers or as part of an activity in which the children are seated at tables. Even when teachers assign table-top activities or particular tasks in centers or work stations, children should have choices, even if only of what to do when their assigned work is completed. Children will not sit for longer than 30 minutes (and early in the year and especially for preschoolers, these sit-down activities will be punctuated with stand-up-and-move activities). Children will have daily small-group lessons in literacy that may be delivered by the teacher or an assistant (and in kindergarten, perhaps by an intervention specialist such as the reading specialist). However, the teacher and assistant should be free from other instructional duties during much of the free choice or center time in order to play with children and engage them in conversations about their activities.

SPACE, MATERIALS, AND CLASSROOM ARRANGEMENT

Effective teachers are thoughtful about the arrangement of space and materials in the classroom. They know that space and materials influence how children behave (Christie, 1991). Children are more likely to engage in inappropriate running or rough-and-tumble play in large open spaces. They are likely to wander in and out of small spaces without sustaining activities when the materials and their arrangement are undefined (Isbell & Exelby, 2001). Children are more likely to engage in mature intentional play in small spaces with materials that suggest a specific theme. The foundation of effective learning is careful arrangement of classroom space, thoughtful selection of materials and their storage, and attention to simple routines for using classroom spaces and materials.

Arranging Classroom Space

Most early childhood classrooms include at least one well-defined large space for whole-class activities such as listening to the teacher read books aloud. This space is typically carpeted, includes a comfortable chair for the teacher, a pocket chart, and an easel for reading big books (enlarged copies of children's books) or displaying chart paper for writing. Many classrooms include small tables where children eat snacks or work on projects. These tables can serve multiple purposes by being part of an art or writing center. All classrooms include accessible storage areas for children's belongings and for classroom materials.

Using rugs, plants, pillows, and lamps softens classrooms that are in institutional settings, provides visual appeal, and can reflect the particular culture of local communities (Isbell & Exelby, 2001). Bringing in unusual and natural materials from the local community and beyond arouses children's curiosity and invites their active exploration of the classroom environment. Displays of photographs of children as they engage in classroom activities also allow children to make personal connections to the classroom.

Children notice when classrooms are appealing and include meaningful activities. Branscombe (1991) describes one young African American boy's reaction to a summer lab classroom where he had many successful experiences reading and writing—unlike his earlier experiences in kindergarten, where he was considered a behavior problem. This classroom was appealing because it included actual butterflies and turtles and colorful nonfiction books about butterflies and turtles that the teacher read aloud and then placed for children's independent exploration in the pretend safari center. The teacher provided opportunities to choose from various activities, including creating a 10-foot construction-paper tree—all on the first day of class.

Centers and Work Stations

Early childhood classrooms that support language and literacy learning usually have several *centers*, small spaces sectioned off from other classroom space that are equipped with materials to encourage children's active involvement. Centers are designed for groups of three or four children to work and play independently or cooperatively. They allow for child-directed play. Kindergarten classrooms may have *work stations* (Diller, 2003), which are similar to centers. These are also small spaces devoted to particular activities. However, the activities found in work stations are those that were previously used in whole-class or small-group instructional activities and are then placed in work stations for children's independent exploration. The purpose of centers and work stations is twofold. First, centers and work stations allow children to practice independently new skills taught previously in instruction. Moreover, self-selection of activities means that children must use self-regulation and other cognitive skills: they plan which centers or work stations to visit, sustain their attention on the activities in the center, and regulate their behaviors and negotiate with other children use of the materials. Second, centers and work stations provide many children with constructive activities that produce gains in cognitive, social and emotional, and physical development, at the same time allowing teachers to provide small-group intentional teaching experiences for other children. That is, while the majority of children are engaging in center activities or at work stations, the teacher or assistant might be providing intentional teaching lessons to a small group of children.

Typical Early Childhood Centers

Typical early childhood classrooms include five to eight centers, depending on space and the number of children served. These usually include Home Living, Block, Art, Sand and Water, Nature and Science, and Math (or Counting) Centers. The Math Center or Counting Center often provides small manipulatives like beads. Teachers select the centers that they will place in their classrooms based on the backgrounds of the children. Most classrooms have children with a variety of developmental levels and background experiences. Meeting children's needs, therefore, requires a range of typical early childhood centers along with some specially designed dramatic play centers and a few unique centers that evolve from the curriculum. Each center includes materials and activities that appropriately challenge children with different levels of knowledge. Materials are labeled and accessible to children. Teachers set rules about the number of children allowed in the center and acceptable behavior and material use based on the size of the space and the nature of activities. Activities in centers are changed on a regular basis in order to maintain children's interest.

Library Center

One of the most important centers for children's language and literacy development is the *Book* or *Library Center*. Figure 2.2 shows a Library Center suitable for preschoolers and kindergartners. The components of a high-quality Library Center (Fractor, Woodruff, Martinez, & Teale, 1993) include:

- Space large enough for three or four children.
- A display of objects and books arranged with their covers visible.
- Accessible storage for 100 or more books (the minimum number of books included in a classroom should be 10 times the number of children, but not all books should be stored in the Library Center—some will be located in other centers).
- Some books grouped into categories (e.g., books about animals, bugs, and favorite characters).
- Equipment for at least two children to listen to recorded books, with storage for 10 or more books and tape bags.
- Attractive wall displays, including photographs of children retelling stories and charts asking children to indicate their favorite animal and storybook characters.
- Soft, comfortable seating.
- A special display place for books recently read aloud by the teacher.

This center offers children several choices for activities, including looking through books, listening to books on tape, browsing books on topics of recent study that their teacher has read aloud (e.g., animals and bugs), or writing on survey charts to indicate favorite characters. While the activities in the Library Center may remain the same, the materials in the center are changed every 2 or 3 weeks. Old books on tape are exchanged for new ones, new objects and book displays are arranged, and books on more recent topics of study replace those on previous topics.

Enhancing Language and Literacy Activities in All Centers

With simple adjustments in materials, teachers can expand the opportunities for children's authentic use of language and literacy during their play in all typical early childhood centers. Familiar settings with authentic objects prompt children to step into dramatic play in which they use reading and writing as they have observed parents and others do in their communities. Children are likely to pretend to read and write during dramatic play at a Home Living Center when the teacher stocks it with authentic literacy

FIGURE 2.2. Preschool/kindergarten Library Center.

props that could be expected to be found in the children's homes. These might include telephone books, food coupons, play money, notepads and pencils, play checkbooks, calendars, cookbooks, recipe cards, pizza delivery menus, envelopes, stationery, and note cards. Teachers can also help children construct their own props for centers. For example, children enjoy making baby albums to place in the Home Living Center by bringing in their own baby pictures and dictating captions. Teachers may help children construct personal telephone books listing the names and imaginary or real (with parent permission) telephone numbers of all the children.

With careful consideration, teachers can add materials and activities that increase the opportunities for language and literacy activities in every center. In the Block Center, teachers can add schematic drawings and blueprints of buildings, large blank sheets for children's schematic drawings and blueprints, clipboards with pretend lumber order forms, and homemade books with captioned photographs of children and their block constructions. Even outdoor play can be altered to include literacy opportunities when teachers provide appropriate materials. Children can become truckers, police officers, and race car drivers as they ride bikes, read maps, and write speeding tickets. They can open a drive-through window for a fast-food restaurant with paper bags, plastic food, credit cards, play money, and a menu. They can set up a car wash with buckets and soap, signs for the cost of a wash, tickets, and play checkbooks.

In addition to enhancing centers with authentic reading and writing materials related to the theme of the center, teachers can also read aloud story and informational books that will extend children's awareness of how to play in the centers. For example, *Building a House* (Barton, 1990) provides an illustration of a blueprint and describes how to construct a house, starting with digging the foundation. This book provides children with new vocabulary and an extended understanding of construction activities that can extend their play in a Block Center.

Dramatic Play Centers

While all early childhood centers can be enhanced with literacy materials, centers that encourage intentional dramatic play are particularly fruitful for stimulating preschool and kindergarten children's language and literacy experiences (Snow et al., 1998). *Dramatic Play Centers* encourage children to take on many different roles in an authentic activity. They are most effective when teachers clearly define a theme and provide a wide variety of literacy materials related to the theme. Play themes that elicit high levels of pretend reading and writing include office, library, veterinarian's or doctor's office, post office, and restaurant (Morrow & Rand, 1991; Neuman & Roskos, 1997). Other possibilities include Camping, Mall, Gas Station, Construction Site, or Beach Centers (Isbell, 1995).

Teachers select themes for Dramatic Play Centers based on the experiences of their children and as related to ongoing curricular activities. Children need some familiarity with the theme in order for it to be effective, but teachers can extend children's ability to play in more complex ways by introducing them to the props included in a center and explaining their possible uses. They can read related books and mention connections between events in the books and possible play activities in the centers. The most effective way to extend children's play in dramatic play centers is to take children to actual sites—a local fast-food restaurant or grocery store. When field trips are not possible, teachers can take children on pretend field trips. They can demonstrate and guide children in dramatic enactments of activities as if they were on a field trip.

Literacy-Focus Centers or Work Stations

Much of young children's literacy learning will occur in three classroom contexts: center activities, including dramatic play centers; specially prepared *Literacy Focus Centers*; and large- and small-group teacher-directed lessons. Literacy-Focus Centers are designed to allow children to explore independently materials and concepts introduced in teacher-directed lessons. These centers put learning materials in children's hands. Independent exploration of materials without teacher direction allows children to connect what they currently understand about literacy concepts with the new strategies and skills introduced by the teacher. Literacy-focus centers will be used more frequently with kindergarten and older preschool children than with younger children.

Table 2.2 provides a list of possible literacy-focus centers, including Computer, Writing, Letter-and-Word, Sound, and Overhead-Projector Centers. This list provides suggestions for materials and activities that might be found in these centers. Activities in these centers both remain stable and change to reflect the objectives and materials used in current literacy instruction. For example, generally children may have access to stationery, a variety of writing implements, small blank books, blank postcards, and alphabet stamps in the Writing center. However, as a result of a particular instructional activity, they may be also encouraged to use clipboards to write a list of names of children in the classroom or to cut words from coupons to use in composing an ABC book of foods.

ESTABLISHING A HIGH-QUALITY LANGUAGE ENVIRONMENT

Classroom environments are more than space and materials. They include interactions among people (children, teacher, aide, volunteers, parents) and the materials in the classroom (Roskos & Neuman, 2001), and such interactions are mediated by language. Although preschoolers and kindergartners have already acquired much competence with their native spoken language, their language development is not complete. They have still to learn many new words and many new meanings of old words. They have still to acquire greater ability with word parts and sentence structures, or *syntax*. Effective preschool and kindergarten teachers help children acquire spoken language, the most critical area of academic focus in the preschool and kindergarten and an essential foundation for reading and writing (Wright & Neuman, 2009).

Language Development and Dialect

At 3, 4, and 5 years of age, young children are acquiring the ability to communicate their meanings in ways accepted as conventional in their language communities. Many

TABLE 2.2. Literacy-Focus Centers

Center focus	Materials
Computer	Text and graphics programs such as Kid Pix, KidWords 2, KidWriter Golden Edition; learning programs such as A to Zap!, Kid Phonics, WiggleWorks, Letter Sounds; books on CD-ROM such as a *Bailey's Book House, Chicka Chicka Boom Boom, Curious George Learns the Alphabet*, the Living Books series, *Mixed-Up Mother Goose, Tales from Long Ago and Far Away, Storybook Theater*; books and stuffed characters or animals to accompany CD-ROM books
Writing	Writing tools such as pencils, pens (with variety of shapes and toppers), markers (of different sizes, scented, and mixable); alphabet materials (stamps, tiles, cookie cutters, sponges, plastic, felt); crayons, chalk; writing surfaces such as clipboards, wipe-off boards, chalkboards, paper (lined, unlined, cut in shapes, various colors and textures), pads (Post-it Notes, pads with printed notes, spiral-bound pads); reference materials (such as photo book with children's pictures and names, words related to themes, visual dictionaries, pictionaries, alphabet chart, copies of menus from local restaurants); environmental print (bags from grocery stores or fast-food restaurants, newspapers, coupons, catalogues)
Letter and Word	Various upper- and lowercase alphabet letters (magnetic, plastic, tiles, cards in different fonts and sizes), ABC charts, clothespins and clothesline, pocket chart, shoe pocket organizers, wikki sticks, alphabet puzzles, words (children's names or theme-related words), paper, crayons, markers, bingo or Concentration alphabet cards, large boxes (for sorting), word books, alphabet books, environmental print (bags from groceries or fast-food restaurants, boxes of food)
Sound	Laminated pictures (words that rhyme, words with the same initial consonants, words with the same final consonants), magazines, scissors, paper, glue, tape recorder and headsets, audiotapes of books with language play (many rhyming words or alliteration, sound games made by the teacher or parents), rhyming books, books with alliteration, pocket chart, boxes for sorting
Overhead Projector	Transparent alphabet letters and words with pattern and word cards, transparent characters and objects for retelling stories, transparent nursery rhymes (with transparent words and alphabet letters to match), blank transparencies and pens, transparent alphabet chart and alphabet letters, small objects and plastic letters (to sort by rhyme or alliteration), transparent children's names and plastic letters

of the at-risk children about whom this book is written speak a dialect different from the mainstream dialect spoken by highly educated members of their communities. Still, speakers of nonmainstream dialects are just as capable of communicating complex, abstract messages as speakers of mainstream dialects.

The purpose of the language activities that we describe in this book is not to require children to speak a mainstream dialect. Rather, it is to expand their ability to use language to express meanings. Children will acquire their community's various ways of speaking—including both mainstream and nonmainstream ways—by being included in conversations and listening to books as they are read aloud. The focus of conversations in preschool and kindergarten should always be on the meaning being conveyed rather than on the form in which meaning is conveyed.

Second-Language Development

Learning English as a second language is accomplished in the same context as learning a first language—in conversation. Learning English is dependent upon many factors, but key is children's willingness to attempt to communicate through English. Language is learned through conversations in which an ELL child attempts to communicate a meaning and a teacher uses gesture, pointing, dramatizations, and repetition to confirm and extend the child's meaning. A teacher's attempt to understand and communicate through simplified language is called *comprehensible input* (Krashen, 1982). Teachers need to focus on making themselves understood and making sure they understand children's attempts to communicate. Just as with dialect differences, the concern cannot be for correctness or conventions of language. Rather, the focus must be on the message. Communicating a message successfully and frequently naturally extends children's ability to use more complex sentences that gradually become more conventional.

There are many concerns related to using English as the language of instruction in preschool and kindergarten, to second-language acquisition, and to language development, in general. What is important here is for teachers to understand that all children are still developing language competence during their early childhood years. Whether children speak English or another language, they need frequent opportunities to engage in conversations with others in order to continue to expand their native language competence. The best opportunities for this occur when teachers are bilingual and are able to talk with children in their home language. In some preschools and kindergartens, aides are carefully selected to provide language resources for the children in the classroom. However, even when teachers and aides speak only English, all children need language experiences in their home language.

When teachers cannot help children further develop their home language, they need to find others who can. They must actively seek ways to bring speakers of other languages into the preschool or kindergarten setting. Parents and community resource persons can help teachers identify people in the community who would be willing to come to school as "conversation partners." Parents and other volunteers can tell stories, help children retell stories in their home language, and talk with children as they play in an Art Center or Drama Center. Teachers also need to find children's books published in the children's home languages for volunteers to read aloud. When these are not available, teachers can draw upon community resources to construct their own books.

CLASSROOM CONVERSATIONS

Rich experience with spoken language means conversation, that is, really talking with children. So among the most important things a teacher can do for preschoolers and kindergartners is to make time to converse with them, to engage them in real talk about their lives, their activities, and their interests. This may seem difficult because of the number of children in a classroom, and because often other matters, especially matters of classroom management, seem more pressing. Having real conversation with all children in a classroom is not easy, but it is necessary. Therefore, teachers must plan for it; they must make time and occasions for it.

Improving the Quantity and Quality of Teacher–Child Conversations

As critical as whole-class and small-group interaction is to children's language development, one-on-one conversations are even more crucial. However, research has shown that many preschool children have little opportunity to talk with adult caregivers or teachers in child-care or preschool settings (Snow et al., 1998; Dickinson & Tabors, 2001). When children did have opportunities to talk with adults, the quality of conversation was found to be low. We describe how teachers can increase the number of conversations they have with each child and improve the quality of those conversations.

Increasing the Number and Quality of Conversations

With responsibility for large numbers of children, preschool and kindergarten teachers are often hard-pressed to find time to talk with individual children. While teachers feel as if they do nothing but talk all day long, most of this talk is directed to groups of children and its purpose is to manage behavior or provide information for groups. Teachers can increase their opportunities to talk with individual children in two ways: set goals for having at least one or two conversations with each child each day, and make teaching in small groups more like conversations (Clay, 1998). Teachers need to be particularly concerned to have conversations with children who are least likely to initiate them: children whose home language is not English or children with poorly developed language who struggle to put thoughts into words. Clay advised teachers to "talk to the ones who are least able to talk. . . . Talk when the going is hard. Listen when the child wants to talk. . . . Reply, and extend the conversation" (1998, p. 11).

The best way teachers can expand the number and quality of conversations they have with individual children is to sit and stay with children and talk with them about their activities in centers or work stations. *Sit and stay* means that teachers will spend lots of time in just a few locations rather than cruising around the room making sure children have materials they need and are engaged in worthwhile activities. *Sit and stay* to talk with children can occur during snack and other mealtimes, when children and teachers are most likely to have high-quality conversations (Dickinson & Tabors, 2001).

As teachers converse with children, they may take opportunities to expand children's language by modeling the use of more complex syntax and demonstrating ways of speaking that are considered more mainstream (Manning-Kratcoski & Bobkoff-Katz, 1998). One of the easiest strategies that teachers can use to expand children's language is to *recast* their responses. If a child says, "doggy bark" the teacher recasts the child's words into an expanded and more conventional syntactic form, "Yes, the dog is barking."

Another strategy is to use *repetition*, in which teachers repeat their recast response, "The dog is barking. The dog is barking loud!" When used carefully, *questioning* is another strategy that can extend children's responses. After giving a response, teachers ask a question calling for the child to provide the same information in a longer and more complex sentence. For example, the child comments, "Doggy bark," and the teacher asks, "Why is that dog barking?" The child may respond with the extended sentence, "Doggy bark at squirrel." Another approach is to use elaboration. *Elaboration* involves using some of the child's own words, but embedding those words in slightly more elaborated sentence structures and adding a bit more related information. For example, a child asked, "When Daddy comes home?" and his mother elaborated, "Daddy will come home soon when it gets dark" (Clay, 1998, p. 8).

Another way of enhancing the quality of conversations is to invite the child to tell more. The more children talk, the more likely teachers are to understand what they are trying to communicate. The more children talk, the more opportunities they have to practice language use. Simply replying with "Mmm" suggests that teachers are listening and ready to hear more. Conversations can be enhanced by letting children have more time to reply. After asking questions, the teacher can wait several seconds to provide children with opportunities to frame a response. One of the best indicators of the quality of a conversation is its length; good conversations involve many give-and-take interactions between two or more speakers. Further, children are encouraged to explain, reason, and argue.

Conversing with children about past events provides particularly rich opportunities to engage them in the sort of talk that is critical for literacy development. When children are asked to describe a past event in which they participated—such as a birthday celebration or a trip to the mall—they must use decontextualized language, that is, words that refer to objects and events not in the immediate context of the speaker and listener. Because written language typically also is decontextualized, coaching children to retell past events is particularly helpful in preparing them for later reading and writing (Dickinson & Smith, 1994; Purcell-Gates, 1988). These conversations are even more powerful when teachers model retelling of past events. As teachers recall what happened, for example, on a trip to the mall, they can use relatively rare and unique words as a part of their conversation, words such as *pedestrian walkway, vendors,* and *saunter.* Effective language instruction occurs when teachers know something about children's backgrounds and interests. Table 2.3 summarizes the methods teacher can use to accelerate children's oral language and vocabulary development.

Using Conversation to Accommodate Cultural Backgrounds of Children

Conversation and instruction that specifically take into account children's culture are called *culturally sensitive* (Diamond & Moore, 1995) or *culturally responsive* (Ladson-Billings, 1994). Culturally responsive teachers have high expectations for all children's learning but are aware that children from different cultural backgrounds may approach learning in different ways. They continually seek knowledge about the cultural backgrounds of their children and enlist the assistance of community members and parents as regular volunteers in the classroom or for special classroom projects.

TABLE 2.3. Ways to Accelerate Children's Oral Language and Vocabulary Development

- Arrange for conversations with individual children and small groups of children daily.
- Sit and stay in centers and talk with children about what they are doing.
- Recast children's simple sentences with more complex syntax (child: "Doggy bark"; teacher: "Yes, the dog is barking").
- Repeat and elaborate by restating the recast response and adding more detail (child: "Doggy bark"; teacher: "Yes, the dog is barking. The dog is barking very loud").
- Ask a contingent question based upon what the child just said and wait patiently for the answer (child: "Doggy bark"; teacher: "Why is the dog barking?").
- Ask children to retell stories and model the use of sophisticated vocabulary words as supports for their retellings.
- Invite children to tell what happened at home and especially in the past.
- Extend and lengthen turn taking by challenging children to explain and elaborate and tell more during conversations.

Seeking Cultural Information from Parents and Community Experts

Learning about children's worlds outside of school allows teachers to adjust the classroom environment and instruction to be more congruent with children's worldviews. The place to begin understanding children's worldviews is with their parents. Parents transmit and interpret culture for their children. "Children learn the habits, traditions, and ways of life of their families" (Gibson, 1999, p. 19). Teachers who show respect for the worldviews of parents are more likely to discover critical information about family and community cultures and to enlist parents' help in supporting children's learning. Respect is obvious when teachers acknowledge parents' high expectations for their children's academic success and their families' sacrifices for the good of the children's educations (Edwards & Danridge, 2001). Teachers also show respect for parents when they "avoid making sweeping generalizations [about children's home or culture] based on skin color or surnames" (Strickland, 1994). Wise teachers are aware that there is a great deal of diversity within every cultural group and among children in a single family.

Making home visits early in the year is an extremely valuable way to establish a respectful and supportive relationship with parents. Teachers who commit to visiting with the parents of every child in their classrooms have found that some parents prefer to meet at a neutral location such as a neighborhood fast-food restaurant, and most parents appreciate very short visits of 15–20 minutes (Edwards & Danridge, 2001). Parents give very insightful information when they are asked a few open-ended questions, such as:

- "Who are the important people in your child's life?"
- "What are the most important things I should know about your child?"
- "What is one of your family traditions [e.g., when someone has a birthday]?"
- "What is something important that you have taught your child to do? How did you teach that?"
- "What is most important for your child to learn this year?" (adapted from Edwards & Danridge, 2001, p. 206)

AN EXEMPLARY CLASSROOM IN ACTION

In this example, Ms. Simpson transformed her preschool classroom into an accelerated prevention program for her at-risk 4-year-olds. Ms. Simpson and her aide teach
18 4-year-olds in a public school preschool for low-income families funded by the state
Office of School Readiness. The school system is located in a rural part of the state where
many parents are only occasionally employed or hold minimum-wage jobs. Ms. Simpson's children have not had extensive experiences beyond their local community. Most
children have never been to the small community library, and most do not own more
than a few children's books.

The Preschool Curriculum and Daily Schedule

In the past, Ms. Simpson's preschool curriculum was not different from that found in
many preschools. She typically focused on several broad themes such as "Fall," "Families," "Plants," "The Farm," "Wild Animals," "Floating and Sinking," and "Favorite
Story Characters." These themes allowed her to cover many content standards related
to mathematics, science, and social studies that she felt were appropriate for preschool
children. She integrated reading and writing with these themes by reading related stories and informational books aloud to her children daily, adding theme-related books
to the Book Center and other centers, and using shared writing (writing on large chart
paper while the children watched) to record information dictated by the children. Her
classroom was organized around six permanent centers: Book, Art, Writing, Home Living, Blocks, and Math/Manipulatives. She frequently added new activities to each of the
centers and often added a new center related to the current theme. She has a large carpeted space for whole-class activities and small tables where children work on activities
such as an art project related to the theme. There is a large playground area that has age-
appropriate equipment, including a climbing structure, large sandbox, and playhouse.
In addition, the children have access to balls, jump ropes, tricycles, and other outside
equipment and toys.

The daily schedule included large blocks of time for children's use of the centers
in the classroom and for outside play (see Figure 2.3), whole-class read-aloud of books,
and whole-class and table-top activities related to the theme. Daily movement and music
were whole-class activities.

Literacy and the Preschool Curriculum

Recently a new federal program in the school system required that reading specialists
be hired and reading assessments regularly administered at all grade levels, including
kindergarten. The reading specialist had been meeting with each grade-level team about
these assessments and then began meeting with the preschool teachers. After examining
the kindergarten data with the reading specialist, Ms. Simpson had a growing concern
over her children's lack of progress once they began attending elementary school. She
discovered that on the state-mandated assessment at the end of kindergarten and first

7:45	Greeting and table-top activities
8:00	Calendar, movement, and music
8:15	Centers (individual free-choice activities)
9:15	Cleanup and restrooms
9:25	Read-aloud
9:45	Outside play
10:30	Theme activities (experiments, cooking, art, viewing or listening)
11:00	Lunch
11:30	Nap
12:30	Restrooms
12:40	Centers (individual free-choice activities)
1:20	Cleanup
1:30	Outside play
2:00	Whole-class daily sharing
2:15	Dismissal

FIGURE 2.3. Ms. Simpson's original preschool daily schedule.

grade, many of her children performed in the bottom fourth of their classes despite their active involvement in the preschool program.

Ms. Simpson was concerned by these results and asked the reading specialist in the elementary school to help her look at the entering kindergarten performance of children who had successfully learned to read by the end of first grade so that she would have a better idea of goals to set for her children at the end of preschool. She discovered that the successful children entered kindergarten writing their first names fluently, recognizing most upper- and many lower-case alphabet letters, and matching pictures with the same beginning sounds. In addition, they knew many letter sounds, and some were inventing spellings after only a few weeks in kindergarten. They were able to retell familiar stories with some detail. This level of skill far exceeded what she had expected of preschoolers. However, she recognized that children entering kindergarten with higher levels of skills seemed to be better prepared to meet the demands of kindergarten and become good readers in first grade. The reading specialist brought in information about the vocabulary gap between children from middle class and lower-SES families (Hart & Risely, 1995, 2003), confirming that at-risk children need to accelerate their learning to catch up with their peers.

Ms. Simpson decided to rethink her preschool curriculum to provide more focused and intentional opportunities for children to develop the higher levels of literacy knowledge displayed by the more successful children. She realized that she had provided many opportunities for children to acquire literacy concepts in her classroom informally—through rhyming word chants and songs during music and movement time, alphabet puzzles in the Manipulatives Center, pretend writing activities in the Home Living Center, and recorded stories in the Listening Center. However, children were allowed to select these activities, and Ms. Simpson suspected that many children had not chosen them frequently enough to extend their literacy knowledge. Further, Ms. Simpson realized that she needed to be more intentional in her teaching. The reading specialist suggested that she begin teaching small groups so that she could provide more individual feedback to children.

Ms. Simpson decided to take a more deliberate approach to literacy in her curriculum. She rearranged her schedule with the help of the reading specialist to have more time for reading and writing instruction (see Figure 2.4). She would continue to use themes and centers as the central part of her curriculum. However, she would add more literacy-focused activities to her classroom routines in ways that would ensure that all children would engage in reading and writing daily. Ms. Simpson decided to add the sign-in procedure (children sign their names to a list clipped to a clipboard) to her routine for the children's arrival. This routine would ensure that each child wrote daily and

7:45	Sign-in, table-top puzzles, and activities
8:00	Whole-class: Greeting, calendar, movement, and music
	8:30 Assistant with small group 1
	8:45 Teacher with small group 2
	9:00 Assistant or teacher with small group 3
8:20	Centers (individual free-choice activities)
9:30	Whole class: Read-aloud, retelling, shared writing and Write On
10:00	Outside play
10:30	Whole-class and table-top: Letter-and-sound activities, word play
11:00	Lunch
11:30	Rest
12:30	Small-group math activities
	Teacher with small group 1
	Assistant with small group 2
12:45	Whole-class and table-top: Integrated read-aloud and hands-on activities (science, social studies)
1:15	Centers (individual free-choice activities) (On many days this includes outside free play.)
2:00	Whole-class gathering
2:15	Dismissal

FIGURE 2.4. Ms. Simpson's revised preschool daily schedule.

would provide numerous opportunities for her to interact with children as they were writing. She also decided to add more retelling activities to her read-aloud program. She realized that children needed more practice deliberately remembering stories. So, she decided she would model and guide children's retelling of at least two books per theme. Retelling would allow them many opportunities to use the vocabulary found in the books she read aloud and to extend their comprehension. To help reinforce alphabet letter recognition, Ms. Simpson would abandon teaching a letter a week. Instead, she would focus on teaching three letters a week and have children learn to write the letters at the same time they learned to recognize them. Two or three times a week she would model writing two or all three of these letters on a large chart. Then she would place the chart in the Writing Center and invite children to practice writing the letters during center time. She also instituted daily small-group instruction in literacy. At three points during the year, she assessed her children's progress in a few key literacy concepts (writing their names, alphabet recognition, telling a story to accompany a sequence of pictures related to a recent theme, and—late in the year—segmenting the first phoneme in a word).

Pulling It All Together

Although Ms. Simpson was concerned about providing her children with opportunities to develop the levels of literacy knowledge that would enable them to become successful readers and writers, she was also concerned that preschool continue to preserve children's natural curiosity about the world in which they lived. She had become increasingly aware that the themes she selected to guide the curriculum were often unrelated to children's real experiences. She decided she would plan activities in which she and the children would collect information from their families and communities and then construct a way to display the information in the classroom. These displays would provide authentic opportunities for writing as the children categorized and labeled information. She also decided to try to help her children conduct surveys and learn to read graphs.

Ms. Simpson was excited about trying out her new curriculum ideas. She decided to begin the school year with the Home and School theme that she had used in the past. During this theme children began the new sign-in procedure as they entered the classroom after breakfast (see Figure 2.5). They collected information through surveys and constructed graphs showing their favorite toys and food at home and school. They read, discussed, and retold *The Runaway Bunny* (Brown, 1942) and *Rosie's Walk* (Hutchins, 1968). During shared writing, they dictated lists of places Rosie went on her walk and things Little Bunny turned into. The children brought photographs of people who lived in their homes and graphed how many people lived there. Because of the children's interest in the photographs of different family members, Ms. Simpson read *Two Eyes, a Nose, and a Mouth* (Intrater, 1995). After reading the book, the children dictated a shared writing list of features found on faces, and Ms. Simpson introduced the Write On procedure. Each child selected a letter on the list that he or she wanted to write. Then Ms. Simpson hung the chart in the Writing Center, and some children added additional letters. Figure 2.6 presents the shared writing and Write On for *face*.

As a result of these changes in her curriculum and interactions with children, Ms. Simpson's children performed much better on the kindergarten and first-grade

★	Sign in
Reem	R 9 9 m
Huy	HUy
Erika	PETI.
Nasrine	00*Us~Ao

FIGURE 2.5. Prekindergarten sign-in sheet.

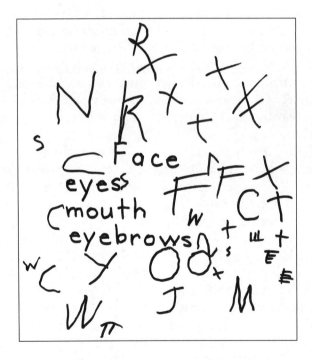

FIGURE 2.6. Shared writing and Write On for *Face*.

assessments. In comparison to previous years, when most children were in the bottom quartile, now most children were performing at or above the class average. Kindergarten teachers noticed the difference in many children entering their classrooms, and the reading specialist asked Ms. Simpson to share with them some of her key literacy approaches. The kindergarten teachers found these especially helpful with their lowest-performing children.

CHAPTER SUMMARY

This chapter introduced seven principles of accelerating literacy learning. Literacy learning emerges from play and social interaction during joint participation in hands-on tasks. Learning is accelerated when instruction is responsive to the needs of the individual learner, is refined through feedback, and is extended through independent practice, and it is more likely when the learner is motivated to engage in literacy tasks. Accelerated learning arises when children can self-regulate and make deliberate use of memory. These principles guide the arrangement of space and materials, and the daily schedule of classrooms. Literacy-rich classrooms have spaces for children to play and to select activities in centers or work stations. They are well stocked with literacy materials and tools. Conversations among children as well as between the teacher and children are considered an integral part of the classroom environment. Teachers engage children in conversation during center or work station activities and are attuned to the possibilities of teachable moments when children are poised to learn a new concept or strategy. Within such classrooms, at-risk children from diverse backgrounds acquire the language competencies and literacy skills they need in order to become highly successful readers and writers.

CHAPTER 3

Keeping the End Goal in Mind

Teaching for Knowledge and Comprehension Gains

The goal of reading instruction throughout a child's life is to build the knowledge, skills, and dispositions that lead to lifelong learning. We are all aware that what we know and can do today is not what adults 20 or 30 years from now will need to know and be able to do. The world is rapidly changing and the future of today's children lies in being seekers and critical users of information.

In very effective classrooms, children do have opportunities to see the ABCs, explore books, and write frequently. However, they are doing so much more—they are engaged in investigations of interesting topics. Knowledge drives the curriculum in these classrooms while letters and sounds are learned along the path of discovery (Neuman, 2006). Thus, much whole-class instruction will be centered around powerful themes. In excellent prevention literacy programs, teachers spend considerable time preparing for theme teaching.

This chapter is about how teachers can help children build knowledge and information. In classrooms where the goal is knowledge and comprehension, teachers guide children's explorations of books, media materials, objects, and investigations rather than merely give children information. Children's discovery of new information is dependent on our skillful sharing of books and other printed or media texts, such as Internet sites, YouTube videos, and apps. We carefully consider the concepts we want children to discover and learn about, building understandings of meaningful themes and developing enriched concepts and sophisticated vocabularies. We want children to grapple with ideas, to think, and to gain new knowledge, not merely to memorize. To achieve this, we help children develop strategies for gaining information and understanding what we share with them through read-alouds and media sharing. We help children to learn new vocabulary words and use them to communicate their own meanings about expanding concepts.

READING BOOKS ALOUD AND SHARING MEDIA: BUILDING TOWARD CONCEPTUAL UNDERSTANDINGS

Interactive Read-Alouds

Interactive read-alouds involve interactions among the teacher's reading, the teacher's comments and questions, and the children's comments and questions. Rather than merely reading aloud, during interactive read-alouds teachers demonstrate how they think while reading and how they pose questions regarding things they are wondering about. From teachers' demonstrations, children learn to make comments that reflect their thinking and wondering. In the following interactive read-aloud, Cindy (a pre-school teacher) and Jeremie read and discuss the pop-up book *Dinnertime* (Pienkowski, 1980). In this story a series of animals, illustrated with large pop-up mouths, announce they will eat another animal, the one the reader has seen on the previous page of the story. The conversation (with the text from the book presented in *italics*) is in both Haitian Creole (Jeremie's home language) and American English (Ballenger, 1999, p. 62).

> Ms. CINDY: (reads first double spread of text) *One day a frog . . .*
>
> JEREMIE: He got mouth?
>
> Ms. CINDY: *. . . was sitting on a log catching flies when down came a vulture.*
>
> JEREMIE: Cindy, he got mouth.
>
> Ms. CINDY: Yes, they all have mouths [reads second double spread of text] *Vulture said to frog "I'm going to eat you for my dinner"* [pointing to vulture] m pral manje ou (I'm gonna eat you) *and that's what he did.*
>
> JEREMIE: Li di li pral manje moun? (he said he will eat people?)
>
> Ms. CINDY: Non, li mem, li di, "m pral manje ou" (no, that one he said, "I will eat you.")
>
> JEREMIE: Manje on frog (eat a frog?)
>
> Ms. CINDY: Yeah, li pral manje on frog (he will eat a frog).

In this interactive read-aloud Jeremie commented twice on the pop-up mouths. Cindy only briefly acknowledged the mouths, then quickly returned to reading the text. She alternated between reading the text in English and repeating the essence of the text in Haitian Creole. Jeremie signaled by asking a question ("he said he will eat people?") that he was confused about whom the vulture intended to eat. It is not surprising that Jeremie was confused. The text refers only indirectly to the frog, which is not illustrated on this page. In order to understand the story, children must infer that the vulture is going to eat the frog that they have seen on the previous page (the text only says "I'm going to eat *you* for my dinner"). Jeremie's question shows that he incorrectly inferred that the vulture will eat people, probably based on his prior knowledge about dangerous animals. To rectify this misunderstanding, Cindy pointed to the animals in the illustrations and made explicit which animal is going to do the eating and which animal is going to be eaten. Then Jeremie asked another question, which served to confirm his understanding that the frog will get eaten, and Cindy's response provided feedback that he was correct. Cindy intentionally expanded Jeremie's language by recasting some of his language ("he got mouth?" and "eat a frog?") into a more conventional response ("they all have mouths" and "he will eat a frog"). The use of interactive read-alouds, including the give-and-take between teachers and children, has been shown to increase children's vocabulary development (Mol, Bus, & De Jong, 2009).

Reading Complex Narratives Aloud: It Takes Three Reads

What Are High-Quality, Complex Narratives and Why Should We Read Them?

Narratives are stories with characters who are placed in particular settings, face problems, and take action to solve problems but are confronted with obstacles. Facing obstacles creates tension and drama, often allowing characters to mature. High-quality narratives are distinguished by richness of vocabulary and language, complexity of character and plot, insightful themes, and interplay between text and illustrations (Sipe, 2008). These qualities provide opportunities to learn about higher level vocabulary (Beck, McKeown, & Kucan, 2013) and use higher-level thinking that calls on integration of content from the story and the child's knowledge (McGinty & Justice, 2010). For example, teachers can say "*Quivering.* That's a good word! Why do you suppose he was quivering when he saw the giant?" or "Oh dear! She has to get to the other side. How do you suppose she will solve that problem?" or "Have you ever heard of a *tchotchke*? What do you think that might be?" or "I wonder why he's hiding from Tony? What do we already know about Tony?" or "I think there's a clue in the picture. What do you see in the picture that tells you why she 'jumped for joy'?" Notice that high-quality narratives allow teachers to draw attention to vocabulary, critical story events, and inferred internal states of characters.

Books that are particularly appropriate for younger preschoolers include characters and activities that are familiar to children, texts with few words, and illustrations with direct relationship to the story line. However, children also love to grapple with books that have complex characters, activities that are unfamiliar and even mysterious, and illustrations that are intentionally in opposition to the story text. For example, *The Tale of Peter Rabbit,* written by Beatrix Potter in 1902, continues to be a favorite even of children living in 21st-century inner cities! High-quality narratives accurately reflect diverse cultures with authentic voices and illustrations (Barrera, Ligouri, & Salas, 1992). Figure 3.1 provides a list of culturally authentic books appropriate for the read-aloud program.

First Read of a Book: Pushing In Ideas and Demonstrating Thinking

The most natural way that teachers read books is to intersperse their reading with questions. Researchers have discovered that questions teachers ask range along a continuum of difficulty (van Kleeck, Vander Woude, & Hammett, 2006). Some questions draw children's attention to details in the illustrations, and these questions are the easiest to answer, requiring only one or two words. Other questions require a few more words to answer but also draw attention to literal information stated in the text or found in the illustrations. They are moderate in difficulty. The most difficult questions require children to infer something based on the text but not explicitly stated or illustrated. These

Marie Bradby (1995). *More Than Anything Else.* Orchard.
Eve Bunting (2006). *One Green Apple.* Clarion.
Yangsook Choi (2001). *The Name Jar.* Dell Dragonfly.
Caron Lee Cohen (1988). *The Mud Pony.* Scholastic.
Niki Daly (1999). *Jamela's Dress.* Frances Lincoln.
Arthur Dorros (1991). *Abuela.* Penguin.
Kristyn Rehling Estes (1999). *Manuela's Gift.* Chronicle.
Carmen Lomas Garza (2005). *Cuadros de familia/Family Pictures.* Children's Book Press.
Lucia Gonzalez (1999). *The Bossy Gallito/El gallode bodas.* Scholastic.
Francisco Jiménez (1998). *La mariposa.* Houghton Mifflin.
Tony Johnston (2001). *Uncle Rain Cloud.* Charlesbridge.
Ellen Levin (2007). *Henry's Freedom Box.* Scholastic.
Grace Lin (2003). *Dim Sum for Everyone.* Dragonfly.
Lenore Look (2001). *Henry's First-Moon Birthday.* Atheneum.
Alejandro Martinez. *La mujer que brillaba aún más que el so/The Woman Who Outshone the Sun.* Children's Book Press.
Pat Mora (2000). *Tomas and the Library Lady.* Dragonfly.
S. D. Nelson (1999). *Gift Horse: A Lakota Story.* Abrams.
Jose-Luis Orozco (2002). *Diez deditos/Ten Little Fingers and Other Play Rhymes and Action Songs from Latin America.* Puffin.
Helen Recorvits (2003). *My Name Is Yoon.* Farrar, Straus and Giroux.
Allen Say (2009). *Tea with Milk.* HMH Books.
Gary Soto (1996). *Too Many Tamales.* Puffin.
Janet Wong (2000). *This Next New Year.* Frances Foster.
Jacqueline Woodson (2001). *The Other Side.* Putnam.
Yin (2003). *Coolies.* Puffin.
Yin (2006). *Brothers.* Philomel.

FIGURE 3.1. Culturally authentic books (realistic fiction or folk tales about underrepresented cultural groups in the United States) for prekindergarten and kindergarten children.

questions call upon higher levels of thinking, and answering them often requires sophisticated and extended syntax. While questions at the lower end are useful in engaging children's attention, only questions at the higher end extend children's thinking and their syntax. Thus, teachers should be aware of the kinds of questions they ask.

Most teachers are used to reading books and stopping along the way to make comments and ask children questions. However, they are often disappointed when only a few children seem to be able to answer questions, particularly if they require higher-level thinking such as inferring a character's motivation or explaining why an event occurred. Often the children who participate the most in interactive read-alouds are those who have had many previous literacy experiences. Unfortunately, especially in programs serving high percentages of children at risk, few children may attempt to answer questions. It may be that children who are relatively passive during book interactions have had few opportunities to listen to books read aloud by adults who expect them to talk. They may need to have the teacher model how to think and talk about the text they have just heard or where to look for information in illustrations. Therefore, a first read of a story for children with few storybook experiences might include more teacher demonstrations of thinking aloud and fewer questions (McGee & Schickedanz,

2007). Teachers can read the same book more than one time so that each read encourages children to take a more active role in talking and later answering questions. A first read of a book might be considered a push-in read, because it is designed to show children that reading aloud involves thinking and talking, that words and their meanings are critical components of understanding and enjoying books, and that using the story problem provides glue to understanding the story as a whole. A first push-in read has five parts. Teachers:

- Give a book introduction that identifies the characters and something about the problem.
- Ask a few lower-level questions.
- Stop to think aloud and talk, making explicit for children the connections between events and revealing characters' thoughts and motivations (demonstrating higher-order thinking).
- Insert information about key vocabulary meanings without interrupting the flow of the story.
- Pose a higher-level question after reading the story that calls for extended explanations around the story as a whole (McGee & Schickedanz, 2007; McGee, 2013).

Giving Book Introductions

Book introductions for storybooks help children focus on the main character's problem. That is, the key to understanding a story is recognizing the problem, which is often not stated directly in the text. By late elementary age, children begin inferring the problem of a narrative immediately upon reading and use this problem as a guide for predicting and understanding events and making inferences about character traits and motivations (Van den Broek, 2001). In contrast, most preschoolers and kindergartners pay almost exclusive attention to characters and their actions without considering how the problem provides psychological motivation, tying the story together and laying the foundation for theme. Thus, a good book introduction prepares children to discover the problem and helps them follow the plan of action toward solving the problem.

In planning a book introduction, teachers read through the book and identify the main characters and their problems. For example, *Do Like a Duck Does!* (Hindley, 2002) is a story about a fox who pretends to be a duck in order to get closer to and capture ducklings to eat. His problem is that Mother Duck suspects he might not be a duck, carefully guards her ducklings, and brings him along on activities that ducks like to do but foxes do not. An introduction to *Do Like a Duck Does!* might be:

> "The main character in this story is a fox, and look, he is trying to act like a duck [using the front cover]. But he has a problem, look here [showing the back cover]. I don't think Mama Duck thinks the fox is a duck. Look, her face shows she is *suspicious* [dramatic demonstration of a suspicious scowl]. Let's find out why Fox acts like a duck and what Mama Duck does. She looks very *protective* of those ducklings. I don't think she will let anything happen to them."

Asking a Few Lower-Level Questions and Talking during Think-Alouds to Support Comprehension Processes

Teachers' comments during the first push-in read are designed to support children's use of higher-level thinking, in which they must integrate information from their previous knowledge with information from the text. Calling upon their prior knowledge allows readers to elaborate on or call to mind additional information about the content that might not be stated directly in the story but which they know from their own experiences. If a book describes a character riding in a car to school, children call to mind what they already know about going to school in a car. They can mentally picture getting in a car, buckling a seat belt, perhaps fighting with a sister or brother, and listening to the car radio. Calling to mind this mental information allows children to make inferences and judgments about characters and their actions. Teachers can demonstrate using prior knowledge, for example, when reading *Do Like a Duck Does!* They can stop and say, "That reminds me of I saw a family of ducks at a pond. One parent was in front of the babies and one in back. If anyone got near, the one in the back flapped her wings and charged toward the person. She looked pretty scary."

Being able to infer what characters are thinking and feeling is critical to understanding a story plot. Teachers can use think-aloud comments to make explicit some of the characters' thoughts and motivations. Teachers should select carefully critical events in the story to stop and talk about. For example, in *Do Like a Duck Does!*, the fox's motivation for acting like a duck is to get right up close to the ducklings, closer than he could if he were acting like a fox. He wants to get up close in order to make eating the ducklings easier. Mother Duck is very suspicious of the ducks and is naturally protective, but she does not send him away at first. Why does she not just send him on his way? Teachers and children must infer her motivation. She may realize she could scare the fox away for one day but he might keep coming back and eventually get a duckling. Thus, she has to scare him away for good. To begin the think-alouds, teachers might comment after reading the third double spread, "Look how mother is protective of her ducklings. They are all under her and she looks mad. I think the fox is trying to get near and I bet he wants to eat one of those little ducklings." After reading the next (fourth) double spread, teachers can comment, "Here is where he pretends to be a duck, but Mama duck notices he doesn't have a beak and his ears are wicked, that means up to no good. And his mouth is wicked, that means up to no good. He is trying to get real close. He is saying to himself, 'I'll just pretend to be a duck and soon I'll pounce on one of those yummy ducklings.'"

However, during the first read, teachers should also engage children's interest by using some, but not many, lower-level questions interspersed through the reading. For example, at the third double spread when the fox first appears, before reading teachers might ask children to identify what animal he is. Later before reading the sixth double spread, the teacher might ask the children to identify what animals watch the ducks as they walk by the farmyard and then at the eighth double spread, to describe the fox (who is licking his chops and casting an evil eye). These questions keep children's attention focused on the action of the story.

Clarifying and Extending Vocabulary

Reading books aloud provides a significant source of new vocabulary for children. Children's books introduce children to more sophisticated words than they are likely to encounter in other language events (Cornell, Senechal, & Brodo, 1988; Hargrave & Senechal, 2000). Before reading a book aloud, teachers can select 8 to 10 vocabulary words or phrases to highlight during reading. The words and phrases selected should be those critical for understanding the story, those that children are likely to encounter in other books, or those that are more sophisticated labels than children usually hear for everyday objects and events (Beck et al., 2013). For example, a kindergarten teacher selected the words *suspicious, protect, waddle, creeping, beak, wicked, muck,* and *zip,* before reading *Do Like a Duck Does!* to her kindergartners. As she read the book, she read the words, turned to look at the children to give a few words of definition or explanation, and then turned back to the text and reread the sentence with the target word or phrase. She also acted out words and pointed to parts of the illustrations.

To exploit these vocabulary learning opportunities, teachers use specific techniques that make it more likely that children will notice the words and learn something about their meanings (Biemiller & Boote, 2006). Teachers can clarify or expand word and phrase meanings in one of four ways:

1. By inserting a short phrase or sentence that defines or explains a word as they read the text (e.g., by saying, "*Protect.* That means she won't let anyone hurt her ducklings. She *protects* them.")
2. By pointing to salient parts of the illustration that help clarify the meaning of a word or phrase (e.g., by pointing to the duck's *beak*).
3. By using dramatic gestures in acting out the meanings (e.g., by demonstrating *creeping* with her arms).
4. By using voice to demonstrate meaning (e.g., by reading with a suspicious voice, "Are you *sure* you're a duck?" and then adding, "I think she is *suspicious.*").

Vocabulary meanings that are offered during the first read provide information about meaning within the context of the story. For example, in *Do Like a Duck Does!, zip* is used to mean move very quickly rather than the more obvious action with a zipper.

Asking Higher-Level Questions after Reading

After reading the entire book, teachers ask a question that calls for children to use extended talk to explain story events. Such questions require that children recall specific events and make connections among them. For example, with *Do Like a Duck Does!*, the teacher might ask, "Why do you think Mama Duck took the fox and ducklings to the mud puddle?" The teacher could help children answer the question by turning to the mud puddle illustration and asking, "Do you think the fox likes eating bugs? How can you tell?" or "Why would mother duck make the fox eat bugs? Do you think she knows he doesn't like bugs?" These questions require extended talk about what happened and why. They are especially important to increasing children's vocabulary, syntax, and story comprehension.

Second Read and Third Read: Pulling Out Ideas and Supporting Thinking

The second read of a narrative should occur within a day or two of the first read. The purpose of the second and third reads is to dramatically increase the amount of talk expected from children while reducing teacher talk. Instead of demonstrating how to think aloud, teachers ask higher-level questions that require children to call upon prior information and make inferences. To begin a second read, teachers ask children to remember the title, identify the main character, and describe the problem. Teachers read the book aloud, expanding the same vocabulary that was emphasized on the first read. At the same spots that teachers selected to stop and talk through a think-aloud on the first read, teachers in the second read stop and ask higher-level questions. For example, after reading the third double spread, teachers might ask, "What do you think fox is thinking?" and after the fourth double spread, "Why do you think Mama Duck is suspicious?" The after-reading question on the second read might remain the same or teachers might ask a different question (McGee & Schickedanz, 2007). Teachers might ask, "Why do you think Mama Duck took the fox to the pond?" or "Why did the fox slink away back home?" The second read is a time to extend children's understanding of the target vocabulary beyond the context of the story (McGinty & Justice, 2010). For example, teachers can reinforce the meaning of *zip* as moving fast, but also draw attention to *zip* your coat, when you move your zipper very fast.

The third read of a narrative should occur within a week or two of the second read, allowing for several days between readings. Now the teacher leads the children in recounting the story and may only read a few pages or sentences. To begin the teacher asks, "Who remembers the title and the problem of this story?" Several children should be encouraged to comment. Then the teacher opens to the first double spread of the book and asks, "What is happening here?" Teachers should ask children to clarify and expand their explanations and provide prompts for using the vocabulary that has been highlighted in the first two reads of the book.

Using Read-Alouds of Narratives to Develop Concept about Stories

Maximum comprehension depends on young children's understanding the structure of stories (Stevens, Van Meter, & Warcholak, 2010). Teachers can strengthen children's awareness of the components in stories by deliberately planning activities that draw attention to particular story concepts (Fitzgerald, 1989), including the following:

- A story has a beginning, a middle, and an end.
- Stories have characters.
- A story has a setting that tells where the story takes place.
- The main character has a problem that needs to be solved.
- The main character takes action to solve the problem. (Adapted from McGee & Richgels, 2000; McGee & Tompkins, 1981; Tompkins & McGee, 1989)

Teachers can introduce the concept of beginnings, middles, and ends of stories by rereading a favorite story, emphasizing each portion of the story as they read. Then they can invite children to retell what happened at each of those three parts of a story. Children can arrange in sequence pictures of story events (cut from an extra copy of the book) and identify which pictures go with the story's beginning, middle, and end. Teachers can introduce the idea of main characters and their problems by reading several books about favorite characters. Children love to read series books about the Berenstain Bears, Franklin, Arthur and D. W., and Henry and Mudge. In each book of a series, the familiar character faces a new problem. Many of the books of a series are set in a familiar story location, but each book also introduces a particular setting. Teachers can draw children's attention to story problems by distinguishing between stories in which characters have a problem with other characters and stories in which characters have a problem within themselves. For example, *Thunder Cake* (Polacco, 1990) tells the story of a girl who is frightened by a thunderstorm. Her grandma helps her conquer her fear by keeping her busy making a cake. In contrast, *Timothy Goes to School* (Wells, 1981) tells of the rivalry between two characters, Timothy and Claude. In this story, Timothy discovers a new best friend, Violet, who helps him ignore Claude's rudeness.

Interactive Read-Alouds of Informational Books

Teachers routinely select stories to read to young children, and most classroom libraries have fewer informational books than storybooks (Duke, 2000; Pentimonti, Zucker, Justice, & Kaderavek, 2010). However, today many high-quality informational books are being published, even for very young children. These books have brief text and engaging illustrations and photographs on topics of interest to children. Some informational books are available in big-book format.

Reading informational books and sharing related experiences are powerful ways to introduce children, particularly children at risk for reading failure, to new concepts and vocabulary (Neuman & Dwyer, 2010; Neuman, Newman, & Dwyer, 2011). Unlike most middle-class children, many at-risk children have had little exposure to experiences that allow them to acquire knowledge or vocabulary about the scientific and technical world around them (Duke, 2000). Reading informational books seems to support especially rich discussion and thinking. Children naturally ask questions and seek information from these books. Their curiosity motivates listening to more difficult books. In fact, children and adults are likely to use higher-level talk when discussing the concepts in informational books (Price, Van Kleeck, & Huberty, 2009). Such talk involves children in:

- Drawing inferences about information not stated in the text or provided in the illustrations.
- Predicting what will happen next based on information provided in the text.
- Comparing and contrasting actions, objects, or characteristics.
- Summarizing, analyzing, or synthesizing information across several pages of text.
- Explaining events or actions, especially making cause-and-effect relationships explicit.
- Making connections among actions, events, or objects based on connections to life experiences (Zucker, Justice, Piasta, & Kaderavek, 2010).

Informational books provide many opportunities to discuss the meanings of new vocabulary and to encourage children to use the new words as they talk about the book. Because informational books are full of technical vocabulary, effective teachers are careful to focus on a few words, the ones central to understanding the concepts presented in the book. During reading, teachers can stop to define a term briefly and then reinforce the meaning of the technical word by saying "This part of the text tells me the meaning of this word. Let me read it to you slowly."

Many informational books explain phenomena—why a volcano erupts or how a spider captures its prey. Embedded in such explanations are events linked by cause and effect. Effective teachers make explicit how the ideas in a text are linked together (Smolkin & Donovan, 2002), using words or phrases such as *as a result of, because of,* and *that causes.* With informational books, teachers may pause frequently to summarize, to link new information with information that has previously been read, and to connect information to children's experiences.

Children's knowledge and vocabulary can be further extended by reading several informational books on a common topic over the course of several days or even weeks (Heisey & Kucan, 2010). Reading several informational books on the same topic is easier now because of the many series of informational books published for young children. Often the books in a series are leveled: That is, the publisher identifies whether the book is intended for very young or slightly older children, based on the amount and complexity of its content. For example, teachers can find many different books about spiders. Some will be intended for very young children; they will include detailed photographs but very little exposition because the text is so short. Other books will be intended for older preschool and kindergarten children; they will include many photographs and some other visual aids such as labeled drawings and will have more text with a few technical words. Still other books will be intended for elementary-age children; they will include a variety of illustrations, including labeled drawings, graphs, charts, tables.

Teachers should read aloud books that are related to content standards in mathematics, social studies, and science. For example, many states have standards related to plants, living things, and history (Pentimonti et al., 2010). In addition to reading informational books about these topics, we recommend that teachers read narrative texts and even predictable or rhyming texts in order to extend children's engagement. For example, teachers can read the story *Bill and Pete* (dePaola, 1996) to accompany informational books about crocodiles (Santoro, Chard, Howard, & Baker, 2008). Or they can read *The Grouchy Ladybug* (Carle, 1996) or *Have You Seen Bugs?* (Oppenheim, 1996) during study of insects (Neuman & Roskos, 2012).

Using Read-Alouds of Narrative and Informational Books to Teach Comprehension Strategies

Children who have had extensive experiences with books and older children can be introduced to using comprehension strategies they will later use as readers. The *Report of the National Reading Panel* (National Reading Panel & National Institute of Child Health and Human Development, 2000) identified particular strategies to teach in order to improve children's comprehension. These include activating and connecting to prior knowledge, visualizing, asking questions, making inferences, and retelling or summarizing. We suggest that during read-alouds, kindergarten teachers explicitly describe such strategies as the following (adapted from Gregory & Cahill, 2010, and Myers, 2005):

- Prior knowledge is all the information already inside your brain. You make connections when something in a book reminds you of something you know. You say, "I connect to that—."
- Visualization is when you make a movie in your brain which shows details, colors, smells, and feelings. You say, "I saw in my brain—"
- Questioning is what you do when sometimes you don't understand something in a book—you wonder why something happened or how it happened. You say, "I wonder—."
- Inferring is when you are able to think about something not in the story or illustrations. You say, "That character is thinking or feeling—" or "This event is connected to that event because—."
- Summarizing is telling the whole book in just a few words. You say, "This story is about _____ [main character] who _____ [problem] by _____ [how problem is solved]", or "This book is about _____ [topic], and it tells _____, _____, and _____ [three important facts]."

Teachers demonstrate how to use one strategy with two or three books before teaching another strategy. When all the strategies are taught, children are invited to use them during pauses in read-alouds or at the end of book readings.

RETELLING AND DRAMA

After reading a storybook to children, teachers can engage them in retelling or dramatizing the story. Or they can help children to tell and then dramatize their own stories. These activities extend children's experiences with the content and words of stories and thus are among the most effective instructional techniques for increasing children's comprehension, vocabulary, and syntax (McGee, 2013).

Guided Story Retelling

Guided story retelling is a blend of retelling and drama (McGee, 2003) through the use of character props. Distributing character props among children assigns them a character.

Guiding Children during Whole-Class and Small-Group Retelling

The easiest books for guided story retelling activities are familiar folk and fairy tales. After children are very familiar with one of these stories, teachers guide them to recount the story, emphasizing what each character says. Then teachers give each child a character prop, such as a paper drawing of the character's face put on tag board. Several children are the same character. For example, the parts of the big billy goat, the middle billy goat, the little billy goat, and the troll are played by several children. Children can sit in a circle for this retelling activity as they will not be dramatizing or moving about. All children in the group participate in guided retelling. At first teachers do the narrating and, by holding up a copy of a particular character's prop, they prompt the children playing that character to say his or her dialogue. Individual children may be silent, say a few words softly, or confidently make up dialogue. All these responses are accepted, as guided story retelling is more like improvisation than saying memorized dramatic dialogue. Because guided retelling of a story is a short activity and is repeated over several days, children's confidence in speaking in character grows over time. On each subsequent day of guided retelling, children should enact different roles so that they become familiar with all of the story's dialogue. Repeated guided retelling is especially beneficial for ELL children. The props help them to remember when to speak and what to say; dialogue is more easily managed because it usually short and repeated; and saying the dialogue in groups provides a natural support for children whose language is not yet well developed. Teachers have found that having a parent or other volunteer read the story in the children's home language and help children retell the story in that language supports their later retelling in English (Roberts, 2008).

Guided story retelling's effectiveness is strengthened when it is accompanied by small-group practice. For example, there are many fine picture book versions of *The Three Little Pigs* and other favorite tales. Teachers might read different versions of the tale to different small groups of children, continuing to use the same props for retelling the story. When retelling in small groups, each child receives a copy of all the character props and practices telling the entire story saying all the character's dialogue. Teachers lead by providing the narration and prompting each characters' dialogue. The teacher's voice fades away as children take the lead in telling the entire story. At this point, teachers should place several copies of the small-group props in the Book Retelling Center or the Library Center.

Independent Book Retelling

Children should be encouraged to reuse small-group retelling props independently to construct new stories or add improvised events to favorite stories (Weisch, 2008). Helping children retell new stories that include the events from familiar stories with new twists and characters provides enormous challenges for language and comprehension (Meier, 2000). Children should also be encouraged to select and make their own retelling props. In order to select objects to represent characters, children must determine qualities that define a character (Rowe, 1998). Thus, allowing children to collect or construct their own props may be more intellectually challenging than providing them. Props include pictures cut from an extra copy of a book, small objects, items of clothing, puppets, and masks. Pictures can be hung on either a story clothesline or a storytelling stick. A story clothesline is constructed by tying a length of clothesline between two sturdy pieces of furniture, such as the teacher's chair and an easel. The best pictures to use on a story clothesline are approximately 6 inches square or larger. A storytelling stick is constructed from a yardstick with several small squares of self-stick Velcro attached to its length. Pictures used on the story stick need to be smaller, but large enough for children to see.

Small objects that represent the characters and important events are easy to obtain. For example, three small bears, three sizes of spoons, three sizes of paper cups (for chairs), and cloths of three different sizes (for beds) can be used to tell the tale of the three bears. *Mirandy and Brother Wind* (McKissack, 1988) is easily told using a jacket, several scarves, an old blouse, an apron, a small quilt, a pepper mill, and a tablecloth. Masks are also easily made book acting props.

Dramatizing Children's Original Stories: Story Playing

Another way to use storytelling in the classroom is to dramatize original stories that children compose. The *story playing* technique (Paley, 1990) has four elements: One child is invited to tell a story, and the teacher writes the child's story. The teacher reads the story aloud, and other children make comments, ask questions, or suggest elaborations. Finally, the child acts out the story, inviting other children to join in the story play to take on any needed roles. One way to organize story playing is to invite a few children to tell a story as they enter the classroom. As the teacher writes a child's story, he or she rereads what the child has said so that the child can see the connection between the talk and the written words. The teacher allows the storyteller to make corrections, additions, and deletions to the written story. The children know that this written copy of the story will be used for their later acting out of the story. During the school day, the storyteller may continue to elaborate on the story. As children become accustomed to the technique, they anticipate the end-of-the-school-day performance by including elements of the story in their dramatic play in play centers. Finally, at the end of the day, the children act out the story as the teacher reads the current written version of it. Some children are in the cast; they are chosen by the original storyteller. The other children are the audience; they are free to contribute to the ever-evolving story with comments and suggestions. In this way, story playing demonstrates revision, a process children will later use in their own writing. Its immediate importance for the preschool and kindergarten child, however, is that it is on-the-spot meaning making; it has immediate connections to the classroom lives of the students, which at this age should include many play opportunities.

PROJECTS, EXPERIMENTS, AND OTHER REAL EXPERIENCES: THE ROLE OF KNOWLEDGE ACQUISITION IN LITERACY DEVELOPMENT

Children learn about animals, space, oceans, and rocks by reading books about these topics. Of course, children also learn about these topics by watching television, visiting zoos, going to the beach, watching YouTube videos, and collecting rocks in nearby streams and rivers. However, as children get older, their learning about topics in science and social studies most often is through books, hands-on experiments, and participating in projects. These experiences are intended to build children's higher-level thinking skills. They are aimed at helping children pose and answer questions, make inferences about cause-and-effect relationships, and think critically. We have already described how reading informational books aloud is a critical component of a high-quality literacy program because it does support children's higher-level thinking. However, effective teachers extend and supplement informational book reading with carefully thought-out units of study that include experiments and projects.

Experiments are a natural part of discovery science and are particularly useful in helping children understand scientific concepts and develop process skills of investigation (Harlan & Rivkin, 2000). As a part of experiments, young children observe, classify, measure, predict, infer, and construct explanations. They use the basic steps of the scientific method, including becoming aware of a problem by asking, "What will happen if . . . ?," hypothesizing or predicting an answer or solution by stating "I think this will happen," finding out by trying out a prediction, and sharing the results with others by telling what happened. These steps are easy to implement, even with young preschool children. Imagine three children standing on a playground in the late afternoon. One child notices his shadow. The teacher urges the child to ask "What if?" questions: "What will my shadow look like if I put my hands over my head?" or "What will my shadow look like if my friend Eddy stands right next to me real close?" or "What will my shadow look like if I sit down?" Each of these questions can be accompanied by a prediction, for example, "I predict my shadow will get smaller if I sit down," and an experiment (actually sitting down to see what happens to the shadow). The results of these experiments can be communicated to all the children later in the day or the next day during circle time. As children share their discoveries and experiments, other children will become interested in pursuing experiments. Teachers should encourage all children to repeat experiments again and again as long as their interest and curiosity are aroused. Many resources, including the Internet, describe science experiments that are appropriate for young children.

The project approach, like discovery science, is another curriculum idea that engages children in posing and answering questions. Generally, projects are constructions created by children after extensive study and observation. For example, children have constructed a veterinary clinic, a dispatch office for school buses, a garden tiller, a bulldozer, an automobile, firefighting equipment, and a fire truck (Helm & Katz, 2001). Before construction, children visit actual sites or observe machines and tools in use. They draw pictures and diagrams, compose lists of materials that will be needed, and make plans for initial construction. During construction, children articulate problems that arise and brainstorm solutions. After constructions are complete, they communicate their project results by drawing and dictating or writing. Children dictate lists of things they learned, construct a big book with photographs and dictated captions, or draw the step-by-step sequence followed to produce their construction.

SHARED WRITING AND WRITING WORKSHOP

Composing written messages is another classroom activity that provides many opportunities for children to extend their concepts and stretch vocabulary and syntax. Children compose by participating in shared writing (in which the teacher has a directive role in both composing and writing) and during writing workshop or journal writing (in which the child composes and writes more independently).

Using Shared Writing

Shared writing is the joint creation of a text by teacher and students; the students provide many of the ideas, and the teacher does the actual writing, usually on a large piece of chart paper or marker board which all the children can see (Payne & Schulman 1998). Shared writing occurs after an experience and extended conversation about the experience. Then teachers make explicit the purpose for the writing. For example, they might tell children that they are writing a summary of what happened on the trip to the orchard to help everyone always remember the great time they had on the trip. Then teachers ask children to help compose. For example, if they were writing a list of the kinds of apples the children saw on the trip, teachers would invite children to name types of apples. Or if they were composing a description of the activities they enjoyed at the orchard, children would be invited to remember what they did. Then, teachers write those contributions on a chart or large white board. The teacher and the children read and reread the resulting text several times together.

Shared writing experiences with younger preschoolers need not be as frequent as those with older preschoolers or kindergartners. Many teachers have found that with young children it is easier to compose lists than more complex text. After reading *Yuck Soup* (Cowley, 1989), one group of 3- and 4-year-olds dictated a list of the ingredients found in yuck soup. Another group of 4- and 5-year-olds compiled a list of animals found in *Over in the Meadow* (Wadsworth, 1992). After writing the lists during shared writing, the teachers hung the lists in the Art Center, and the children were invited to draw or paint pictures of the animals or yucky ingredients. Later, the shared writing charts, decorated by cutouts of children's art, were placed in the preschool hall where parents picked up their children, and children were reminded to read the charts to their parents.

Making Shared Writing a Daily Activity

With kindergartners, shared writing should occur daily. Many teachers have used the *morning message* (see Payne & Schulman, 1998) to accomplish the daily writing goal. Morning message is sometimes called daily news or class message because it is usually written early in the morning, and topics that are written include the date, a greeting, upcoming school events, or anticipated activities. Many teachers have a rotation schedule so they select two or three children who dictate the morning message each day. Most teachers use one or two phrases that are repeated daily and then invite children to add additional sentences. Teachers help children remember the repeated message included in the news every day. Then they either help the selected child compose a sentence or guide children as they compose a message together. A typical morning message may include the following:

Good morning kindergartners!
Today is Tuesday.
Marie is going to her grandmother's house.
Joseí is going fishing with his uncle.

Another way to incorporate daily shared writing, one we actually recommend over daily message, is to compose texts for a class *memory book.* Teachers can take photographs of important classroom events or have children draw pictures—such as a picture of the sorting room children visited on their trip to the apple orchard. Then teachers can help children compose messages to accompany the photographs or pictures. For example, a teacher might help children compose the caption "Our apple orchard field trip." Then they would remind children of the purpose for writing: "That will help me remember that you drew these pictures after our field trip to the apple orchard. Oh, look, here's Mark's picture of the sorting room. Mark, what shall we write under your picture so people will remember the sorting room?" The children already know that the memory book displays their pictures of the apple orchard, and they may even recognize Mark's picture, but this teacher talk reinforces the record-keeping function of written language.

Making Shared Writing Purposeful

Shared writing offers many opportunities to share with children the many kinds of printed texts we read and write. It allows teachers to make explicit the nature of language used in particular kinds of texts and their purpose. For example, want ads in the newspaper and birthday present wish lists serve the instrumental purpose of satisfying needs and wants. All children enjoy composing lists of hoped-for birthday presents, but they are also interested in how people use want ads: to obtain help for yard work or to locate a jersey worn by a favorite hockey player.

Teachers can seize opportunities to use shared writing to read and then compose texts that serve real purposes. For example, they can read aloud several of their own e-mails to relatives and then help children compose an e-mail to a classmate who has moved away or to a distant grandparent. When a child is absent from school, teachers could have on hand several get-well cards to read as models. Then they can help children compose their own card. Teachers can extend experiences with get-well cards by placing them in the Writing Center along with specially cut paper and envelopes for children's pretend writing.

Teachers can introduce children to yard-sale signs, party invitations, grocery lists, telephone books, maps, and directions in order to enrich play in the Home Living Center. They bring in examples they have gathered from their homes or found in their neighborhoods, share them with children, and then place them in the center. Each of these print items can become a shared writing activity or an activity for the Writing Center.

Teachers can capitalize on opportunities to demonstrate using writing purposefully as they arise during classroom activities. When children have completed an especially complicated structure from blocks, teachers may invite them to dictate a DO NOT DISTURB sign. Later, the teacher would read the sign to the children and talk about what it means. Leaving the sign and block construction in place for a day or two emphasizes its regulatory purpose. Later, teachers can photograph the children, their block construction, and the sign and add it to the class memory book, using this as still another opportunity for shared writing.

Using Shared Writing to Display Information

Shared writing can be used to collect and display information gathered during a social studies or science unit. During a unit on plants, children can dictate for a whole-class science journal their daily observations of a sweet potato's growth in a glass jar. Later, teachers can help children compose a list of things they have learned about plants. *Venn diagrams* (two circles drawn so that they overlap) or *comparison charts* can be used to compare information about similar objects or events. For example, teachers can help children compare a maple leaf to an oak leaf and then use the information from their discussion to compose a Venn diagram.

Another way to use shared writing to display information is by constructing surveys. Classroom events suggest many topics for surveys, which can be answered with the words *yes* or *no* or by having children write their signatures under columns labeled "Yes" and "No." A child's recent trip inspired the survey "Have you been to Disney World?" A child who came to school one day with a cast over a broken bone helped to construct the survey "Have you ever had a cast?" A rainy day sparked the survey "Did you wear boots today?" The answers to even simple questions such as "Do you like red?" provide many opportunities for displaying information. Once a survey is completed, teachers can help children compose summary statements such as "Three children wore boots today. Twelve children did not." After learning how to take surveys, many children enjoy creating their own during center time. To encourage survey taking, teachers can stock a Writing Center with a few clipboards and pencils.

Journal Writing and Writing Workshop

While shared writing involves more teacher direction (selecting the topic of the writing and the genre—a list, recipe, description, want ad, etc.—and writing the message), journal writing or writing during writing workshop allows children to decide topics and genre, and compose and write their message more independently.

Journal Writing, Sharing, and Conferencing in Preschool

Writing is usually a daily occurrence in preschool, at least for some children, as they pretend to write in the Home Living Center, Dramatic Play Center, or Writing Center. That is, many children effortlessly incorporate writing into their pretend dramatic play or attempt writing at the Writing Center, especially when teachers or assistants model writing and invite children to write with them. Teachers also encourage children to write by asking them to place their writing in a basket or special chair and after center time allow each child to talk about his or her writing. Other teachers encourage writing by displaying many examples of children's writing around the classroom or by inviting children to hang their own writing where they choose.

However, teachers who notice that many of their children do not choose to write may schedule a separate daily writing time of 15 to 20 minutes. They might call this time journal writing or writing workshop. In elementary school, writing workshop includes short mini-lessons, free writing when children write independently, writing conferences in which children confer together and with their teacher about their writing, and sharing, when children read their writing to the other children and solicit comments and feedback. In preschool and kindergarten, the writing workshop can be modified to meet the developmental needs of the writers in the classroom and across the school year.

In the beginning of the year, preschoolers and kindergartners compose in journals made of several pages of paper stapled together. The paper can be blank or have the bottom half lined. Teachers can demonstrate how to draw a picture and then write a word, a phrase, or a sentence to label the picture. Then they can model how to compose by merely speaking, without writing; by using scribble writing; by making strings of letters; or by inventing spellings. Teachers model invented spelling by saying words slowly, listening for sounds, and then writing letters that represent those sounds. As children finish their drawing and writing, they can come to the teacher or assistant and dictate their story for the teacher or assistant to write quickly at the bottom of the page. Teachers help children reread their stories, not worrying if the words are exactly the same as the dictation. At the end of writing time, children can be invited to sit in a special chair to read their story and to walk slowly around the circle to show the illustration to the other children (King, 2012). As children walk around, other children are allowed to comment or ask questions.

Meanwhile, as journal writing is getting under way, teachers can prepare children for writing longer texts—writing stories or other informational texts that extend across six to eight pages and take more than one day to compose (Ray & Glover, 2008). Teachers can use one of their read-aloud times to focus on reading for becoming a writer. That is, during read-aloud time, teachers comment on and share with children how authors and illustrators find topics to write about, how they extend their ideas across several pages, and how they select words for the text and images for the illustrations. For example, teachers can point out that picture books:

- Contain words and illustrations.
- Have words and illustrations that change from page to page.
- Are about something(they stick to a topic and one or two characters).
- Are composed of carefully selected words and images (Ray & Glover, 2008, p. 132).

Teachers can help children think about topics that authors choose to write about. Teachers read aloud books that demonstrate how authors decide what to write about. Authors write about:

- A place they like.
- An activity they like to do or want to remember.

- Their families or friends.
- How they are feeling.
- How to do something.
- A topic that interests them.

Children can also be encourage to write about topics related to their own experiences. They can write about an art project they completed, a pretend episode from the Dramatic Play Center, a game they played outside, or an object that the teacher has brought in to share. Children can also write about content topics they are studying, such as living things, plants, or history.

Finally, picture books can be read aloud to share with children interesting language, different font sizes and shapes, or dialogue. Teachers can point out illustrators' use of color, perspective, borders, and detail.

When children have been taught a little about picture books and how they work, teachers can replace journals in which they are expected to write a page a day with empty books of six to eight pages in which they are expected to write an extended story with an illustration and text on each page (of course, many children will continue to rely on dictation to create their written texts).

Conferences with advanced preschoolers and kindergartners are opportunities to promote children's understanding of invented spellings and to provide feedback about the quality of children's compositions. Some teachers prefer at first to provide daily topics for writing, but later to allow children to select their own topics (Bergen, 2008). Teachers have found that conferences with one or two children in which they provide feedback at children's levels of need about both spelling and composition are more effective than the whole-class mini-lessons that typically occur in elementary school. Most teachers have found they can confer with each child about once a week

AN EXEMPLARY CLASSROOM IN ACTION

As an example of how teachers can make information, understanding, and knowledge the center of their preschool and kindergarten program, we describe how a prekindergarten teacher, Ms. Simpson (introduced in Chapter 2), used a theme to provide a rich informational background in which she embedded a wide variety of literacy, language, and math activities. She wanted to teach considerably more than the narrow range of skills that are targeted in many packaged literacy programs. She wanted to develop themes that would be more interesting to the children and provide more opportunities for investigation. One afternoon an idea for a new theme occurred to her while she supervised her children as they were boarding the school buses and being picked up by parents for their trips home from school. She decided to plan a theme around automobiles—the most frequent form of personal transportation. In the past she had used focused on all forms of transportation—by land, water, and air. However, she realized that the theme of automobiles was far more closely related to the children's lives and potentially offered more opportunities for investigation than the more general theme of transportation. She knew she could integrate this theme with social studies standards around history and economics.

Developing the Theme

To prepare for the theme, Ms. Simpson researched automobiles using the Internet. She found information about the history and significance of the Model T and other models of automobiles, including the 1949 Ford Coupe and the Mustang. She located information on current makes and models of automobiles, and she took a virtual tour of the Henry Ford and Rolls Royce Museums and viewed photographs of old cars rebuilt by collectors. She found many Internet sites devoted to restoring antique cars and to car clubs. As she studied the information on these Internet sites, Ms. Simpson became keenly aware of how the automobile had changed not only the way goods are produced and sold, but also the very nature of society. However, she realized many of these abstract ideas were not appropriate for her young children. She did think that her children would be highly motivated by the topic and could learn a great deal about history as a part of this theme.

Ms. Simpson visited the local library to locate children's books related to automobiles, using keyword searches. She also used online bookstores to locate more resources for the theme. By using the library, buying a few new books, and using a few books from her previous transportation theme, Ms. Simpson found nearly 25 books she could use for the automobile theme (see the list of books as part of Ms. Simpson's planning web in Figure 3.2). She quickly read the books, jotting down the major ideas presented in each. She realized that none of the books she had selected for the theme came in big-book format. However, she noted that several used rhyming phrases. She decided to copy portions of *Duck in the Truck* (Alborough, 2001) and *Pigs in the Mud in the Middle of the Rud* (Plourde, 1997) on large charts to use for shared reading.

After reading all the books she had selected for the unit and browsing the Internet sites, Ms. Simpson thought about the major concepts and vocabulary she might help her children learn. She decided that several major ideas were appropriate learning outcomes for 5- and 6-year-olds. They could learn that there are many makes (manufacturers) and models of automobiles; automobiles have many parts—some designed for safety and some mechanical; automobiles have changed over time; automobiles influence the way we live; automobiles are manufactured from raw materials such as steel, sold at businesses called car dealerships, bought by families, and repaired at service stations; and families have to balance their needs with their wants when they purchase an automobile.

Planning Theme Activities

Now Ms. Simpson decided she would need to gather old family photographs from her family that featured her family's car; pictures from the Internet on the history of the Ford Model T, 1949 Coupe, and Mustang; and copies of brochures from several car dealers. She knew her children could not go on long field trips, so she decided she would visit the nearby Mercedes manufacturing plant and take photographs of the assembly line in order to take her children on a virtual tour. She gathered old photographs of automobiles from the Internet and asked her father for back issues of *Motor Trend* magazine. Finally, she gathered miniature cars for the Block Center. She would use these artifacts, photographs, and toys to initiate conversations with her children about their knowledge of automobiles and to develop new concepts about the makes, models, and parts of

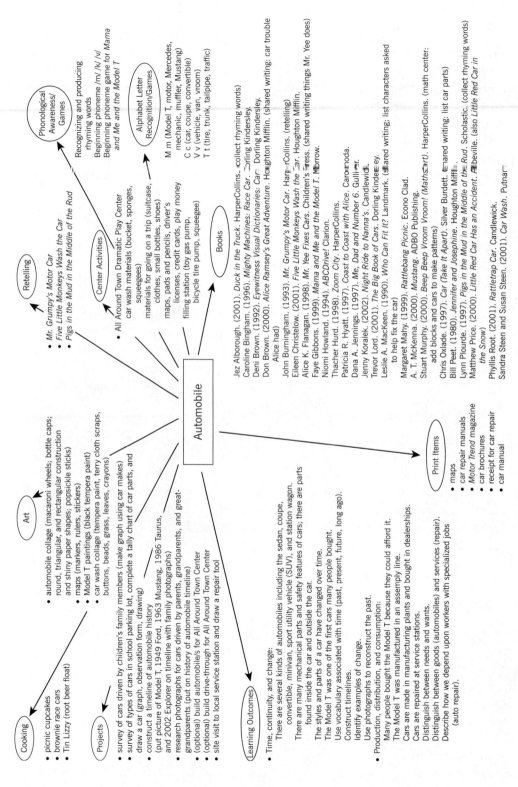

FIGURE 3.2. Automobile theme planning web.

58

automobiles. These resources would also provide a visual introduction to the manufacturing of automobiles and to changes in automobiles over time.

Then she brainstormed car-related cooking and art activities and thought about projects that children could do to collect data for graphs, charts, and other displays about cars. She planned a special dramatic play theme center, All Around Town, in which children could pretend to wash cars, go on car trips, order fast food at a drive-through, and buy gas or get a car fixed at the gas station. She thought about the props she would need to gather for the All Around Town center. She selected three books that would be appropriate for retelling and considered props to use in this activity.

Involving Parents and the Community

All preschool classrooms in Ms. Simpson's building host parent meetings once a month. She decided to write a letter to parents about the automobile theme prior to the upcoming meeting. She wanted parents who owned cars to have the option of visiting school with their cars. She stressed that having a variety of cars for children to explore would be especially fun, but she was careful not to convey an assumption of car ownership or an expectation that all children's families would visit the school with their cars. She also invited parents to bring in car repair tools and old car parts. Because two of her children spoke Spanish at home, Ms. Simpson asked the elementary home–school liaison to write the letter in Spanish for those parents. At the parent meeting she described the theme and talked about ways parents could support it at home, including ways that did not depend on owning a car, for example, by making lists of cars observed in the neighborhood. She stressed the importance of using lots of vocabulary words related to cars. The parents brainstormed a list of over 50 words related to automobiles. Ms. Simpson shared with parents the importance of using these words in their everyday conversations with children. As they left the meeting several parents made commitments to bring their cars to school.

Ms. Simpson also visited a service station that was located near the school to find out whether the children could come to observe a car being repaired. She convinced the mechanic (who had worked on her previous car) that her children would like to see him roll under a car, change the oil, and fix a flat tire. She discussed safety issues and set the day and time for the visit.

Teaching the Automobile Theme

Ms. Simpson was ready to make weekly plans for teaching the automobile theme. In her weekly plan, Ms Simpson listed books for read-alouds, other print items that could be read for information or introduced for center activities, resources to use in theme activities, books for retelling or drama, art and cooking activities, music, and the text used for shared reading.

Introducing the Theme

Ms. Simpson began her theme by introducing the children to the miniature cars she brought for the Block Center. The children talked about their toy cars at home, their families' cars, and favorite cars. She discussed the word *automobile*, wrote it on a strip of poster paper, and placed it in the Writing Center. She also showed children the copies of *Motor Trend* magazine she had found and placed some of these in the Writing Center, some in the Art Center, and some in the Home Living Center. She encouraged children to write about or draw automobiles during center time that day.

Finally, Ms. Simpson read *Beep Beep, Vroom Vroom!* (Murphy, 2000) aloud. In this story a little sister tries three times to arrange her big brother's miniature cars in the same pattern that her brother uses. As she read, Ms. Simpson commented on the story, and many children talked about their miniature cars, brother–sister relationships, and hating to be "too little" to play with good toys. Ms. Simpson pointed out the pattern of the colors of cars lined up on one page of the story. She wrote the color words on a large sheet of chart paper in the pattern illustrated in the book. She named each letter of a color word as she wrote it, then read the word and invited children to read the words. Ms. Simpson reread the chart several times, inviting the children to join her. Then the children were invited up to the chart to identify an alphabet letter or a word they would like to write on the shared writing chart. Ms. Simpson hung the chart in the Writing Center and reminded the children that they could write more letters or words on the chart during center time. She encouraged children to bring their miniature cars to school to use in the Block Center. She suggested visiting this center to make more patterns. She reminded children they could make patterns with the paper, blocks, or any other manipulatives in that center. She also taught many explicit math lessons on making patterns.

Theme Activities

Ms. Simpson planned to read portions of the new car brochures the next day. This would make a good transition between toy cars and real automobiles. It would introduce children to the concept of the difference between make and model of cars and start a discussion about the parts of cars. Later in the week she would show a picture of herself and her current car and three pictures she had found of cars her mother, father, and grandfather had previously owned. One of these photographs showed her grandfather's 1949 Ford. This would begin the study of automobile history and serve as a springboard into one of the projects: finding photographs that included cars, including family photos and photos from magazines. The children used Ms. Simpson's and their own photographs during many writing workshop activities. They wrote ads for cars, stories about riding in cars, and information about car parts and their purpose during shared writing (and Ms. Simpson encouraged them to use these topics during journal writing).

As the theme unfolded, Ms. Simpson's children acquired much information about automobiles and their history. They learned the difference between the make of a car and model. In one shared writing experience, children listed the three most popular makes of cars. Children also collected information about the parts of cars. Figure 3.3 presents Jamaica's tally of car parts she found when she observed and drew a picture of Ms. Simpson's car in the parking lot (adapted from Helm & Katz, 2001). They learned vocabulary words such as *vehicle, automobile, Tin Lizzy, Model T, sedan, coupe, convertible,*

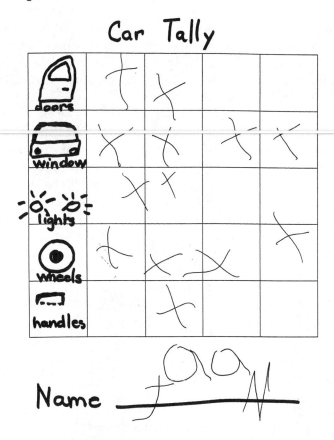

FIGURE 3.3. Jamaica's tally of car parts.

SUV, bumper, windshield, wipers, glove box, hood, tailpipe, muffler, chrome, steering wheel, dashboard, gearshift, upholstery, tachometer, odometer, oil gauge, gasoline, highway, overpass, tunnel, intersection, pedestrian, traffic, passenger, license tag, Ford, Chevrolet, Toyota, BMW, Mercedes, Mustang, Corvette, Viper, motor, manufacturer, assembly line, dealership, service station, repair, wrench, mechanic, motorcar, running boards, starter, and *pedal.* They collected family photographs showing cars from the past and used them along with pictures they found on the Internet to construct a 100-year timeline from 1902 to 2002. Several children built three automobiles for the All Around Town Dramatic Play Center out of cardboard boxes and other household items.

The children also engaged in many reading and writing activities as part of the theme. Ms. Simpson read several times *Mr. Gumpy's Motor Car* (Burningham, 1993) and *Pigs in the Mud in the Middle of the Rud* (Plourde, 1997). Then she prepared laminated construction paper animals and characters for retelling the stories. All of the children visited the Book Center and retold these stories numerous times. They constructed street signs for roadways that they built in the Block Center. They listened to and discussed an alphabet book about cars, stories that took place in cars, fictionalized accounts of real automobile adventures, and informational books about cars. As part of these book experiences, children talked about automobiles from the past and the stereotype of girls not being allowed to drive cars. They recalled rhyming words they heard in *Duck in the Truck* (Alborough, 2001) and then played rhyming word games with picture cards.

During the theme, Ms. Simpson introduced four phonemes (/m/, /v/, /k/, and /t/) by modeling and talking about how to articulate each phoneme. Children practiced articulating a phoneme and deciding whether a spoken word had that phoneme. They matched pictures that had the target phoneme and sorted pictures according to beginning phonemes. They played a game based on *Mama and Me and the Model T* (Gibbons, 1999) in which children drove a Model T around the game board by matching pictures with the same beginning phoneme. Some children cut pictures of objects and made phoneme charts as part of a center activity. Ms. Simpson modeled writing both the upper- and lowercase alphabet letters for *M, V, K, and T* on Alphabet Write Ons, and all the children wrote dozens of alphabet letters on the Write Ons during center activities. The children wrote checks for food (see Figure 3.4), ordered food at a pretend drive-through (a puppet stage converted to a "Burger Barn"), and wrote speeding tickets. They read maps as they played in the All Around Town dramatic play center and made maps in the Art Center.

Reflecting on the Success of the Theme

Near the end of the theme, the reading specialist visited the classroom and noticed that many children had made progress in recognizing alphabet letters and being able to segment beginning sounds both in instructional activities and when they invented spellings. Several children pretended to read books to themselves in the Book Center, often choosing books with rhyming words. Most children pretended to write as they played in the Dramatic Play Center and composed stories and information books during writing workshop. They were talking more during book reading and other media-sharing experiences, often making elaborated comments using the sophisticated vocabulary they had been exposed to during the theme. The children's parents commented on how much the children talked about cars as they traveled.

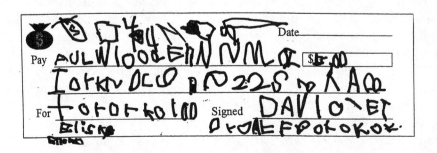

FIGURE 3.4. Check for a drive-through order.

CHAPTER SUMMARY

In this chapter we discussed the critical importance of keeping knowledge acquisition at the forefront of curriculum development for exemplary prevention programs. Children learn literacy in the service of gaining new knowledge and understanding. We described several methods of reading aloud to children depending on children's experience listening to and talking about books at higher levels of comprehension. For example, children with fewer book experiences and young children may need a deliberate approach to reading narratives that includes three reads of the same book. The first read, a push-in read, consists mainly of teacher-demonstrated talk. The teacher begins with a book introduction that identifies the main character and problem. The teacher also emphasizes and extends the meaning of 8 to 10 vocabulary words while maintaining the flow of the story. After reading, children are challenged to answer a high-level question that requires extended explanation. The second and third readings, pull-out reads, engage children in answering questions and recounting on their own the events of a story. Information books should also be read aloud, especially in themed units where teachers share parts of many different books about the same concepts. Vocabulary learning should be tied to the concepts being learned. Children with more book experiences and older children can benefit from narrative and informational book read-alouds that focus on comprehension strategies such as retelling or summarizing, clarifying vocabulary, asking questions, and visualizing. Understanding of books read aloud is extended by guided drama and retelling activities in whole-class, small-group, and independent contexts. Concepts are extended through projects and experiments, shared writing, and journal or book writing. Teachers can demonstrate the variety of purposes for writing by demonstrating writing get-well cards, surveys, and Venn diagrams. Through all these activities, teachers create daily opportunities to extend children's concepts, vocabulary, and understandings of complex picture books and other media and content topics. Classrooms with rich experiences associated with in-depth study of topics provide for assessing individual children and grouping them to provide differentiated instruction that accelerates learning.

CHAPTER 4

Literacy Development and Its Assessment

In this chapter we describe some of the many expected literacy accomplishments of young children, whether they are considered at risk or not. Our discussion is intended to provide a broad overview of literacy development during these early years, keeping in mind that children who have been shown to be at risk for learning to read and write generally demonstrate lower levels of literacy achievement than their peers who are not at risk (National Early Literacy Panel, 2008). Some children as young as 3 years old are considerably behind in vocabulary development (Hart & Risely, 1995), and the gap persists at school entry. Because this book is intended to describe prevention and intervention programs to eliminate such gaps, we present information about assessing children in order to pinpoint their development and craft instruction that will accelerate them toward successful reading and writing.

DEVELOPMENTAL CONTINUUM OF LITERACY ACQUISITION

Experts in literacy development have described phases of literacy development that capture the interplay between unconventional and more conventional reading and writing attempts. One such description is found in a joint position statement of the International Reading Association (IRA) and the National Association for the Education of Young Children (NAEYC) called *Learning to Read and Write: Developmentally Appropriate Practices for Young Children* (IRA/NAEYC, 1998; Neuman, Bredekamp, & Copple, 2000). This statement describes five phases of literacy development. Children in preschool and kindergarten usually fall somewhere on the early part of this continuum—in the first phase, Awareness and Exploration, or the second phase, Experimental Reading and Writing. We expect that some kindergartners might reach the beginning of the third phase, Early Reading and Writing. Yet, most children do not begin this phase until after they have entered first grade, and many children are still within this phase in second grade.

Although the statement about the literacy continuum (IRA/NAEYC, 1998) attaches grade-level designators to each phase, the authors emphasize, "Children at any grade level will function at a variety of phases along the reading/writing continuum" (1998, p. 200). Their use of the word *phases* rather than *stages* is consistent with an important caution about any such continuum: Children do not proceed along the continuum in a lockstep manner. The continuum is a guide; it gives teachers rough indicators of a group of children's current notions about literacy and their skills with reading and writing. It suggests potential next steps for children under appropriate supportive conditions, the sorts of conditions that this book will present. The authors stress that teachers should be mindful of the need to assess the unique achievements and needs of individual children rather than trying to place children within a phase.

AWARENESS AND EXPLORATION

The first phase, Awareness and Exploration, describes the learning that children do as they take their first steps in literacy development. *Awareness* suggests a new kind of attention to the phenomena of written language to which children in most modern cultures are everywhere exposed. They become aware of print written on T-shirts and graffiti written on subway walls. They notice captions on television programs and print in children's books. *Awareness* implies a conscious knowing that print itself is a special category of marks different from other visual displays. From parents' reactions to print, children become aware that print carries a message, is related to certain activities, and serves specific purposes. For example, on a trip to Kmart a parent might exclaim, "Look at that big *K*!" Children know that the "big K" is related to the activity of going to Kmart and that the printed *K* is related to the word *Kmart*. Through these and other activities, children become aware of print, that print conveys a message, and that its message is related to previous experiences.

In this book we recognize (along with others, e.g., Schickedanz & Collins, 2013) that this Awareness and Exploration phase of learning is long. It begins when babies are read their first book or toddlers are given their first set of markers. Younger children, including toddlers and 2-year-olds, in this phase are emergent readers and writers who are just beginning to learn about the world of print, the roles of stories and information books, and how to make their arms and hands produce intentional marks. These early explorations are important and playful. Most children with adequate literacy experiences begin to notice alphabet letters as unique marks with special significance. They learn about their written names and often are invited to write their signatures. They learn to listen to books read aloud to them and when and how to talk about interesting things found in books. They react to the rhythms created by the language patterns in nursery rhymes, poems, and chants. Older children in this phase are still emergent readers and writers, but they have learned some conventional knowledge and are more aware of the details in print. Table 4.1 presents an overview of the range of knowledge we can expect from early (younger) and later (older) emergent readers and writers in the Awareness and Exploration phase. Later, we will devote separate chapters to activities for early (Chapter 6) and later (Chapter 7) emergent readers and writers.

TABLE 4.1. Overview of the Accomplishments in Four Phases of Reading and Writing Development That Are Possible in Preschool through Kindergarten

Awareness and exploration: early (younger) emergent readers and writers	Awareness and exploration: later (older) emergent readers and writers	Experimental reading and writing: almost readers and inventive spellers	Early reading and writing: first-grade-level readers and writers
Oral comprehension and meaning vocabulary			
Understand and make comments and answer questions about books read aloud; acquire vocabulary from books; attempt telling about illustrations	Understand and make a minimal retelling with a few details of easy narratives and informational books; acquire and use vocabulary from read-alouds	Understand and make a somewhat elaborated retelling with some details of narratives and information books; acquire and use some Tier Two vocabulary from read-alouds	Understand and make a more elaborated retelling with many details of more complex narratives and information books; acquire and use Tier Two vocabulary from read-alouds
Retelling checklist	Retelling checklist	Retelling checklist	Retelling checklist
Name writing			
Write name with letter-like forms and some legible letters	Write first name with many legible letters; a few reversals and/or omissions	Write first name with all legible letters; attempt to write last name	Write first and last name with age-appropriate size, proportion, and alignment
Observation and name sample (name-writing assessment)	Observation and name sample (name-writing assessment)	Observation and name sample (name-writing scale)	Observation and name sample (name-writing scale)

Concepts about print			
Demonstrate book-handling and some directionality concepts	Demonstrate directionality; move from tracking with sweeps or taps to attempting one-to-one matching during fingerpoint reading of familiar pattern text	Demonstrate concepts about letters and words; demonstrate consistent use of one-to-one matching in familiar easy text and later in unfamiliar very easy text level 1–3	
Concepts about print assessment	**Concepts about print assessment; fingerpoint reading assessment**	**Concepts about print assessment; fingerpoint reading assessment**	
Alphabet knowledge			
Identify a few alphabet letters and develop motor skills to control lines used in letter writing and drawing	Recognize many alphabet letters; write some to many letters in legible form	Recognize most upper- and lower-case alphabet letters; write many to most letters in legible form	Recognize letters quickly; write letters quickly without attention to letter formation; write letters within words with appropriate size, proportion, and alignment
Alphabet assessment	**Alphabet assessment**	**Alphabet assessment**	**Observation and writing sample**
Phonemic awareness			
Learn nursery rhymes and poems and respond to rhythm and rhyme	Know many nursery rhymes; may identify and produce rhyming words; segment a few beginning phonemes	Segment most beginning consonant phonemes; segment and blend single phoneme onsets and rimes; identify and generate rhymes; segment ending phonemes	Segment and blend two- and three-phoneme words
	Segment beginning phoneme assessment; rhyme assessment	**Segment onset and rime assessment; rhyme assessment**	**Segment two- and three-phoneme words assessment**

(continued)

TABLE 4.1. (continued)

Awareness and exploration: early (younger) emergent readers and writers	Awareness and exploration: later (older) emergent readers and writers	Experimental reading and writing: almost readers and inventive spellers	Early reading and writing: first-grade-level readers and writers
		Alphabetic principle: invented spelling	
	Emergence of the alphabetic principle shown by invented spelling of a few words with one sound–letter correspondence of a highly salient sound (usually at the end of this phase)	Invent spellings that have one sound–letter match and later with two sound–letter matches (boundary phonemes)	Invent spellings with most to all phonemes spelled (fully phonemic spelling); spell high-frequency suffixes (-ed, -s, -ing)
		Spelling assessment; TWR (Richgels, 2013)	**Spelling assessment; TWR (Richgels, 2013)**
		Phonics: decoding and conventional spelling	
	Know a few consonant letter-sounds	Know most consonant letter-sounds; spell and read new words by substituting consonants to familiar rhyming words	Know letter–sounds for consonant digraphs and blends, short vowels; use these in decoding and spelling single-syllable regular words
		Consonant letter–sound assessment; spelling assessment; TWR (Richgels, 2013)	**Spelling assessment; TWR (Richgels, 2013)**
		Sight vocabulary for reading and writing	
		Recognize 15–30 high-frequency words in reading; spell 10–15 high-frequency words	Recognize 200–300 high-frequency words; learn meanings of Tier Two words encountered in text reading
		High-frequency word reading; 10-minute word writing	**High-frequency word reading; 10-minute word writing**

Fluency			Reread familiar text with phrasing and fluency
Text complexity and level: comprehension	Read with support (remember and chant with a group) the words of familiar poems or songs printed on charts	Fingerpoint read familiar texts; read with accuracy and understanding texts at the easy, preprimer 1 level (levels 1 through 3/4 or C) with teacher support	Read with accuracy and understanding all first-grade levels (levels 4 through 16/18, C–I/J); use reading strategies while reading to fix-up word recognition errors and monitor comprehension **Running records**
Writing composition: text writing	Make representational drawing of a person (tadpole); may use scribbles or mock letters in writing attempt **Draw a picture and write about yourself**	Make representational drawing of person (tadpole) with a few details; may use mock letters, or random letters in writing; may copy words; may attempt to spell a label or word with one sound–letter correspondence **Draw a picture and write about yourself**	Make representational drawing of person with a body and some details; use invented spellings to write words, a phrase, or a simple sentence. **Draw a picture and write about yourself**	Make representational drawing of person with a body and many details; write two or more connected sentences with invented and conventional spellings **Draw a picture and write about yourself**

Note. Suggested assessments are in bold.

Oral Comprehension and Language Development: Engagement with Books and Other Printed Texts

During the Awareness and Exploration phase of literacy development, children learn how to respond to a variety of printed texts, from storybooks to grocery lists, from informational books to McDonald's signs. Most 3-year-olds cannot read a McDonald's sign, but they do understand the significance of the big yellow arches. Children's awareness of the print in their environment and how it is used often is reflected in their dramatic play. Children pretend to read a telephone book and call a friend as part of their play in the Home Living Center of a preschool.

Our culture organizes texts in particular ways. One way that preschoolers become better at understanding storybooks or informational books is by becoming aware of such text organizations. For example, children acquire a rudimentary awareness of the ways that stories are organized (Stein & Glenn, 1979). By listening to many stories, children gradually acquire a *concept about story* that includes the notions that stories have characters and that those characters are present throughout the story. Children learn that stories have actions or events that lead to an ending. Later, children's concept about stories is refined to include an understanding that story characters have problems, that they attempt to solve their problems, and that settings can influence problems and their solutions. Their growing concept of story is demonstrated when they attempt to retell a favorite story. Gradually, their retellings shift from mere repetition of a story's words or phrases to description of salient objects in pictures, to telling the sequence of actions in the story using simple sentences.

Children also develop concepts about informational books and how they are organized (Duke & Kays, 1998). For example, stories are about specific characters such as Tacky, a penguin in *Tacky in Trouble* (Lester, 1998). Informational books, on the other hand, are about generic rather than specific characters, such as "the penguins" in *The Penguin: A Funny Bird* (Fontanel, 1989). Stories are told in the past tense ("Tacky waddled ashore . . ."; Lester, 1998, unpaged); informational books are told in a timeless present tense ("The penguins leave the ocean . . ."; Fontanel, 1989, p. 6). When asked to pretend to read or retell informational books, kindergartners use language structures found in these books rather than using story-like language (Pappas, 1993).

Children's retellings of both stories and informational text can be analyzed using a *retelling checklist*. Appendix C presents a retelling checklist developed for the book *Owl Moon* (Yolen, 1987). As shown in this checklist, the main ideas and important details found in the story are divided into short phrases, leaving out most descriptive phrases. Teachers note where elements of children's retelling match the events and information on the checklist. Teachers can make note of when children make insightful inferences not included in the checklist or when they include literary language such as similes or metaphors. This indicates an abstract level of comprehension not usually measured in a retelling checklist. Over time, children recall more information from both informational books and storybooks (Pelligrini & Galda, 1982), and their retellings follow the order of events and use the language features as they are presented in the book (Duke & Kays, 1998; Newkirk, 1989; Purcell-Gates, McIntyre, & Freppon, 1995). Children's retellings shift from remembering just a few ideas in random order to recalling many ideas in a well-connected sequence.

The preschool years are a time of vocabulary explosion; children acquire thousands of vocabulary words. The particular vocabulary children acquire is related to their language experiences at home and school (Dickinson & Tabors, 2001). Children whose parents and teachers frequently share books with them develop a larger and more varied vocabulary than children who have little exposure to books (Wells, 1986). Books have more unique words, words that appear infrequently in everyday spoken language. Therefore, books allow children to develop understandings about words they do not hear while listening to television or engaging in everyday conversations. Perhaps because of differences in frequency of book experiences, as early as 3 years of age, children from low-income families have smaller vocabularies than children growing up in middle-class families (Hart & Risley, 1995). Clearly, one of the important tasks of all phases of literacy development is expanding vocabulary—learning new words and new meanings for known words. One preschool teacher had read aloud *Rosie's Walk* (Hutchins, 1968) several times as part of a farm theme with her group of 3- and 4-year-olds. She listened to the children as they talked about the illustrations in the book to determine whether they used vocabulary from it and other books included in the theme. She found some children, but not all, used such words as *chicken coop, hen, beehives, haystack, goat, rake, tines,* and *tractor.* She had used these words when talking about *Rosie's Walk.*

In addition to learning new vocabulary, children also acquire the ability to talk using more sophisticated sentence structures: they use more words in sentences and combine words in more complex structures such as in independent and dependent clauses. Children's *mean length of utterance* (MLU) is the average number of morphemes (roughly equivalent to words) that children use in a thought unit (roughly equivalent to a sentence). A morpheme is a unit of meaning. A word can be one morpheme, such as *happy* or *walk*; but words can have more than one morpheme with the addition of prefixes or suffixes, as in *unhappily* (three morphemes) or *walked* (two morphemes). MLU is a powerful indicator of language sophistication.

A conversation between Leslie, Delores, and Daryl as they played in their preschool Office Center illustrates how MLU and thought units provide a measure of language sophistication. In the transcript (Neuman & Roskos, 1993, p. 111), the thought units are separated by slashes. Daryl is stamping papers while Delores is pretending to write. Leslie picks up the phone:

LESLIE: Cops?/ Come and get Daryl and Delores/ . . . Bye /(Looks at others) Cops comin' to get you and Delores./

DARYL: Uh-uh

LESLIE: Is/

DARYL: Uh-uh

LESLIE: Yes./Yes they IS! /(Picks up telephone receiver).

DELORES: They gonna come get me?/ They gonna come get you 'cuz youse bein' BAD!/

LESLIE: I'm calling the cops on you again./

DARYL: No you aint!

LESLIE: Yes I is./ 1.2.3.4.5.5.6.6.9.9 (Dials some numbers)

In this short conversation Leslie says a total of 30 words (not counting the numbers) in nine thought units. Three of the words (*comin'*, *I'm*, and *calling*) have two morphemes each, making the total number of morphemes 33. The MLU is 3.67 (33 ÷ 9). Delores says fewer words (14) than Leslie; four of them (*gonna, gonna, youse,* and *bein'*) have two morphemes each, for a total of 18 morphemes. However, she combines these words into two sophisticated thought units, so her MLU is 9.0 (18 ÷ 2). Delores's MLU is much longer than Leslie's, reflecting the more complex sentence structure she uses. Different tasks and settings often result in different measures of language sophistication. For example, having children talk about stories or pictures or retell favorite storybooks or familiar informational books may allow them to demonstrate more sophisticated language use.

Teachers can make their own wordless books to use when analyzing children's language and vocabulary development. Richgels (2013) provides photographs that can be used to make such a book with a far-away-and-up-close pattern. He describes using the book as part of Talk, Write, and Read, a method for sampling emergent literacy skills. Teachers explore the wordless book with children, inviting them to identify and talk about the objects in the photographs. For example, they ask, "Oh look, what do you see in this picture from far away?" and for the next page, "Now what can you see up close?" (Richgels, 2013, p. 382). Some children may give only one- or two-word responses even when prompted to tell more. Other children may provide phrases and asides with personal connections while also using sophisticated vocabulary, such as identifying *vans* rather than *cars*.

Name Writing

Among the first printed words that children attend to are their own names. Parents and teachers begin to teach children about their names by writing them on their drawings. Most preschools have prominent displays of children's names and pictures. Children notice the beginning letters of their names in printed signs, and often these are the alphabet letters that children first recognize and write (Justice, Pence, Bowles, & Wiggins, 2006). Children frequently notice words in stories that begin with the same letter as their names. One preschooler insisted that Marcus read with him. When his teacher asked why, he explained, "There's all these words with *M* and Marcus has to be there for his words."

Children's first attempts to write their names often are uncontrolled scribbles. Later they make more controlled scribbles that have some linearity (alignment in a line). Next, they write individual round or angular scribbles, but with little resemblance to actual alphabet letters. Eventually, children pay more attention to letters and notice such features as straight, curved, and diagonal lines that connect in various ways. This coincides with their making letter-like forms called mock letters. Finally they make legible letters. As children gain even more control, their writing shrinks in size, and they pay more attention to the alignment of letters within words. Researchers have used samples of children's name writing to develop a *name writing scale* (Bloodgood, 1999; Hildreth, 1936): (0) no response, (1) scribble, (2) linear scribble, (3) separate units (but no letters formed), (4) mock letters (letter shapes that are not conventional but share some features with actual letters) or a mixture of mock letters and a few conventional letters, (5) first

FIGURE 4.1. Kimberly's signature (first signature in November, second signature in December, third signature in January, last signature 1 week later in January).

name generally correct (although all letter formations may not be well formed or have correct orientation), and (6) consistently well-formed name (smaller-sized letters with good legibility). Figure 4.1 presents Kimberly's signature from November to January of her preschool year. Her signatures demonstrate a common preschool progression of name writing from level 2 to level 5.

Concepts about Print

Being aware of print and exploring it through reading and writing allow children to construct *concepts about print*. These concepts are related to the visual characteristics, features, and properties of written language. Concepts about print can fit broadly into three categories: book handling, directionality, and concepts about letters and words. Book handling refers to understanding how to look at a book and turn pages and knowing the top from the bottom and that print, not illustrations, is what is read in a book. Directionality refers to children's awareness and control of left-page-to-right-page sequencing, left-to-right reading within a line, and return sweeping to begin a new line. Finally, as children develop concepts about letters and words, they distinguish letters from words and recognize words as units of print bordered by spaces. During the phase of awareness most children develop book handling and the beginnings of directionality.

Teachers can learn more about children's concepts about print by using informal measures similar to Clay's (2007) *concept about print assessment*. Earlier we described a teacher-made wordless picture book with far-away and up-close photographs. The "read" portion of the Talk, Write and Read assessment (Richgels, 2013) gives children an opportunity to demonstrate concepts about print using a teacher-made with-text picture book illustrated with the same far-away and up-close photographs. Appendix

B provides instructions for creating another hand-made book for assessing concepts of print, using the familiar song "Itsy Bitsy Spider." Teachers can use these books to ask children to perform book-handling tasks such as "Show me the front of this book. Show me the back. Now point to the top of the book. Now show me the bottom." Other tasks for analyzing children's understandings of book handling and directionality are presented in Appendix B.

As children learn to write their names, they discover many concepts about print and learn about alphabet letters. They become aware that words are composed of alphabet letters written left to right and in a particular order. Figure 4.2 presents 3-year-old Eric's signature. The letter-like forms in his signature are not conventional, but they have some features of conventional alphabet letters. These *mock letters* are found in many children's name-writing attempts. Eric's signature suggests that he does not yet understand several concepts about print: that a signature should have linearity and that each prescribed letter need be written only once. Nonetheless, his name writing demonstrates a growing fine-motor control that has enabled him to produce recognizable letter features.

Older preschool children signal an understanding about directionality when they move their hands below a line of text as they retell a story. *Fingerpoint reading* (retelling a story from memory while pointing at text from left to right and top to bottom) demonstrates children's awareness of the directionality of print. At first, children's ability to track print is very global. They sweep their hands across the lines of text without attempting to point to individual words, or they merely tap at the text. Later, with experience and feedback from a teacher or parent, children attempt to point to each word while reciting a memorized text. Both teacher-made books described above (the with-text far-away-and-up-close picture book [Richgels, 2013] and the "Itsy Bitsy Spider" book [Appendix B]) can be used to analyze children's fingerpoint reading. A teacher reads the book, familiarizing children with the words, so that they can recite them.

FIGURE 4.2. Eric's signature.

Then the teacher demonstrates saying the words while pointing to them. Finally, the teacher asks the child to read by reciting and pointing and notes whether the child makes a word-for-word, spoken-to-written match. Appendix B includes guidelines for assessing children's fingerpoint reading.

Alphabet Recognition

Learning to recognize all the alphabet letters by name and to write them is a major accomplishment of the Awareness and Exploration phase of literacy development. Young children take one, two, or sometimes even more years to master letter naming and writing (Bloodgood, 1999). Many children begin this process as they learn to write their names. Eric's use of mock letters rather than conventional letters in his name writing (see Figure 4.2) demonstrates his attention to features of letters. Features of alphabet letters are what distinguish one letter from another. For example, the only difference between an ɑ and a d is the height of the vertical line. Attention to such features drives children's alphabet learning; they become able to name letters and discriminate between visually similar letters.

There is no particular sequence to alphabet learning. A child often recognizes early on the first letter of his or her name. Children also learn early the letters in other family members' names or in the names of friends. Once children recognize some letters, they use them in writing. However, during Awareness and Exploration, children do not understand the role of alphabet letters in representing sounds in spoken words. Instead they hold many unconventional concepts about the relationship between alphabet letters and messages. For example, at age 3, Tatie, a bilingual Haitian child, hid in her cubby all the plastic and magnetic letter *T*'s from her classroom, presumably because they were *her* letters (Ballenger, 1999).

Alphabet knowledge is usually assessed by presenting children with the upper-case and then the lower-case letters typed in random order on a card (Appendices B and C present directions and scoring sheets for both upper-case and lower-case *alphabet recognition assessments*). In general, children are expected to learn the names of many upper- and some lower-case alphabet letters in preschool, especially the letters in their names. Children who begin kindergarten knowing many of the alphabet letters are at an advantage (Snow et al., 1998). In fact, researchers have shown that at the end of preschool, children who know fewer than 18 upper-case and 15 lower-case letters are at risk for later reading difficulties in first grade (Piasta, Petscher, & Justice, 2012). At the end of kindergarten, children should be able to name quickly and without hesitation all the upper- and lower-case alphabet letters (Adams, 1990).

Another component of alphabet assessment is to determine how well children can write alphabet letters. Teachers name a letter, and children write the letter. Appendix B includes directions for administering this task. Teachers judge whether the letter is similar in form to the expected shape; some orientation problems are acceptable. Teachers can observe whether children are able to write the letters quickly and accurately or confuse letters and have some orientation problems. Children can write letters in either upper- or lower-case.

Phonological and Phonemic Awareness

Phonological awareness includes the ability to pay attention to the sound properties of spoken language apart from its meaning. This ability begins early for some children. Parents of toddlers sometimes comment how their children rock back and forth along with the beat produced by the accented syllables in favorite nursery rhymes. Children as young as 3 memorize parts of favorite nursery rhymes (Maclean, Bryant, & Bradley, 1987). Enjoying and memorizing nursery rhymes may not reflect conscious awareness that words can be segmented into syllables or that words rhyme. However, ability to say a new rhyming word at the end of a rhyming poem indicates conscious awareness of sound units in spoken language (IRA/NAEYC, 1998).

Response to *alliteration* (the presence in words of identical *beginning phonemes*), is evidence of a subcategory of phonological awareness that develops for some children during Awareness and Exploration. This subcategory of phonological awareness is called *phonemic* awareness because its focus is phonemes. One child made up the following chant as she hopped on her neighborhood playground hopscotch grid: "Boogle, bumbum, boo—bee, boogle, bumbum, boo—bee." This child showed her sensitivity to /b/ by making up nonsense words that begin with that phoneme. A more deliberate application of beginning phoneme knowledge—one that is critical for children's later reading and writing achievement but is not yet evident in the Awareness and Exploration phase—is being able to match pictures by beginning phoneme, for example matching pictures of a bat, a balloon, and a book with a picture of a ball rather than with a picture of a telephone. A phonemic awareness achievement that lies between alliterative chanting and beginning phoneme matching and that can occur late in the Awareness and Exploration phase is segmenting (isolating and pronouncing) beginning phonemes, such as saying "/b/" for the word *bat*. Appendix B presents an assessment that can be used to document children's ability to segment 16 high-utility consonant phonemes at the beginning of words.

Appendix B also presents a rhyming assessment. Children may or may not develop rhyming awareness as emergent readers and writers, and rhyme does not need to be taught prior to learning to segment beginning phonemes (McGee & Dail, 2010). At some point children do need to understand the properties of rhyming words in order to become successful first-grade readers and writers. For some children this understanding comes much beyond the Awareness and Exploration stage when they learn the sound patterns of rhyming words by noticing the patterns of their spellings.

Alphabetic Principle: Inventing Spellings, Learning about Letter–Sounds, Acquiring Sight Words

The alphabetic principle refers to the concept that both reading and writing depend on the systematic use of letter–sound correspondences. Most experts agree that a prerequisite to acquiring the alphabetic principle is the ability to segment a single consonant onset in a single-syllable word (e.g., /b/ in *bat*) and to associate that sound with a letter (for example, /b/ with *b*) (Byrne & Fielding-Barnsley, 1991). Most children first demonstrate full attainment of the alphabetic principle in their writing when they attempt to write words by listening carefully to at least one sound in a word and then deliberately selecting a letter to spell that sound. This careful listening to phonemes and selecting of letters to spell them is invented spelling. The letters children select for their invented spellings often are not the same as in conventional spellings, but they are, nonetheless, a good-sense match with sounds. For example, children may spell the word *wagon* with the letter *y* because when they say the letter name for *y*, they hear the sound /w/. Inventive spelling of at least a few words with letter–sound matches is typical of the end of the Awareness and Exploration phase.

Inventing spelling signals another important literacy understanding, concept of written word. After all, what children are attempting to spell are words. Not surprisingly, invented spelling co-occurs with another indicator of concept of word, fingerpoint reading (Morris, 1983). Richgels (2013) includes directions, record sheets, and scoring procedures for using the "write" and "read" components of Talk, Write, and Read to sample children's invented spellings and their fingerpoint reading as they first spell words to fill blanks in the with-text version of a teacher-made picture book and then reread the book.

Text Writing

Writing during the phase of Awareness and Exploration often is representational. That is, children intend to draw a person, and what they draw looks like a person. Early *representational drawings* of people usually consist of a big round circle for a head with lines radiating off the circle for arms and legs, a figure often called a tad-pole. Children's ability to make representational drawings is related to their growing awareness that pictures in books are representations rather than merely interesting shapes, colors, and lines (Wu, 2009). As children gain control over the basic lines and shapes (up and down, across, diagonal, and around, for example), they become better at adding details to their drawings. At this time, they begin making letter-like shapes (Kellogg, 1969). That is, emergent writers may draw a person and add letter-like shapes or cursive-like scribbles to tell the story of their pictures. At other times, emergent writers may just make marks on paper, exploring the kinds of lines a new set of markers may make, rather than making a representational drawing or intending to write a story.

Figure 4.3 presents 3-year-old Marie's self-portrait and signature. Her drawing is easily distinguished from her writing. As she was writing, her teacher observed that she was making the linear mock cursive, moving from left to right and thus demonstrating her awareness of directionality. When asked to read her writing, Marie replied, "It says Marie." Marie's writing and reading of her writing demonstrate the important concept of *intentionality*. She intended to write, and she intended her writing to say something. Teachers can sample children's text writing by asking them to draw pictures of and write about themselves (McGill-Franzen, 2006). Appendix B presents a rubric for analyzing such drawing and writing.

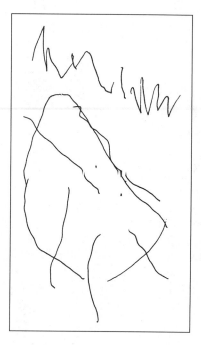

FIGURE 4.3. Marie's self-portrait and signature.

EXPERIMENTING READERS AND WRITERS

With supportive home and classroom activities, children gradually begin to operate with print in more sophisticated ways that suggest a new level of conceptual understanding about written language. Teachers will notice that children show increased involvement in literacy activities by frequently pretending to read and write during play, answering questions and making comments more readily and more frequently during book read-alouds, and attempting to fingerpoint read familiar texts with nearly one-to-one, spoken-to-written word matching. This new level of engagement and attention usually indicates that children are moving into the phase of Experimental Reading and Writing. Table 4.1 presents an overview of what is expected to emerge in the Experimental Reading and Writing phase of development.

The Experimental Reading and Writing phase of literacy development is similar to what we have described elsewhere, also using the word *experiment* (McGee & Richgels, 2000). We have argued that the key to experimenting is an even keener awareness than in the previous phase. Now young readers and writers are not only aware of literacy around them, but know more about the processes of reading and writing: they know letters and words are important and they can recognize and write most letters (the alphabet recognition assessment would provide information about which few letters these children need to learn). They know about the directionality of print (left to right and top to bottom), and they realize that what readers say as they read has some relationship to the print on the page (fingerpoint reading assessments will continue to be useful to determine how close children are coming to one-to-one fingerpointing).

Oral Comprehension and Vocabulary Development

Experimenting readers and writers, because of their experiences with constructing meaning from books during Awareness and Exploration, can construct more complex understandings and produce more detailed retellings of stories and informational books. They begin to employ a wider range of strategies for understanding what is read aloud to them, including asking questions, making inferences, noticing details in texts and illustrations, predicting, and connecting book information with their lives or with other books. They also develop a keen interest in new and interesting words, especially when their teachers highlight words during book read-alouds. Retelling checklists and the *talk* component of the Talk, Write, and Read assessment continue to provide critical assessment information.

Concept of Written Words and Learning Sight Words

Experimenting readers develop a fine-tuned sense of directionality, and when they fingerpoint read, they deliberately and carefully attempt to point to one written word for each word they say. As children deliberately point to each word in a printed text, they demonstrate an awareness of how words are marked—with spaces. Early on children miscalculate how to point when spoken words have more than one syllable and may use the ends of text lines to self-correct. This self-correcting is an early form of monitoring that will come into play more critically as children begin to read conventionally.

In order to reach this level of understanding about print, children must memorize small bits of text. This is a simple task for children who have had numerous experiences with pattern books that have repeated words and phrases. As experimenters frequently reread *Silly Sally* (Wood, 1999), for example, they see the word *went* and hear themselves say "went" dozens of times. They gradually realize that the written word *went* coincides with the spoken word "went." Thus, children acquire *sight words*. Sight words are words that children recognize and can say immediately upon seeing them, without using memory of an entire text. Children recognize sight words even when they are taken out of familiar context. Although experimenting readers and writers do not acquire many sight words, their ability to read some words in a conventional manner indicates their growing sophistication with written language. Teachers may want to use a list of high-frequency words found on the Internet to track children's acquisition of sight words. Appendix B provides a sample list. Another assessment teachers may want to consider is to ask a child to write all the words he or she knows how to spell, starting with his or her name (Clay, 2002). This *word writing task* allows teachers to track children's known spellings.

Phonemic Awareness and Inventing Spellings

Children in the Experimental Reading and Writing phase have an increased awareness of phonemes as shown by their ability to manipulate small sound units in spoken words. For example, when asked to say the first sound in the word *Bob,* they say "/b/." Most children acquire this level of phonemic awareness because their teachers have provided playful games and activities that draw attention to sounds in words. Teachers may carefully elongate beginning sounds in words that begin with continuants, that is, sounds whose pronunciations can be prolonged. For example, they may emphasize the continuant /m/ at the beginning of *Marcel* by saying "Mmmmmmmmarcel." Teachers may emphasize stop consonants, sounds whose pronunciations cannot be prolonged, by popping those sounds at the beginning of a word, for example, emphasizing /t/ by saying, "T-T-T-T'quele."

Children in the Experimental Reading and Writing phase also learn to match reliably a phoneme with the conventional letter that spells it. For example, children who have had many opportunities to see their teacher or parents write the words *boy, baby,* and *birthday* eventually realize that the letter *b* that appears at the beginning of those written words is related to the /b/ phoneme that they hear their teacher pop at the beginning of the spoken words. Some children easily discover letter–sound relationships because their teachers frequently write words, say their beginning sounds with either elongation or popping, and then tell children what letters spell those sounds. Other children notice that many letter names include the phoneme associated with that letter (for example, the letter *d*'s name, "dee," begins with /d/). Other children need to have teachers point out these relationships during shared writing and during small group instruction that focuses on phonemic awareness. We suggest that teachers assess whether children know the sounds of high-utility consonants (*b, c, d, f, g, h, j, k, l, m, n, p, r, s, t, v,* and *w*) by adding to alphabet recognition assessment an invitation to say the sounds that these letters make. Appendix B includes a description of a task for determining which of these consonants children are able to identify by sound.

Once children learn several consonant sounds, teachers can introduce them to word building from familiar rhyming words. A new word *sat* can be spelled using part of the spelling of the familiar rhyming word *cat,* that is, by removing the onset *c* and adding a new onset *s* to the rime *at.* (The onset is all the sounds before a syllable's first vowel; the rime is the first vowel and following sounds.) Teachers can invite children to play other games that tap different types of phonemic awareness. They may say words divided between their onsets and rimes, for example, "p-ay," "pl-ay," or even "spr-ay." Then children guess the word. When children become familiar with hearing words divided this way, they can be invited to divide the words themselves, saying the onsets and the rimes. Appendix B presents an assessment of the high-level phonemic awareness skill of segmenting words by their onsets and rimes.

Children's increasing sophistication in phonemic awareness and knowledge of consonant letter sounds influence their spelling. At the beginning of the experimenting phase, children may only hear one phoneme for a word and so spell the word with a single letter. For example, Kyung wrote, "My favorite ride is the roller coaster" (presented in Figure 4.4). His writing does include many sound–letter matches (*m* for *my, f* for *favorite, z* for *is,* and *r* for *roller coaster*). However, Kyung ignores word spaces, only spells one of the most salient phonemes for each word, and includes many letters that are merely *place holders* (they do not represent sounds in the words). Nonetheless, with practice, experimenting writers' invented spellings will expand as they represent boundary phonemes (first and last sounds in words).

FIGURE 4.4. "My favorite ride is the roller coaster." M (my) fREtf (favorite) RT (ride) Z (is) RDEf (the) RKHCDR (roller coaster).

Teachers can assess children's growing sophistication in spelling using the "write" portion of the Talk, Write and Read assessment (Richgels, 2013), which has the advantage of occurring during the experience of reading a picture book with predictable text. Children's invented spelling can also be assessed with an activity presented as a game whose goal is not correct spelling but rather to see how many letters children can use to spell each word (Bear, Invernizzi, Templeton, & Johnston, 2008). Teachers can analyze spellings for word parts represented, including initial consonants, final consonants, and vowels (at a later phase of development this assessment taps children's ability to use blends, digraphs, and long-vowel markers). Talk, Write, and Read targets the words *car, boat, sign, bus, duck, bench, flag,* and *train* and provides sample invented spellings and scores. Appendix B includes a spelling assessment with the words *bud, ham, jet, fin, log, note, skip, train, sheep,* and *chair.* Children may spell these words with random letters, indicating they know that words have letters but not which letters match with sounds in words. Alternatively, children might spell a word with some consonant letters in initial or final positions, indicating a beginning ability to hear sounds in words and use sound–letter knowledge to spell some parts of the word. Sometimes children produce spellings using the expected, *conventional* letters (for example, spelling the word *fan* with an *f*). However, with early invented spellings, many children spell words with letters that have reasonable but unconventional relationships to phonemes (such as spelling the word *wagon* with a *y*).

Early Text Reading

Early in the Experimental Reading and Writing phase, experimenters benefit from fingerpoint reading. When children fingerpoint read, they already know the words of the text because it is memorized and are merely trying to match what they say with the words. This early form of reading allows children to fine-tune their one-to-one, speech-to-print matching and to learn a few sight words. However, as experimenting readers gain a few sight words and learn several consonant letter–sound matches, they can benefit from their one-to-one matching of print and awareness of spaces between words by reading new text rather than memorized text. That is, these children are almost conventional readers (McGill-Franzen, 2006). Experimenting readers with good one-to-one matching and use of some sight words can read highly patterned little books. These little books have only one or two lines of text per page, and most words are repeated in a predictable pattern. The illustrations are closely related to the text. For example two pages from a highly patterned text might be:

> Page 1: The girl likes to run.
> Page 2: The girl likes to jump.

Experimenters are likely to know the words *the* and *to* and will learn the word *likes*. They could figure out the words *girl* and *run* or *jump* using picture clues and first letters. All children are expected to read books like these by the end of their kindergarten year. Teachers can analyze children's reading of predictable, patterned texts by taking running records of easy books read only one time previously (this assessment will be described in more detail when we discuss the Early Reading and Writing phase of reading). Many kindergartners go beyond reading level 1 or 2 texts to being able to read at levels 3, 4, 5, or even higher, that is, at beginning-of-first-grade levels. Reading texts beyond level 3 and spelling with vowels and consonant blends indicate performance beyond the experiemental phase.

Text Writing

Experimenting writers are capable of writing text that is more conventional because they can use invented spelling. However, not all experimenting writers will use invented spelling, especially when they compose stories that are personally important. When the story is long and exciting, it is too difficult to focus on spelling words one by one. So then experimenters often return to earlier strategies of writing with random letters

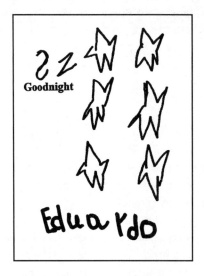

FIGURE 4.5. Eduardo spells *stars*.

or mock cursive. As they gain more experience and knowledge about consonant letter matches, they can write labels for pictures and later one short sentence per picture. Figure 4.5 presents Eduardo's drawing and writing in response to the book *Goodnight Moon* (Brown, 1947). He drew stars and labeled his picture with the invented spelling *sz* for stars, indicating that he can segment first and last phonemes (boundary phonemes) and match them with letters. Even though the word *stars* ends with the conventional letter *s*, its sound matches with the letter *z*, which Eduardo uses.

READERS AND WRITERS

We do not expect all children to reach the Early Reading and Writing phase (conventional, first-grade-level reading and writing) before they enter first grade (and some struggle to do so even in the course of first grade). Nonetheless, many children will begin the Early Reading and Writing phase near the end of kindergarten, thus achieving above grade level. We discuss what children will do as they enter this phase in literacy development. Some 7-year-olds may be characterized as conventional, first-grade-level readers, just as some 5-year-olds may be; all that matters is that their abilities and performances are characteristic of the benchmarks of this phase. Table 4.1 presents an overview of the outcomes expected of conventional readers and writers in the Early Reading and Writing phase.

Phonemic Awareness, Decoding, and Spelling

Conventional, first-grade-level writers are proficient at using consonant letter–sounds. They learn to decode and spell short vowels, especially in frequently occurring, familiar word families. For example, they know the short -*a* sound in the *ad*, *an*, and *at* families (see Appendix A for more information about these elements of phonics and for a phoneme pronunciation key). Their spellings reflect an awareness that every word includes a vowel, although the vowel they use in spelling may be unconventional. As shown in Figure 4.6, Ryan wrote, "Jim gave the giant a wig" in response to *Jim and the Beanstalk* (Briggs, 1970); he spelled the word *wig* as *weg*. Notice that Ryan has control over word spaces, and in addition to inventing spellings, he uses conventional spellings for high-frequency words. He spells the short -*i* sound with the letter *e* because he notices the similarity in articulation when saying that sound and saying the name of the letter *e* (the shape of the mouth and the amount of tension in the voice are the same for both). Spelling at this level is called *alphabetic spelling* (Bear, Invernizzi, Templeton, & Johnston, 2000). Children who spell alphabetically include a letter for every phoneme in simple words, as Ryan did. Such spellings are called *fully phonemic* because the complete phonemic structure of the word is represented. Children who can construct fully phonemic spellings are also likely to use *fully phonemic decoding* when reading; they decode a written word by producing a phoneme for each letter or letter combination. Fully phonemic spelling and decoding require a high level of phonemic awareness: children must be able to segment and blend three- or four-phoneme words including words beginning with continuant consonants (easiest to segment), single-stop consonants (moderately easy),

FIGURE 4.6. "Jim gave the giant a wig."

and consonant blends (most difficult). Appendix B includes an assessment of children's ability to segment two- and three-phoneme words.

Text Reading

Conventional, first-grade-level readers are more prolific and fluent than are experimenting readers. They have acquired a sufficient number of *sight words* (words read automatically, on sight, without sounding out or otherwise deliberately analyzing) so that they can read many easy-reading texts. Most of such sight words are *high-frequency words*—words such as *the, was, are,* and *can* that appear frequently in all texts. Texts for early reading instruction have many high-frequency words, words that are repeated, and words that children are capable of decoding. *Decodable words* use expected relationships between letters and sounds (see Appendix A, "A Primer on Phonics for Teachers"). As children read and reread these texts with the support of their teacher, they acquire several hundred sight words (teachers can track children's sight word knowledge using a *high-frequency word list* such as the one found in Appendix B). They become more fluent in decoding words and using comprehension strategies such as predicting, asking questions, and rereading.

For example, consider the easy text *Danny and the Dinosaur* (Hoff, 1958), which has long been a favorite. Page 18 of this book presents an illustration of Danny riding on the neck of his friend, a dinosaur. The text is

> "Bow wow!" said a dog,
> running after them.
> "He thinks you are a car,"
> said Danny. "Go away, dog.
> We are not a car."

In order to read this text successfully, children must know many of its words by sight, including *said, a, after, them, He, you, Go, We,* and *not. Bow wow* may be decodable if children know the sight word *how,* use what they know about this word, and apply sound–letter correspondences. Context will help with the words *dog* and *car;* most readers know that what says "bow wow" is a dog, and many readers know that what dogs sometimes bark at is cars. Knowledge of word structure may help with decoding the word *running;* readers may notice the word part *run,* recognize it as a sight word, and also recognize *-ing* as a common, readable word ending. Children in the Early Reading and Writing phase can read books leveled for difficulty for first graders. They read with accuracy, understanding, and fluency.

The assessment most commonly used to document such reading is the *running record.* A running record is a recording of the miscues that children make as they read. Using a copy of the text the child is attempting to read, the teacher writes words that children substitute (for example, reading "yard" for *garden*), omit, or insert. Teachers also note children's decoding attempts (attempting to read *garden* by saying /j/ for the beginning letter *g*). Teachers note when children self-correct their miscues, and self-corrected words are not counted as miscues. After reading, teachers ask children questions in order to assess comprehension. Then, teachers calculate the *accuracy rate:* the percentage of words read correctly (determined by subtracting the number of miscues from the total number of words in the passage and dividing this number by the total number of words). Finally, teachers determine the level of comprehension by calculating the percentage of questions answered correctly. When books are read at the independent level, children can read the words with 98% or better accuracy and answer 90% or more of the comprehension questions. At the instructional level, children read words with 90–95% accuracy and answer 70–90% of the questions. Texts read with less than 90% accuracy and 70% comprehension are considered at the frustration level. Running records can be used on any text that children are capable of reading.

Text Writing

Conventional first-grade-level writers can produce a coherent text that is two or three sentences or longer. They use conventional spellings and invented spellings, and they search for spellings using resources in the classroom, including books and word displays on classroom walls. Ryan wrote only one sentence in response to *Jack and the Beanstalk* (Briggs, 1970; see Figure 4.6), but his picture and sentence capture the essence of that story. Conventional, first-grade-level writers often produce other kinds of texts, including informational texts and descriptions. Figure 4.7 presents a complex plan for making an incubator produced by two kindergartners. This list reads: bolt 2 inches, nut 2 inches, 3 light bulbs, 18 inches plastic cover with holes, stand, wire 10 inches, all clear, 3 inches screws, cotton fluff. The only idea out of sequence is their comment about "all clear," which was intended to go with the plastic cover. The text includes many conventionally spelled words (*bolt, inches, holes, stand, all clear,* and *screws*) along with several sophisticated invented spellings (*nt* for *nut, pltk* for *plastic,* and *wyr* for *wire*). Teachers may want to assess children's growing knowledge of conventional spelling with the 10-minute writing words assessment in Appendix B.

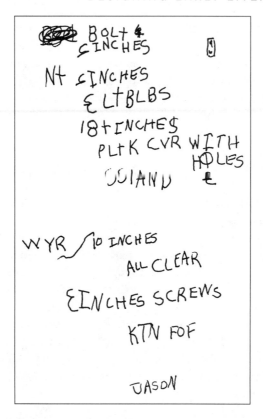

FIGURE 4.7. Jason's and Freddy's plans for making an incubator. From Richgels (2002, p. 592). Copyright 2002 by the International Reading Association. All rights reserved. Reprinted by permission.

THE LITERACY CONTINUUM REVISITED

Children acquire dozens of benchmark concepts as they progress through the phases of emergent readers and writers, experimenting readers and inventive spellers, and conventional, first-grade-level readers and writers. However, this progress is not accomplished in a lockstep manner. We know that later concepts arise from earlier concepts, but not all children acquire all the benchmark concepts we have described. Instead, acquisition of a critical mass of concepts within one phase seems to facilitate taking on the challenges of the next phase.

Overlap from One Phase to Another

We hope that our descriptions of the early phases of literacy development show that they are not discrete; rather, one phase overlaps with the next. In both the Awareness and Exploration and the Experimental Reading and Writing phases, for example, children are expected to develop rudimentary forms of phonemic awareness. Likewise, in both the Experimental Reading and Writing and the Early Reading and Writing phases, children are expected to acquire knowledge of sound–letter correspondences and some sight words. Development of sound–letter correspondences and fluency in word reading from the earlier to the later phase is a matter of degree. It is important to remember, too, that development is elastic; children will move back and forth between neighboring phases, influenced by the amount of support they receive in a reading or writing event and by such other factors as their purposes and the number of other, competing demands on their effort and attention.

The Importance of Assessment for Accelerating Learning

Assessment is especially important to sound instructional decision making. Children from diverse backgrounds are likely to come to preschool or kindergarten with diverse understandings about the nature of print and its use. All children's understandings are products of their family and cultural experiences. Early developing concepts are likely to be nonconventional. For example, Tatie (mentioned earlier in the chapter), walked around her classroom making the shape of the letter *T* with two fingers. When her teacher asked her what she was doing, she replied, "That's me" (Ballenger, 1999, p. 45). While Tatie did not seem to know the name of the alphabet letter *T* nor its function of representing the sound /t/, she did demonstrate an awareness that letters have something to do with meanings. Identifying unconventional, not fully developed concepts such as Tatie's is an important starting point for planning classroom experiences that will make sense to children.

Issues of Appropriateness, Reliability, and Validity

As important as assessment is for instructional decision making, it can be tricky. Children ages 3–5 are still in the early stages of language development and may have difficulty understanding directions and expressing what they know. Thus, assessments of young children may not be highly reliable; the results may not reflect what the children actually know.

Consider the challenges of assessing Tatie's understanding of alphabet letters. Imagine giving her a sheet of paper with all the alphabet letters printed in random order and asking her to name the letters. This alphabet letter identification task has been used frequently with young children and is considered a valid assessment of early literacy. In fact, children's knowledge of alphabet letters before entering school is related to their reading at the end of first grade (National Early Literacy Panel, 2008). What might Tatie do when presented with this assessment task? Suppose she merely shrugs her shoulders? Does this mean that she does not have a concept of alphabet letters or that she does not understand the task? We already have seen that Tatie does have some concept of alphabet letters, so using the alphabet letter identification task alone, although valid, would not be a very reliable assessment of Tatie's early literacy concepts.

As teachers assess individual children, the best practice is to form tentative conclusions about children's literacy awareness and then refining those conclusions with multiple additional assessments. Teachers who wish to make the best analyses of children's current levels of development and record their growth over time combine observation of naturally occurring classroom events with administration of specially devised assessments like those presented in Appendix B.

EFFECTIVE ASSESSMENT PRACTICES

Effective teachers continually observe the relationship between the nature of classroom events and children's responses during those events in order to adjust their minute-by-minute interactions with particular children. However, in order to be most powerful, assessment should be more systematic than the informal observations teachers normally make as they interact with children. Assessment is most effective in helping teachers make instructional decisions when it is systematic, when it is guided by knowledge of a broad overview of literacy development such as we have provided in this chapter, and when it is used to make plans for future instruction and classroom adaptations.

Developing a Systematic Assessment Plan

Systematic assessments are planned to meet specific objectives; teachers have in mind particular literacy concepts that must be assessed, such as the benchmark concepts described in Table 4.1. Once they decide which concepts to assess, teachers select a valid and reliable method of assessment that provides the best information about children's development of those concepts. Finally, teachers schedule assessments to make sure information is gathered in a timely manner.

Teachers might want to schedule particular assessments early in the year, again at midpoint, and then toward the end of the year. For example, using a name-writing scale to analyze children's signatures (Villaume & Wilson, 1989) at the beginning of preschool provides information about several literacy concepts that then can be used to plan more responsive instruction and classroom activities for 3- and 4-year-olds. In addition, teachers might want to plan observations of naturally occurring classroom events once a month for each child. Perhaps these observations would be taken on Tuesday. The first week of the month the teacher would designate four or five children for observation. During center time, the teacher could observe each child for approximately 8–10 minutes. During the second, third, and fourth Tuesdays of the month, other children would be designated for observation. So by the end of the month, all the children would have been observed and the cycle could resume again.

Observations that guide instructional decisions and reflect children's growth over time require detail, accuracy, and objectivity (Rhodes & Nathenson-Mejia, 1992). Teachers write anecdotal records about children's language and behaviors without making inferences about children's thoughts or about what their behaviors might mean. These records allow teachers, parents, and others even months later to know what children were doing and saying. Anecdotal records use the fewest possible words to describe the classroom setting of an event and the children's critical actions; they use as many of the children's words as possible.

Figure 4.8 presents one teacher's anecdotal records about a play event that occurred in the Home Living Center as three children pretended to go grocery shopping in the

Jamie, Mary, and Tomika are playing in the Home Living Center. Jamie says, "I need some milk and eggs and bread and cookies." He gathers packages of food from the Home Living Center and writes a list. Mary says she's going shopping, too. She writes a list and says, "I'll buy candy." She gets a cart and goes to the Grocery Store Center. Tomika writes a list. She takes her list and gets a cart.

Jamie's grocery list and the teacher's reflection.

LIPTON
FRIDS
CAMAT

Jamie recognizes that print communicates specific messages related to the activity. He uses a strategy of thinking about what could be bought at a grocery store to plan what he intends to write. His strategy for writing is to select printed words from familiar food items to copy onto the list. However, he does not match the words that he says he will write with the words he does write. His writing demonstrates awareness of directionality and linearity, list format, words as composed of groups of letters, and recognizable (although not perfect) upper-case alphabet letter formats.

Mary's grocery list and the teacher's reflection.

Mary recognizes that print communicates messages and uses her knowledge of food items in a grocery store to assign meaning to her writing after she has written. Her writing demonstrates awareness that writing consists of discrete symbols. No conventional letter formats are discernable although the number 5 is included.

Tomika's grocery list and the teacher's reflection.

Tomika is willing to join in the activity of writing with other children. She knows that writing carries a message, but does not use her knowledge of grocery items to assign a specific message to her writing. Her writing consists one line of linear mock cursive.

FIGURE 4.8. Anecdotal records of observation at the Home Living and Grocery Centers.

nearby grocery store Dramatic Play Center. The anecdotal records describe the setting and the three children's behavior and language as the teacher observed them play. Later, the teacher gathered the three children's writing samples (also shown in Figure 4.8) and placed them along with copies of her anecdotal records in the three children's assessment files.

It is at this point that the teacher makes inferences about the significance of each of the children's language, behaviors, and writing—not as part of making the anecdotal record, but rather as part of reflecting about the record and related artifacts. This is when the teacher can make inferences about underlying cognitive strategies and understandings (Clay, 1998). The teacher's reflections shown in Figure 4.8 include tentative hypotheses that are about specific documented language and behaviors of the children and that are consistent with what she knows in general about children's literacy development. Finally, the teacher places her written reflection for each child in an assessment notebook.

Using Insights to Plan Responsive Instruction

Once teachers have written tentative hypotheses about their students' literacy concepts, they make decisions about instructional activities that will provide children with opportunities to push forward. Teachers consider how to use what children already know to provide bridges for the development of more complex concepts. They consider adjustments in current instructional activities, changes in materials and activities for particular centers, or alterations in classroom routines. They may decide to prepare particular instructional activities for some children or to spend a few minutes each day with one or two children in a particular center. For example, after observing Jamie, Mary, and Tomika play in the Grocery Store Center, their teacher decided that Jamie and a few other children would benefit from fingerpoint reading to expand awareness of written words and to strengthen understanding of the relationship between spoken and written words. She decided to spend time with Mary and Tomika as they wrote their names for morning sign-in to support their attention to linearity and conventional letter features and formation.

CHAPTER SUMMARY

In this chapter, we have given an overview of literacy development using the first three phases of the IRA/NAEYC's (1998) continuum: Awareness and Exploration, Experimental Reading and Writing, and Early Reading and Writing. In the phase of Awareness and Exploration, children turn conscious attention to print. They acquire concepts about print such as linearity and directionality. They learn to write their names and recognize and write alphabet letters. They develop early phonological awareness through playing games with rhyming words and alliteration. They learn to listen to and talk about books that are read aloud to them. They construct understandings about a variety of kinds of books and print in the environment and begin developing a concept about story. Their vocabulary grows as they acquire understandings of new words through their experiences, including experiences with books. As experimenting readers and writers, children develop a concept about written words and acquire the alphabetic principle. They discover sound–letter correspondences and use them to invent spellings. They use fingerpoint reading to acquire a few sight words. Children in the Early Reading and Writing phase use sight words to read easy text conventionally, and they use knowledge of more sophisticated sound–letter correspondences to decode unknown words. They write using conventional spellings of some words, and they show understandings about vowels and awareness of the complete phonemic structure of words. As these phases of literacy development suggest, learning to read and write is a gradual process requiring the orchestration of many foundational concepts. Effective teachers use a combination of specially selected assessment tasks (such as those presented in Appendix B) and systematic classroom observation to make hypotheses about individual children's literacy growth. They write clear and precise anecdotal records and later write reflections on what the observations suggest about children's literacy knowledge and development. They use these to plan more responsive instructional activities for individual children.

CHAPTER 5

Using Assessment to Plan Differentiated Instruction

In this chapter we describe how to use assessment data to make decisions about differentiated instruction for children at varying levels of literacy development. We discuss how to analyze the results of a broad array of assessments in order to make instructional decisions for individuals and groups of children. First, we present information about screening assessments and why teachers would want to use them. We describe popular standardized screening assessments used in preschool and kindergarten and provide information about ranges of benchmark scores that have been calculated for these measures to determine whether children are at risk or on target for later successful reading and writing.

Then we compare the standardized screening measures and benchmark scores to the continuum of literacy development and assessments we laid out in Chapter 4. Using the information from Chapter 4 about the variety of levels in literacy development expected in preschool and kindergarten, we consider how to interpret the results of assessments in order to make decisions about appropriate instructional activities.

We describe how to select children for small-group instruction and to determine which domains of literacy to target for instruction. In the meantime, this instruction is embedded in classrooms rich in exploration of content topics (such as described in Chapters 2 and 3). Within such classrooms, children have ample opportunities to listen to and talk about stories and informational texts and other media in whole-class groups and in center time. They study and explore interesting topics, such as mammals, reptiles, insects, history, and plants. They have experiences with dramatic play related to the curriculum and engage with their teachers and other children in pretend play. They have opportunities to engage in music, movement, art, and cooking experiences and observe their teachers write on shared writing charts as a part of gathering information and communicating that information to others both inside and outside the classroom.

The majority of their classroom experiences consist of these engaging and intellectually rich activities.

Within the context of such exemplary classrooms, at-risk children often still need the added value of small-group literacy instruction that is targeted specifically to their strengths and needs. Children who are the most at risk for reading and writing failure need the best and most intensive, differentiated instruction teachers can provide in order to accelerate their learning and close the gap with their peers who are on track for success. They may need small-group instruction that is supplemental to the normal, ongoing, small-group lessons provided to all children. The focus of this chapter is analysis of assessment data for the purpose of planning small-group instruction—both ongoing small-group lessons planned for all children and supplemental lessons planned for children considered more at risk. Thus, we consider small-group instruction both as part of good classroom teaching (Tier 1 instruction) and as part of more intensive, supplemental intervention (Tier 2 instruction).

IDENTIFYING CHILDREN NEEDING ADDITIONAL SUPPORT IN DEVELOPING EARLY LITERACY

The National Early Literacy Panel (2008) demonstrated that skills in alphabet knowledge, print concepts, phonological awareness, and vocabulary and syntax (oral language) measured in preschool or kindergarten predicted children's later elementary school reading outcomes in both decoding and comprehension. Other studies have shown that children with high levels of literacy knowledge in preschool and kindergarten continue to display high levels of reading achievement in elementary school (Storch & Whitehurst, 2002). Note that low levels of early literacy knowledge do not necessarily mean that children will become struggling readers. They, too, can become successful readers and writers, but usually only if they have more opportunities to learn and practice in supplemental, small-group instruction.

Certainly children bring to preschool and kindergarten varying literacy experiences and diverse concepts about reading and writing. Many children begin kindergarten equipped by literacy knowledge gained in preschool to succeed in kindergarten. Other children may begin kindergarten with very low levels of literacy knowledge. Still others may not make sufficient progress in preschool or kindergarten despite good classroom instruction. All children should have access to small-group instruction in preschool and kindergarten. Children entering kindergarten who are identified as at risk by their low levels of knowledge or by their lack of progress need additional small-group instruction. All children benefit from careful observation and assessment that pinpoint their instructional needs. Teachers may make informal observations during classroom activities or more careful and systematic observations as part of targeted assessment tools, or they may administer standardized screening assessments (Lonigan, Allan, & Lerner, 2011). Screening instruments are typically brief and intended to provide a snapshot of children's current literacy knowledge rather than a broader or more in-depth picture. They are used to determine which children are performing as expected in literacy development and which relatively poorly.

Screening Assessments

Three standardized screening assessments can be used in preschool. The Get Ready to Read! Revised Screening Tool (GRTR-R; Whitehurst & Lonigan, 2002; Lonigan & Wilson, 2008), a short, 25-item assessment, primarily targets print knowledge and phonological awareness. Individual Growth and Development Indicators (IDGIs; McConnell, 2002) measures alliteration, rhyming, and picture naming (oral language). These two assessments are quickly administered to individual children and provide indications of whether they are performing with generally good or generally poor early literacy skills. They do not provide specific information about the wide range of specific components of early literacy with which children may have difficulty (Lonigan et al., 2011). In contrast, the Phonological Awareness Literacy Screening—PreK (PALS-PK) takes longer to administer. It assesses a wide array of literacy skills, including name writing, alphabet knowledge, beginning sound awareness, rhyme awareness, and nursery rhyme awareness. It identifies children's specific literacy needs and strengths and can be used to identify both children who are on target for success and those who are at risk.

Two screening tools are widely used in kindergarten: Dynamic Indicators of Basic Early Literacy Skills (DIBELS; Good & Kaminski, 2005) and Phonological Awareness Literacy Screening—Kindergarten (PALS-K; Invernizzi, Justice, Landrum, & Booker, 2004–2005). DIBELS assesses kindergartners' knowledge of initial sounds (saying the beginning sounds of words and matching words to beginning sounds), upper- and lower-case letter naming, phoneme segmentation (with two- to five-phoneme words), and nonsense word deciphering. DIBELS provides information about whether children are performing generally well or generally poorly, but because of its short duration (1 minute for each of the tasks) and limited domains, it does little to help teachers identify specific instructional needs. In contrast, PALS-K takes 25–30 minutes to administer and includes assessment of rhyme, beginning sounds, alphabet recognition, letter–sounds, spelling, concept of word (fingerpoint reading and locating words in text), and sight word reading. It provides information about children who are at risk as well as on target for success and specific information about components of early literacy that need targeted instruction.

Some screening instruments, such as the GRTR-R and DIBELS, can identify children likely to need further support. However, teachers need to perform diagnostic assessments if they wish to determine which among the broad array of skills and knowledge in early literacy are strengths and weaknesses of individual children. Diagnostic assessments take longer to administer but provide more in-depth information. PALS-K and PALS-PK can be used both as screening and diagnostic assessments. The assessments provided in Appendix B and *Talk, Write, and Read* (Richgels, 2013) that are described in Chapter 4 can also be used both as screening and diagnostic assessments.

Benchmarks That Point to Success or Likely Failure in Later Reading and Writing

All screening instruments have benchmark scores or ranges of scores. Often they provide two benchmarks. A score at or above the higher benchmark usually indicates children are likely not to experience any difficulty later in learning to read and write. A score at or below the lower of the two benchmarks usually predicts difficulty in further learning (Invernizzi et al., 2004–2005). The goal is that all children reach the benchmarks indicating probable success, and differentiated instruction is warranted for children who have not yet reached those benchmarks. Children who score below the benchmarks indicating risk are likely to need additional, supplemental, small-group instruction.

PALS-PK's high- and low-end benchmarks for end of preschool are shown in Table 5.1. They indicate as risk factors knowing fewer than 9 of 26 lower-case letters, 4 of 26 letter–sounds, 5 of 10 beginning sounds, and 5 of 10 rhyming matches. PALS-K provides for kindergartners only an overall at-risk benchmark of 28 for the summed total score. An analysis of the performances of entering kindergartners who scored at or below 28 (17,792 children out of 83,099 children who took the assessment) yielded mean scores of 5 of 26 lower-case letters, 1 out of 26 letter–sounds, 4 of 10 beginning sounds, and 5 of 10 rhyming matches. Most of these children did not attempt to spell words or read words. Notice that three of these means are lower than the at-risk benchmark scores for end of preschool, so performance at these means probably indicates very high risk for entering kindergartners. Certainly, scores by entering kindergartners that are higher than these means, but at or lower than the end-of-preschool at-risk benchmarks, would still indicate risk.

The state of Wisconsin requires all kindergarten teachers to assess children with the PALS-K at midyear and has set statewide benchmarks (*www.palswisconsin.info/faqs. shtml*). These are also provided in Table 5.1. Notice that the at-risk indicators for mid-kindergarten are much higher than those for end-of-preschool (and so also would be much higher than for beginning-of-year kindergarten). Midyear kindergartners who know fewer than 23 lower-case letters (compared to 9 at the end of preschool) and fewer

TABLE 5.1. PALS-PK End-of-Year and PALS-K Midyear Benchmarks Indicating At Risk Compared to No Risk

Benchmarks	At risk	No risk
Preschool end-of-year benchmarks: PALS-PK		
Upper-case recognition (26)	<12	>21
Lower-case recognition (26)	<9	>17
Letter–sounds (26)	<4	>8
Beginning sounds (10)	<5	>8
Print awareness (10)	<7	>9
Rhyme (10)	<5	>7
Kindergarten midyear benchmarks: PALS-K (Wisconsin)		
Lower-case recognition (26)	<23	26
Letter–sounds (26)	<17	26
Beginning sounds (10)	<9	10
Rhyme (10)	<9	10
Spelling (20)	<10	20
Word list (20)	<3	>10

than 17 letter sounds (compared to 4 at the end of preschool) are considered at risk in Wisconsin.

DIBELS also provides high- and low-end benchmarks at the beginning, middle, and end of kindergarten (see Table 5.2). Only letter-naming speed (number of upper- and lower-case letters identified within 1 minute) is given all three times. Initial-sound identification (number of first sounds identified in 1 minute) is given in the fall and at midyear, where it is expected to be established (only children who do not reach the high-end benchmark are given the assessment at year end). Phoneme segmentation and nonsense word deciphering are assessed at both the middle and the end of the year. Unlike the PALS assessments, all of the DIBELS assessments sample only 1 minute of performance (although the initial sounds assessment may take a child less than or longer than a minute, the score is converted to correct responses in 1 minute). Table 5.2 shows that children must make marked increases in performance to make end-of-year benchmarks, compared to fall and midyear benchmarks. At year end, a kindergartner must correctly identify 40 alphabet letters, segment 35 phonemes or smaller-than-word segments of spoken words, and articulate at least 25 phonemes from printed nonsense words, all within 1 minute, to be considered likely to succeed in learning to read and write in first grade and beyond. While these levels of achievement are considerable, research has shown that 80% or more of children who score at these levels do become good readers and writers (Good, Simmons, Kame'enui, Kaminski, & Wallin, 2002).

The benchmarks may seem confusing, given the different ways literacy is measured and the different tasks children are asked to perform. However, it is clear that by kindergarten entry, children who go on to be good readers and writers already are able to name more than half the alphabet letters, say the sounds of many consonants, and segment the beginning sounds of many words. By the middle of kindergarten, they can do considerably more: name all or nearly all the alphabet letters, identify nearly all consonant letter sounds, segment the beginning sounds of most words, and invent spellings with

TABLE 5.2. DIBELS Beginning-of-Year and Midyear Kindergarten Benchmarks Indicating At Risk and Not at Risk

Benchmarks	At risk	Not at risk
Kindergarten beginning-of-year benchmarks		
Initial sounds	<4	>8
Letter naming	<2	>8
Kindergarten midyear benchmarks		
Initial sounds	<10	>25
Letter naming	<15	>27
Phoneme segmentation	<7	>18
Nonsense words	<5	>13
Kindergarten end-of-year benchmarks		
Letter naming	<29	>40
Phoneme segmentation	<10	>35
Nonsense words	<15	>25

one to two conventional or unconventional letter–sound matches. Especially by the end of kindergarten, children increase the speed with which they can perform these tasks.

The usual approach for children who have been identified as at risk is to provide supplemental instruction in the specific areas in which they exhibit low levels of literacy knowledge. For example, for children who score below benchmark on alphabet recognition, teachers provide small-group instruction on learning to name alphabet letters. For children who do not score at benchmark level for phoneme segmentation, teachers provide small-group instruction on how to isolate beginning sounds. Instruction is usually targeted at only the one area in which children scored below benchmark. Children who score below benchmark for more than one area belong to more than one targeted instructional group. Children then frequently receive monitoring assessments, usually every 2 weeks, to determine whether or not they have benefited from targeted instruction. Monitoring assessments may be intended to provide broad indicators of growth (such as by using one of the DIBELS measures repeatedly), but they are more effective when they align with the curriculum and thereby provide specific information about the targeted domain of instruction. For instance, if a child receives intense alphabet instruction aimed at recognizing and writing letters, subsequent monitoring assessment tests for identification and production of both letters that were taught and those not yet taught.

Developmental Milestones versus Benchmarks

So far in this chapter we have outlined a screening and benchmarking approach to assessment and instruction that may seem in many ways at odds with the developmental stance that we have taken in this book. In Chapter 4 we presented a continuum of literacy development recognized by reading and early childhood professional organizations. For more than 30 years, researchers have recognized and documented the importance to children's growth into literacy of both their conventional and their unconventional knowledge and performance (e.g., Schickedanz & Collins, 2013). Most children move along a developmental continuum that includes the unconventional and end up reading and writing within acceptable ranges in first grade and beyond. But increasingly, federal mandates have directed our attention to the children who do not move along the continuum as expected and end up struggling to learn to read and write. These children continue to read with significantly less success as they progress through all levels of schooling and often fail to achieve employment or remain underemployed for life. It is critically important, then, to identify and provide effective instruction for children who do not progress as expected into literacy. This, however, in no way warrants abandoning a developmental perspective that recognizes the value during development of unconventional knowledge and performance. A comparison of the developmental milestones presented in Table 4.1 with the benchmarks presented in Tables 5.1 and 5.2 reveals that the domains of reading and writing found in the former are more extensive than what is tapped by any of the screening measures found in the latter. For sure, many of the domains in Table 4.1 are assessable with standardized measures and can be benchmarked across preschool and kindergarten as presented in Tables 5.1 and 5.2. These include alphabet recognition, segmenting beginning sounds, recognizing rhyming words, identifying letter–sounds, spelling, and word reading. However, among the elements presented in Table 4.1 that are missing from the screening measures in Tables 5.1 and 5.2 are children's oral comprehension and their ability to retell stories and repeat information read aloud to them, their ability to compose texts with varying structures and purposes, and the watershed accomplishment of their one-to-one, speech-to-print matching during fingerpoint reading.

A critical consideration about a developmental continuum with milestone accomplishments is that children who receive rich literacy experiences from their culture, family, or preschool develop knowledge across a wide array of literacy domains *simultaneously*. They do not learn to recognize alphabet letters, then learn nursery rhymes, then acquire a concept about a word, and so forth. Instead they make progress in acquiring more complex understandings across all of these domains of literacy development as they participate in a wide variety of literacy activities. Most naturally occurring at-home activities and well-planned school activities provide opportunities to learn a variety of literacy concepts. As a child watches his mother help an older sibling write his name and then attempts to write his own name (e.g., see Eric's signature in Figure 4.2), he learns that print "says" or communicates a message, that print consists of letter-like forms with particular features and directionality, and that letters make up words. Thus, they are learning concepts about print *and* alphabet knowledge. As a teacher reads aloud a book about a runaway bunny and then writes a list of all the places the bunny went, children learn about characters and their problems. They learn about character motivations and how they affect solutions to story problems. They observe their teacher recall and write about information from the story. They observe her start to write at the top of the page and move left to right as she writes words. They notice she leaves a space between words and often writes letters children recognize. Sometimes the teacher articulates sounds at the beginning of words and remarks that she knows what letter spells that sound. Opportunities to learn simultaneously within several different domains of early literacy usually are embedded in rich and meaningful activities like these that are not focused exclusively on print learning. When reading about a runaway bunny and writing a list of places the bunny goes, a teacher may intend to focus on oral comprehension; however, her lesson includes opportunities for children to learn much more. As children acquire comprehension skill, they also learn concepts about print, phonemic awareness, and growing alphabetic awareness, all in a period of 20 minutes.

Embedded Experiences in Literacy and Developmental Phases

We have shared examples of instruction about concepts of print and phonemic awareness that is embedded in reading a story and writing about its events. These examples illustrate the important principle that embedded literacy instruction always includes meaning making. Even as children learn about print concepts including alphabet knowledge, phonemic awareness, and sound–letter relationships, they must never be misled into thinking that knowing about those concepts is what reading and writing are all about. Print concepts are necessary but not sufficient for becoming effective readers and writers. Readers and writers do not use print concepts alone; they also employ concepts about the functions of written language and about determining its meaning. For this reason, instructional activities designed to help children focus on print, attend to sounds, and match sounds to letters should frequently take place in meaningful and functional contexts, with texts that make sense to children and serve evident purposes in their home and classroom lives. Research documents that children whose embedded literacy experiences have taught them many concepts about print and imparted much knowledge about how print functions acquire conventional reading and writing skills more easily and more quickly (Purcell-Gates & Dahl, 1991). When children have experienced embedded and meaningful opportunities to learn literacy concepts across a wide array of domains, their development in one domain is likely to affect development in other domains.

Consider the continuum of literacy development presented in Table 4.1. Children we would characterize as older emergent readers and writers have had experiences listening to stories and attempting to retell them, they have learned how to write their names with some readable letters, and they are beyond random sweeps across print as they pretend to read by attempting one-to-one, speech-to-print matching. They can recognize and write many alphabet letters, know and recite many nursery rhymes, and are attuned to the rhythm and sounds in songs and chants. They have a bundle of knowledge across a broad array of literacy domains because of their experiences in interrelated and embedded literacy experiences. We have found that some children may be delayed in a few domains of the continuum within their developmental phase, but generally most children within a particular developmental phase approximate the milestones in Table 4.1. For example, most children in the early emergent reading and writing phase may not yet draw representational people, but with multiple experiences using markers and other drawing utensils, they will learn to do so. They may recognize no alphabet letters by name, but they will learn to do so. This movement from unconventional levels of knowledge to conventional knowledge would be expected for young 3-year-olds and even for some 4-year-olds who have had few home literacy experiences. On the other hand, we would expect 4-year-olds who have had several months of exemplary preschool experiences to exceed this level of conventional knowledge. That is, we would expect them to have developed more enriched understandings through their experiences in preschool literacy activities. Further, we know that entering kindergartners who have very few early literacy concepts are very much behind their peers.

USING DEVELOPMENTAL MILESTONES AND BENCHMARKS TO IDENTIFY CHILDREN NEEDING ADDITIONAL SUPPORT IN DEVELOPING EARLY LITERACY

We present case studies of four children in order to consider their progress along the continuum of literacy development. Each of these children was administered the assessments we provide in Appendix B. Because our assessments are similar to those used in PALS-PK and PALS-K, we also use the benchmarks from those assessments to consider the progress and instructional needs of the four children.

Eric

Eric was enrolled in a state-funded public school prekindergarten in a small town in Alabama when his teacher assessed his early literacy concepts in January. His teacher, Ms. Warren, was considered outstanding by the local school district leadership. Many parents requested that their children be assigned to her room. A majority of children, including Eric, qualified for free lunch and the next year would be attending kindergarten in the lowest-performing elementary school in the district. The children begin attending the all-day prekindergarten program the first week of August. Ms. Warren and her assistant teacher assessed all of the children in January. As part of the assessment, the teacher collected the children's signature writing from one of their regular sign-in sheets (all children wrote their name on small slips of paper that they placed in an attendance pocket chart). Ms. Warren also planned a special Writing Center activity for the month of January in which children were expected to draw a picture and write a story about themselves. At the end of center time, children who had completed this task placed their work in the teacher's rocking chair and later shared their writing with the class. Ms. Warren took notes as the children shared their compositions about themselves, collected the writing sample, and used the sample and her notes as part of her assessment. She also read the book *Owl Moon* (Yolen, 1987) 3 days in a row, and on the third day she and her assistant asked children to retell the story during center time or during nap. Then all children were given the upper-case letter recognition, alphabet letter writing, concepts about print, and fingerpoint reading assessments. Some children were given additional assessments if they performed at the high ends of these assessments.

Table 5.3 presents the results of Eric's assessments (a copy of his Literacy Assessment Scoring Record is found in Appendix D). When Eric was asked to retell the story *Owl Moon,* he shrugged his shoulders. When asked who was in the story, he again shrugged. Then the assistant who was recording the retelling opened the book for Eric to use in talking about the story (see the assistant's notes following Eric's Retelling Checklist in Appendix D). He mainly labeled the actions in the illustrations (e.g., "walking") and imitated the owl sound. He wrote his name with three non-letter-like shapes (see Figure 5.1), knew seven concepts about print, tapped randomly at each page when asked to fingerpoint read, and recognized four alphabet letters. He refused to write alphabet letters. His drawing of himself was nonrepresentational although he drew a round shape, lines, and dots that could be a very unorganized tadpole. His writing was mock cursive, and he did not offer a story when sharing with the class, but merely said about his drawing, "This is me." (See Figure 5.2.)

Ms. Warren recognized that Eric was operating with the knowledge of a child within the early emergent reader and writer phase of development (see Table 5.3 for the developmental milestones expected in early emergent reading and writing). While he displayed little conventional knowledge, Ms. Warren noted that Eric had made progress since the beginning of the year. He did engage in telling about the book's illustrations, and while he only labeled actions and made the owl sound, these were important in the story. He refused to write his name in the beginning of the year and then adopted an uncontrolled scribble. His use of individual shapes in this assessment was progress toward writing individual letters, an early emergent milestone.

TABLE 5.3. Developmental Milestones of Early Emergent Readers and Writers Compared to PALS End-of-Year PK and Beginning-of-Year K Benchmarks for Eric and Sarah

Early emergent readers and writers	Developmental milestones	PALS benchmarks: end-of-year PK, beginning-of-year K, indicating at risk (and on target)	Eric	Sarah
Oral comprehension and vocabulary	(May have no, or little, experience sharing books); makes or learns to make comments and ask questions about books; acquires vocabulary from books; attempts to describe book illustrations	Not included in benchmarks	Labeled pictures	Minimal retelling with few details
Name writing	(May write no, or only a few, letters in signature); learns to write name with letter-like forms and some legible letters	Not included in benchmarks	3 non-letter-like forms	All legible upper-case letters
Alphabet knowledge	(May identify no, or only a few, alphabet letters); learns to recognize and write a few alphabet letters; develops motor skills to control lines used in letter formation and drawing	<12 (>21) upper-case <9 (>17) lower-case	4 upper-case	3 upper-case 0 lower-case
Phonological and phonemic awareness	(May demonstrate no conscious phonological awareness); learns nursery rhymes and poems and responds to rhythm and rhyme	Note: Early in emergent reading and writing, phonological awareness is likely not to be measured.		
Concepts about print	(May demonstrate no, or only a few, concepts about print); begins to demonstrate book-handling concepts and some directionality	<7 (>9) out of 10 print concepts	7 concepts out of 20	9 concepts out of 20
Text writing	(May not draw a representational drawing); learns to draw or draws representational drawing of a person (tadpole); learns to use or uses scribbles or mock letters to write	Not included in benchmarks	Nonrepresentational drawing with scribble writing	Representational drawing of tadpole with many details, mock and real letters in writing, no evidence of alphabetic principle

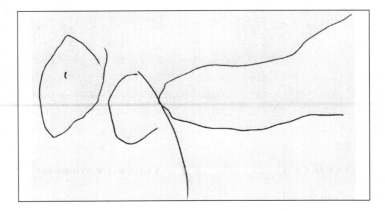

FIGURE 5.1. Eric's signature.

Table 5.3 also presents the end-of-year PALS-PK at-risk and on-target benchmarks that Ms. Warren used to review Eric's performance. She recognized that these benchmarks are for the end-of-the-year prekindergarten, while all her children were only mid-year in prekindergarten. Still, she decided it would be a good idea to consider how well children were progressing toward reaching the on-target end-of-the-year benchmarks. While Eric only knew four alphabet letters, he did recognize the first letter in his name. This was considerably below the on-target benchmark for the end of the year (>21 upper-case letters) and even below the at-risk benchmark (<12 letters). He did enjoy nursery rhymes at this time of year and even could recite several independently. However, Ms. Warren knew that Eric needed to make more accelerated progress in order to reach on-target levels in alphabet knowledge, beginning sound awareness, and rhyme at the end of preschool.

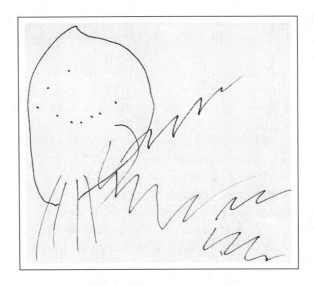

FIGURE 5.2. Eric's text writing.

The January assessment in Ms. Warren's classroom showed that most children in her classroom, unlike Eric, could identify 10 or more alphabet letters (and many could identify 26 or more upper- and lower-case letters) and could write a nearly recognizable name. Most were drawing at least simple tadpole people. Thus, Ms. Warren decided that all children would continue to receive one small-group literacy lesson daily as they had been doing since early in the school year. She and her assistant had divided the class into two groups of nine children, and each taught a small-group lesson for 15 minutes. However, she decided that Eric and three other children could benefit from additional small-group instruction. With these four children, she would focus more intensely on name writing, alphabet letter recognition, listening to and reading charts of nursery rhymes (with matching words and letters), and retelling easy folktales. This extra small group would meet at least three times a week. When the four children's alphabet knowledge increased, she would begin teaching how to segment beginning phonemes.

Sarah

Sarah attended an all-day kindergarten in a midwest state that began classes in mid-August. Her kindergarten was located in a middle-income neighborhood that included some apartments as well as many single-family homes. Only 20% of the children were on free or reduced lunch. Sarah's teacher, Mrs. Meier, knew that Sarah had not attended a preschool, but rather a local day-care center since she was a baby. Mrs. Meier assessed her children the last 2 weeks of September with the help of a retired teacher hired by the school district. She used a whole-class activity to collect samples of text writing and photocopied a signature from one of the children's activities for the name-writing sample. She assessed upper- and lower-case alphabet recognition, concepts about print, and fingerpoint reading individually with each child but collected alphabet letter writing from children in groups of three. Mrs. Meier read *Owl Moon* 3 days in a row, and the retired teacher asked all children individually to retell the story and recorded their retellings. Some children were also given the beginning phoneme segmentation, rhyming, and consonant letter assessments if they showed high levels of performance on the first set of assessments (because of her low scores on the first set of assessments, Sarah was not given these assessments). Appendix D includes a copy of her Literacy Assessment Scoring Record. Based on her scores, Mrs. Meier decided that Sarah was operating in the phase of early emergent reading and writing. Sarah's scores on the assessments provided in Appendix D are also found in Table 5.3 along with the expected milestones for children within this phase of literacy development.

Sarah wrote her name in legible letters although all letters were upper-case (see Figure 5.3). She knew nine of the concepts about print but merely swept her hand across the page in fingerpoint reading. She recognized three upper-case letters, *A, E,* and *O,* and randomly named the other letters *S, H, P,* and *Q.* She recognized none of the lower-case letters and wrote no letters, instead saying she could draw pictures. Her drawing of herself was a representational tadpole with many details, and her story was written with mock and real letters (see Figure 5.4). When asked to read it, she said, "This is me, and I'm going to the store." Her retelling was minimal, with only three ideas.

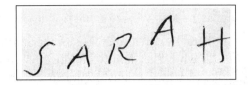

FIGURE 5.3. Sarah's signature.

Mrs. Meier compared Sarah's scores to the relevant end-of-preschool PALS-PK benchmarks (also presented in Table 5.3) and was concerned about indications of risk. She realized Sarah was operating with some knowledge beyond the early emergent reading and writing phase: she attempted a retelling, her name writing was legible, and she drew a representational tadpole with many details. However, Mrs. Meier also knew that recognition of only 3 alphabet letters was below the at-risk level of 9 and far below the on-track level of 22. Still, her many years of teaching experience told her that many kindergartners enter school with this level of knowledge and that with good teaching that included focused, small-group instruction, most go on to be successful readers and writers in first grade

Mrs. Meier decided to include Sarah in a group of five children with similar levels of knowledge for a daily 20-minute small-group literacy lesson. First she would focus intensively on alphabet letter recognition and writing, and then when the children knew more than 10 alphabet letters, she would begin teaching how to segment beginning phonemes. Once children had learned 15 alphabet letters and could segment some sounds, she would provide direct instruction about consonant letter–sounds corresponding with the phonemes children were learning to segment. The children would also practice fingerpoint reading on very short poems containing either alliteration or rhyming words.

FIGURE 5.4. Sarah's text writing.

Marceli

Marceli attended all-day kindergarten in a small city in the South. She had attended the local Head Start program, for which her family qualified based on income. When she entered Head Start, she spoke very little English. Spanish was spoken at home, although her father could speak understandable English. The Head Start center was a model center for this southern state, and Marceli's teacher was known for her ability to send children to kindergarten with noticeably high levels of literacy. Marceli began kindergarten in early August; in September she was assessed by a preservice teacher enrolled in the nearby state university. A summary of her results is found in Table 5.4, and a copy of her Literacy Assessment Scoring Record is found in Appendix D.

Marceli retold *Owl Moon* (1987) with some elaboration although her ideas were randomly ordered (see Appendix D). She wrote her name in all readable letters and knew many concepts about print (see Figure 5.5). She was able to fingerpoint read with accurate one-to-one, speech-to-print matching 50% of the time. She identified a total of 33 upper- and lower-case letters and wrote 14 letters (see Figure 5.6). However, she could not segment beginning phonemes (only repeated the entire word) and refused the consonant letter assessment. She did draw a representational person with a body (legs and toes). She did not use the alphabetic principle in her writing (see Figure 5.7).

Her teacher recognized that Marceli's performances in some areas of literacy knowledge placed her in the experimenting reading and writing phase. These were her name writing, letter identification, fingerpoint reading, and drawing. However, her upper- and lower-case alphabet recognition scores were between the at-risk and on-target end-of-preschool benchmarks from the PALS-PK (see Table 5.4). She lacked the level of phonological and phonemic awareness expected of emergent readers and writers; her segmentation of phonemes and identification of consonant letter–sounds are below at-risk benchmarks for end-of-preschool.

Overall, Marceli would probably not be considered at risk at the beginning of kindergarten, but her assessments clearly suggest she needs small-group, targeted instruction to acquire more sophisticated phonemic awareness, learn sound–letter correspondences, and develop the alphabetic principle. Her teacher decided to include her in a small group of eight children whom the teacher knew needed direct instruction in a combination of phonemic awareness and sound–letter knowledge, practice in stretching out words to spell in guided invented spelling, and fingerpoint reading of longer texts. This group could also benefit from making and breaking familiar rhyming words.

Jacob

Jacob attended kindergarten in a school district with a mixture of low- and middle-income families in which 92% of children were on free and reduced lunch. He had attended a local church-affiliated preschool as a 3- and 4-year-old with after-school care. His mother reported to his teacher that he loved books and drew all the time. The results of his early literacy assessments in September are summarized in Table 5.5, and his Literacy Assessment Scoring Record is found in Appendix D.

TABLE 5.4. Developmental Milestones of Later Emergent Readers and Writers Compared to PALS End-of-Year PK and Beginning-of-Year K Benchmarks for Marceli

Later emergent readers and writers	Developmental milestones	PALS benchmarks: end-of-year PK, beginning-of-year K, indicating at risk (and on target)	Marceli
Oral comprehension and vocabulary	Does a minimal retelling with a few details of easy narratives and information books; acquires and uses vocabulary from read-alouds	Not included in benchmarks	Somewhat elaborated retelling with more details (7 ideas), but not ordered sequentially
Name writing	Writes name with some legible letters, some reversals, omissions	Not included in benchmarks	All legible letters, includes lower-case
Alphabet knowledge	Recognizes many alphabet letters; writes some to many alphabet letters in legible form	<12 (>21) upper-case <9 (>17) lower-case	18 upper-case 15 lower-case 14 letters written
Phonological and phonemic awareness	Knows many nursery rhymes; may hear some beginning phonemes or segments in words; may identify and produce rhyming words	<5 (>8) beginning sounds <5 (>7) rhymes <4 (>8) letter–sounds	0 segmented beginning sounds, refused consonant letter assessment
Concepts about print	Demonstrates some directionality; moves from tracking with sweeps or random taps to attempting one-to-one matching during fingerpoint reading of familiar pattern text	<7 (>9) out of 10 print concepts	11 out of 20 print concepts 6 out of 12 fingerpoint reading
Text writing	Makes representational drawing of person (tadpole) with a few details; may use scribbles or mock letters to write	Not included in benchmarks	Representational drawing with body and some details; letters used in writing, but no evidence of alphabetic principle

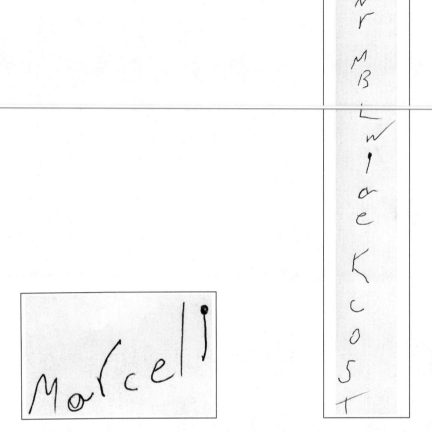

FIGURE 5.5. Marceli's signature.   **FIGURE 5.6.** Marceli's letter writing.

FIGURE 5.7. Marceli's text writing.

TABLE 5.5. Developmental Milestones of Experimenting Readers and Writers Compared to PALS End-of-Year PK, Beginning-of-Year K, and Midyear K Benchmarks for Jacob

Experimenting readers and writers: Almost readers and inventive spellers	Developmental milestones	PALS benchmarks: end-of-year PK, beginning-of-year K, indicating at risk (and on target)	PALS-K benchmarks: midyear K, indicating at risk (and on target)	Jacob
Oral comprehension and vocabulary	Does a minimal retelling with some details of narratives and information books; acquires and uses some Tier 2 vocabulary	Not included in benchmarks		Somewhat elaborated with more details (6 ideas recalled)
Name writing	Writes first name with all legible letters	Not included in benchmarks		All legible letters
Alphabet knowledge	Recognizes most upper- and lower-case alphabet letters; writes many to most letters in legible form	<12 (>21) upper-case < 9 (>17) lower-case	<23 (26) lower-case	25 upper-case 23 lower-case 22 letters written
Phonemic awareness	Segments most beginning phonemes	<5 (>8) beginning sounds	<9 (10)	8 segmented beginning phonemes
Phonics	Knows most consonant letter sounds	<4 (>8) letter-sounds	<17 (26)	5 consonant letters
Decoding and spelling using phonics	Learns to make and break rhyming words (segment onset and rime)	<5 (>7) rhymes	<9 (10)	
Spelling using phonics	Learns to invent spellings		<10 (20)	8 words spelled with one letter–sound match at beginning or end (would be score of 8)
Concepts about print and early text reading	Tracks print one to one during fingerpoint reading of familiar text	<7 (>9) out of 10		15 out of 20 7 out of 12 fingerpoint reading
Sight vocabulary	Learns some high-frequency words in reading and writing		<3 (>10)	
Text writing	Makes a representational drawing of person with a body and some details; writes with invented spellings	Not included in benchmarks		Representational drawing of body with many details; used invented spelling to write a sentence: I (I'm) pn (playing) w (with) m (my) f (friend)

Jacob's teacher decided that he operated within the phase of experimental reading and writing (see the milestones of this phase of reading and writing in Table 5.5). Jacob provided a somewhat elaborated retelling and drew a detailed representational drawing of himself and his friend. In his composition about himself, he wrote a sentence using invented spelling with mostly one-letter sound matches (see Figure 5.8). He knew 75% of the concepts about print and could fingerpoint read with one-to-one, speech-to-print matching on over 50% of the text, even self-correcting at the end of one line when he noticed he had pointed where no word was left to point to. He could write 22 letters, some upper- and some lower-case (see Figure 5.9). He segmented many beginning phonemes and knew some consonant sound–letter matches, although his spelling demonstrated he knew more than he demonstrated on this task (see Figure 5.10). When Jacob's teacher considered the end-of-preschool PALS-PK benchmarks, she noticed that on every assessment Jacob was on target. In fact, Jacob had reached performance expected at midyear kindergarten on many assessments. Nonetheless his teacher grouped Jacob with six other children with whom she met three times a week. She focused instruction on identifying high-utility consonant letter sounds, spelling boundary phonemes and vowels, breaking and making familiar rhyming words, fingerpoint reading in little books, and reading and writing a few sight words.

CONSIDERATIONS WHEN PLANNING SMALL-GROUP INSTRUCTION

Raising Children's Consciousness

Much, though not all, of what Eric, Sarah, and Marceli need to learn is related to print-processing skills (learning alphabet letter names, signatures, directionality of print, and sounds that make up spoken words). In order to teach these domains of early literacy, teachers must help children to pay attention to these aspects about print. This involves a change in the children's approach to language. "Paying attention" involves a consciousness that usually is not necessary with spoken language, but often is necessary for gaining mastery of written language. Much of what children like Eric, Sarah, and Marceli already know about language is in the form of unconscious knowledge. Consider, for example, the sentence *Joe fell down the stairs*. Even 3-year-olds can easily make that into a question, *Did Joe fall down the stairs?* Now, consider how speakers of English come up with the word *did* at the beginning of such a question. They know without knowing that they know it—that is, unconsciously—that *fell* is equivalent to *did fall* and that making a question requires moving the *did* part of the verb *did fall* to the beginning of the sentence. In contrast, reading and writing call upon conscious knowing. One of the greatest hurdles for learning to read and write is the new necessity of acquiring conscious language knowledge that is unnecessary for spoken language, not knowledge about *did* and its role in questions, but about such things as phonemes and directionality.

This consciousness raising can occur for many children during whole-class instruction when teachers make remarks about alphabet letters or words as they write on large charts, point to where they will start reading a big book, or frame a familiar word on a pocket chart with their fingers. But to be truly effective in raising individual children's consciousness about print, teachers have to be experts at three things. First, they must

FIGURE 5.8. Jacob's text writing.

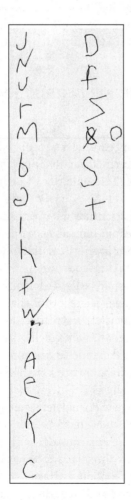

FIGURE 5.9. Jacob's letter writing.

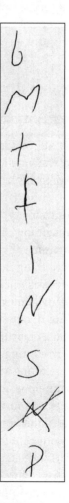

FIGURE 5.10. Jacob's spelling.

know the continuum of literacy development very well (we have referred to Table 4.1 many, many times as an example of this continuum). Second, they must know the literacy development of each and every child in their classroom (we have provided four case studies of how teachers might assess children and analyze the results to make instructional decisions). Finally, they must be masters at knowing just the right teachable moment for a particular child or a small group of children to insert a comment about print processing within ongoing whole-class routines and center activities. Knowing each child's developmental level allows teachers to be systematic, to fine-tune their plans for teaching, in order to take into account children who have more or less developed print skills. When teachers are masters at knowing "teachable moments," they are able to draw a child's attention to a new print concept when that child is ready to learn it. However, this expertise in teaching is most realized in small groups in which teachers personalize instruction for a group of children with particular strengths and needs.

When teachers develop the level of teaching craft advocated and illustrated in this chapter and elsewhere in this book, they need not resort to using commercial programs with sequenced activities and directions for what to say and do with children. We have outlined a continuum of development and provided screening assessments for identifying instructional needs appropriate to each level of development along the literacy continuum. With these tools, teachers can craft their own instructional programs that are flexible enough to meet the needs of their particular children.

Direct, Systematic Instruction

We recommend teaching deliberately and systematically, so that when the need arises, teachers can provide small-group instruction that is explicit but also playful and connected to other ongoing reading and writing activities. This will be especially true for kindergartners.

By deliberate we mean that teachers know the literacy milestones that children can be expected to reach for a broad array of literacy domains (see Tables 4.1, 5.3, 5.4, and 5.5). They plan activities that allow children to use their current level of knowledge, but also provide support for children to take the "next step" in acquiring new knowledge, knowledge that moves children toward more conventional skills. Teachers make concepts explicit during demonstrations of reading and writing. This means that they name the concept, define it, demonstrate it, and state why it is useful in reading and writing. For example, when reading books with many rhyming words, a teacher says, "These words are called rhyming words, and rhyming words sound alike at the end, like in the words *hat, sat, rat, cat*. Knowing rhyming words helps readers remember words when they read and can help writers find words they want to write."

By systematic, we mean that teachers use ongoing monitoring assessments to keep track of each child's literacy development. When children seem to be at a standstill—not developing more sophisticated understandings—teachers consider whether to provide instruction that is supplemental to the small-group instruction they are providing as a regular part of the classroom curriculum. By explicit we mean that teachers draw children's attention to salient concepts both inside and outside the reading and writing context. In this way, teachers provide instruction that highlights concepts as they are embedded in meaningful activities. However, teachers also plan instruction that focuses only on one domain of early literacy. For example, teachers can prepare alphabet-learning games to draw attention to specific letters that children are confusing or construct phonological awareness games using pictures of rhyming words, some related to rhyming words found in familiar poems and books recently read aloud to the whole group and some not. As teachers play alphabet letter games or engage children in matching rhyming pictures, they make explicit connections between letters or rhymes children are learning in the game and letters and rhymes that have been discussed in other reading and writing activities. For example, teachers might remark "There's that *L*, like in Lakisha" when playing an alphabet game or say, "Mittens, kittens, those were rhyming words in *Goodnight Moon*," when playing a rhyming game.

CHAPTER SUMMARY

In this chapter, we described the use of screening instruments and benchmark scoring to identify children for targeted instruction in early literacy. The urgency to identify children earlier than ever is based on research demonstrating that without intervention, children who have low levels of skills in preschool and kindergarten go on to become struggling readers and writers. However, as we have shown in Chapter 1, research has clearly demonstrated that intervention instruction can make a difference in whether children continue to struggle or make accelerated progress and reach average or higher levels of literacy achievement.

We recommend screening children in the middle of the prekindergarten year, at kindergarten entry, and midyear in kindergarten. Such screening allows teachers to make decisions about small-group instruction and which children might need more intensive, supplemental, small-group lessons. All children benefit from small-group instruction that meets their current levels of development and pushes them to the "cutting edge" of learning. However, children who demonstrate very low levels of knowledge or who are not making expected progress should receive small-group instruction in addition to, supplemental to, small-group instruction received as a part of the regular curriculum. Their learning should be monitored. Yet instruction should always be playful and engaging for children.

We provided case studies of four children with results of their screening assessments, and we discussed these results in light of benchmarks scores. Further, comparing their performance to developmental milestones suggested directions for instruction. In the following chapters we provide more information about instructional activities that advance the learning of preschool and kindergarten children at various points along the continuum of literacy development.

CHAPTER 6

Small-Group Differentiated Instructional Activities for Early Emergent Readers and Writers

In this chapter, we describe small-group instructional activities that are designed to help early (younger) emergent readers and writers in the Awareness and Exploration phase develop a broad array of literacy concepts including name writing, alphabet knowledge, phonological and phonemic awareness, and concepts about print. Occasionally small-group activities might also include activities focused on oral language development, oral comprehension and vocabulary, and text writing. However, many of these activities are addressed in whole-class and center activities discussed in Chapters 2 and 3. The activities we describe in this chapter are targeted specifically for children at this early period of their awareness and exploration. In Chapter 7, we describe activities for later (older) emergent readers and writers in the Awareness and Exploration phase, and in Chapter 8, we discuss activities for experimenting readers and writers.

CONSIDERING WHAT EARLY EMERGENT READERS AND WRITERS KNOW AND CAN DO

Early emergent readers and writers in the Awareness and Exploration phase may show no or very little conventional knowledge about literacy. Recall Tatie, the 3-year-old Haitian child who gathered up all the magnetic letter *T*'s in the class room and put them in her cubby. She also frequently walked around the classroom with her figures crossed in a T shape. When her teacher attempted to assess some of her children using assessment tasks like those found in Appendix B, Tatie refused the alphabet recognition assessment. Her teacher was not surprised or concerned. Rather, she knew Tatie was merely displaying a lack of conventional understanding about alphabet letters expected for young 3-year-olds with few mainstream home literacy experiences. Table 6.1 presents the characteristics of early emergent readers and writers at the beginnings of this phase of learning and suggests what they might learn within this phase. It presents instructional

TABLE 6.1. Characteristics of Early Emergent Readers and Writers at the Onset and End of This Period of Development, with Recommended Instructional Activities

Early emergent readers and writers	Characteristics at onset of this period	Instructional activities	Outcomes of teaching; characteristics at end of this period
Oral comprehension and vocabulary	May have no, or little, experience sharing and talking about books	Interactive read-alouds; drama and retelling; retelling and book acting in centers (see Chapter 3)	Make comments and ask questions about books; acquire vocabulary from books; attempt telling about book illustrations
Name writing	May write no, or only a few, letters in signature	Sign in by locating name; sign in by writing, using name model and teacher support; name games such as matching names, matching letters in names, learning to recognize first letter of names, clapping syllables in name, naming letters in signature; guided writing of first letters in names; transition activities with names and first letters, syllables, and sounds in names	Write first name with letter-like forms and some legible letters
Concepts about print	May have no, or only a few, concepts about print	Shared reading of big books with teacher talk about concepts about print; shared reading of a sentence related to read-alouds; shared reading and word matching with cut-up sentence	Use book handling and some directionality concepts
Alphabet knowledge	May identify no, or only one or two, alphabet letters	Shared writing from read-alouds and step up to locate letters and frame words; singing of alphabet song and matching of letters while singing; guided drawing using letter strokes; learning upper-case letters in writing and in games	Identify a few alphabet letters; develop motor skills to control lines used in letter writing and drawing
Phonological and phonemic awareness	May demonstrate no conscious phonological awareness	Read-alouds of rhyming and alliteration books, later with teacher talk about sounds; shared reading of nursery rhyme and song charts; dramatic finger plays and motions for nursery rhymes; sounds in motion	Learn nursery rhymes and poems and respond to rhythm and rhyme
Writing composition: text writing	May not draw a representational drawing or attempt to write	Drawing activities to accompany book read-alouds, shared writing, and other classroom events (see Chapter 3)	Make a representational drawing of a person (tadpole); use scribbles or mock letters in writing attempts

activities suggested for children at this level of literacy development, and provides outcomes that teachers can expect after several weeks and months of instruction. Children in this phase of development range from 2 to 5 years old. Two- and 3-year-olds in this phase are on target and likely progressing along the literacy continuum without difficulty. Four-year-olds who are at this stage reflect they have had few opportunities to learn conventional concepts about literacy. They need many experiences across all domains of literacy knowledge in whole-class, small-group, and center activities in which teachers interact with them one-on-one. With good teaching and adequate opportunities to engage in a wide variety of literacy experiences in an effective preschool program or in a highly literate home, these children typically move through this phase in less than a year. When children have had 6 months or more in a rich preschool classroom with more than adequate opportunities to learn and yet remain in this phase, teachers are concerned and make closer observations. Following careful observation and perhaps assessment and analysis, teachers may decide to initiate supplemental small-group instruction for children who seem "stuck" in this phase. Children who are 5 years old and beginning kindergarten with this level of knowledge should have both regular and supplemental small-group instruction fairly soon after kindergarten entry. Without accelerated learning, they are at risk for struggling to learn reading and writing.

Notice that in Table 6.1 the desired outcomes of the literacy activities suggested for early emergent readers and writers are not fully conventional understandings. Instead, children are expected to make progress toward more conventional knowledge across a wide band of concepts.

NAME WRITING

Often the first place to begin instruction that targets more conventional performance is children's names. Recall Tatie's interest in the letter *T*, no doubt based on her awareness of this first letter of her name. A consistent finding in research is the "my name advantage." Among the earliest letters children identify are those at the beginning of their names or family members' names (Justice et al., 2006; Trieman, Cohen, Mulqueeny, Kessler, & Schechtman, 2007), and early invented spellings often include those letters (Both-deVries & Bus, 2008). That is, children find the written artifact of their names meaningful. It is perhaps the first print to which children ascribe a particular meaning and to whose individual parts (letters) they attend. Thus, learning to identify the first letter of one's own name, learning to recognize one's own name from a group of other names (especially names with the same beginning letter), and attempting to write one's name are extremely potent opportunities for acquiring several critical early literacy concepts: concepts about print, alphabetic knowledge, and eventually phonemic awareness.

Using Attendance and Job Charts

Posting children's names in the classroom is a start—children's names should appear on their cubby or other locations used to store their belongings, classroom job charts, sign-in attendance bulletin boards, and welcome displays. However, teachers must intentionally draw attention to names and their beginning letters in order to for children capitalize on and learn from these classroom displays. We recommend using interactive attendance charts. These can be created by purchasing peel-and-stick library pockets, which come in manila and a variety of bright colors. Teachers attach a pocket for each child to sturdy tagboard and print each child's name on a pocket. Then teachers make a name card for each child printed on a sentence strip. As a daily routine, teachers spread children's name cards on a table, and as children enter the room, they locate their name cards and place them in their pockets on the attendance chart. During the first days of school, teachers can help children locate their name cards, using beginning letters and then help children locate their name pockets on the chart. Figure 6.1 presents portions of a class attendance chart made from library pockets. As a part of the daily, beginning-of-day, whole-class activity, teachers read each child's name by pointing and underlining the name from left to right (rather than merely pointing at the word) then pointing back to the first letter. Teachers can then say, "Shanesh'a is here. *S* is her first letter. Tyrelle is here. *T* is his first letter." As this routine becomes familiar, all the children chant with the teacher. Later, a class job is to read the names as the teacher supplies the beginning letter or each child says his or her own beginning letter. As days pass, teachers use different strategies to get children involved in reading names and identifying beginning letters, with the goal that all children be able to read all the names and identify all of the beginning letters.

Another way names and beginning letters can be used is during transitions from one activity to another. As teachers dismiss children to line up for lunch or for going outdoors, they can use a set of name cards with children's names printed on them. The teacher says, "Watch for your name. When you see it, you can line up." Again, teachers should point to the name from left to right. Later, teachers can merely use a set of capital letters and say, "Watch for the first letter in your name. When you see it, you can line up." Children who have friends with the same first letter can line up together.

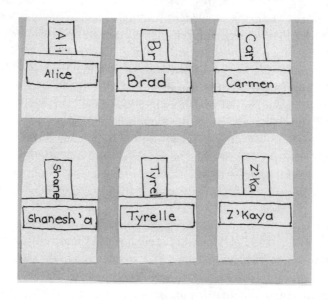

FIGURE 6.1. Classroom attendance chart.

Playing Name Games in Small Groups

Capitalizing on children's names should also be part of small-group activities. Teachers can cut three-piece puzzles from sentence strips and glue on one puzzle piece a child's photograph, on another piece the child's name printed with a computer font, and on a final piece the child's hand-printed name. The three pieces of the sentence strip can be cut apart using a variety of jagged and curved lines. These puzzle pieces can be used in a variety of game-like activities. Teachers can give each child his or her photo puzzle piece and scatter the computer printed puzzle pieces in the center of the table. Children search through the puzzle pieces to locate their own names. Then teachers scatter the hand-printed puzzle pieces, and again children search. Teachers can also place magnetic letters that spell a child's name on a small flat pan or in a plastic baggie. Each child has the letters spelling his or her own name. Children place their letters on the table above their handwritten names and then arrange the letters left to right to spell their names. Teachers can show children how to scramble up the letters so they can practice several times arranging their letters left to right in correct order to spell their names. Then teachers can play games such as "Whose name begins with *S*?" "Whose name begins with *W*?" "Whose name has three letters? Four letters? Eight letters?" The identified child holds up his or her name card and all children read the name. That child holds up the magnetic letter at the beginning of his or her name or counts the number of letters. Teachers can prepare center activities by placing each child's photograph, printed name, and magnetic letters in a baggie and putting the baggies in a special name box. During center time, children enjoy locating their names and names of their friends, matching alphabet letters to printed names, and arranging letters left to right in order to spell names. Or teachers can make an interactive pocket chart activity by placing letters across the top of the pocket chart and children's name cards in a baggie. Children take out their name cards and place them under the appropriate beginning letters.

Another name game is to select a child of the day. For example, one day it might be Amari's day for the name game. The teacher would prepare a name game sheet shown in Figure 6.2a for each child in the group and one for the teacher. The teacher writes Amari's name across the top and bottom of the name game paper. As shown in Figure 6.2a, the letters across the bottom are placed in squares and teachers will cut these out and place them in an envelope. To play the game, each child and the teacher has the cut-out letters spelling the name in an envelope and the name game sheet with the name printed at the top. To play, the teacher and children remove their letters from the envelopes and spread them out on the table (we recommend using different colors of paper so the children do not mix their letters with children sitting next to them). The teacher demonstrates selecting and placing the beginning letter of the child's name, for example, for *Amari*, placing the cut-out *A* over the letter *A* printed at the top of the sheet. Teachers monitor children's actions to make sure they select the correct letter and match it appropriately. There are many opportunities to name letters as children select and match each of the letters of the name of the child of the day. After matching and naming all the letters in the name several times, children can draw pictures of the child. Often teachers invite children to attempt to write the name: "You can write Amari's name if you want to." The teacher can staple the pictures together and send them home with the child of the day.

The focus of this name game during early emergent reading and writing is learning to search for and distinguish among letters, name letters with support, match letters, and practice left-to-right orientation. Children have exposure to both upper- and lowercase letter formations and say most of the letter names as each child's name is used. Figures 6.2b and 6.2c present two children's drawing and writing during Amari's name game activity. His teacher helped children draw by calling attention to Amari's eyes, nose, mouth, hair, eyebrows, and ears.

Another name activity that helps children learn alphabet letter names is to say a child's name and chant all the letters in the name. Teachers should point to the letters (the name can be printed in large letters on a sentence strip placed in a pocket chart). First, teachers say the name and underline the name left to right, and then they chant each letter as they point to it. Children should chime in saying the name and chanting the letter names. In order to spice up this routine, teachers might have children use different

FIGURE 6.2. Name game activity. (a) name game sheet. (b and c) Two classmates' drawing and writing during Amari's name game activity.

voices: whisper voice, cat purring voice, monster growling voice, mouse squeaking voice, and so forth, One teacher we know adapted the BINGO song and game to chanting the letters in children's names. For example, to the tune of BINGO, children would sing, "S-T-E-V-E, S-T-E-V-E, S-T-E-V-E, and Steve is his name O." This teacher just elongated and repeated sounds for children's names with fewer than or more than the number of letters in BINGO. Marquette's name, for example, was a challenge to get in tune to the song!

Some name activities focus on phonological or phonemic awareness rather than alphabet knowledge or concepts about print. For example, teachers can demonstrate and have children clap the syllables in names. Later teachers can demonstrate saying the name and then just the first sound, "Brett begins with the sound /b/-/b/-/b/-/b/. Amari's name begins with the sound /uh/-/uh/-uh/." Both first syllables and first sounds can be made into guessing games. A preschool teacher used a drawstring bag to play this game. First she placed in it photos of all the children, attached to sturdy tag board. To play the game, she drew out a picture of one child without showing it. Then she pronounced the first syllable of the child's name and had children guess who it was, then showed the picture to confirm. Later, when syllables were familiar, the teacher said just the first sound, being careful to keep the sound exactly as it is pronounced in the name, and had children guess. If no one could guess correctly, she would give the syllable.

Guided Drawing as a Precursor to Children's Name Writing and Alphabet Writing

One of the best ways to learn letters is to learn to write them. This draws attention to the features that make up letters: vertical, horizontal, diagonal, and curved lines of different lengths joined at different places along the lines. For example the capital letter *A* is comprised of two diagonal lines that touch at the top and one horizontal line that stretches from the middle of one diagonal line across to the other. That is, the capital letter *A* could be considered to be made up of lines that slant back, slant forward, and go across. Naming lines in letters is called *letter formation talk* and can help children to write readable letters. Figure 6.3 presents letter formation talk for all the capital letters. Notice that one of the critical lines is described as "down," for the vertical line created by moving from top to bottom, such as the first line written in the capital letter *E*. Many letters begin with this down stroke: *B, D, E, F, H, I, J, K, L, M, N, P, R, T,* and *U.* Thus, learning to draw a vertical line from top to bottom (down) is a critical component skill in writing readable letters. Another critical line is the one described as "across," meaning a horizontal line created by moving from left to right. Only the letter *Z* begins with this stroke, but the letters *E, F, H, I, L,* and *T* include at least one across line. "Curve back" is when a circular shape is drawn by moving counterclockwise, as is done in writing the letters *C, G, O,* and *Q* and the first curve of *S.* "Curve forward" is when a curved line is drawn clockwise, as in the letters *B, D, P,* and *R* and the second curve of *S.* Slants occur in the letters *A, K, M, N, R, V, W, Y,* and *Z.* Slants move down and to the left or down and to the right. Other minor lines include the curve back on *J,* curve forward on *U,* and little lines in *G, I,* and *Q.* Figure 6.3 groups letters by major type of line rather than in alphabetical order. Children find downs and acrosses easier than curves, and curves easier than slants (because of slants' tricky connections to other parts of a letter).

T	Down, across at the top,	L	Down, across at the bottom	E	Down, across 1, across 2, across 3		
T	Down, across at the top	F	down, across 1, across 2	H	Down, down, across		
L	Down, across at the bottom	I	Down, little line across, little line	E	Down, across 1, across 2, across3	F	Down, across 1, across 2
D	Down, big curve forward	B	Down, curve forward, curve, forward	I	Down, little line across, little line across		
P	Down, little curve forward	H	Down, down, across	D	Down, big curve forward	B	Down, curve forward, curve forward
J	Down, curve back	U	Down curve it up	P	Down little curve forward		
O	Circle back	C	Circle back stop	G	Circle back stop, little line in		
C	Circle back stop	Q	Circle back, little line out	S	Circle back and curve forward		
A	slant back, slant forward, across	W	slant forward, slant up, slant forward, slant up	V	slant forward, slant up		
Z	across, slant down, across	Y	little slant, little slant, little down	V	slant forward, slant up		
M	UP, slant down, slant up, DOWN	N	UP, slant down, UP	K	down, little slant in, little slant out	R	Down, curve forward, little slant out
K	Down, little slant in, little slant out	V	slant forward slant up	M	UP, slant down, slant up, DOWN	X	Slant forward, slant back over

FIGURE 6.3. Letter formation talk and groups of letters for instruction.

Many children who come to school with no or little skill in drawing hold markers in their fists rather than using the standard three-finger (thumb, first and second finger) grip, and their drawing usually consists of scribbles. They have not yet learned to control their arms and hands to make circles, lines, and dots. Children in highly literate homes typically have 1 to 2 years' more experience with drawing than other children. To accelerate children's drawing growth and help them learn to make basic shapes and lines, teachers can use guided drawing (McGee, 2007). Guided drawing is simply a teacher's telling a story and making marks on a piece of paper to accompany it. The marks on the paper are lines, dots, and circles. Children make marks on their papers as they watch their teacher. Often their marks are approximations of what the teacher has created rather than copies. After guided drawing, children are encouraged to make their own drawings.

One guided drawing activity is simply to make fences. Teachers tell children they are helping farmers make fences to keep in the cows (or whatever animal might be interesting to children). Teachers demonstrate how to make down and across lines. Then they help children turn their papers in landscape orientation and demonstrate how to make fences. First they draw many downs from top to bottom using various colors of marks. After making the downs, children make across lines to complete their fences. Figure 6.4 presents two examples of 3-year-olds' fences. Not all the children made downs as demonstrated, but their approximations are to be expected. They are no cause for concern; many children intersperse other shapes and lines with their fences. Many teachers cut paper into thin strips to use in this activity. After drawing their fences on several strips of paper, children tape the ends of the papers together, making a long fence. Finally, they

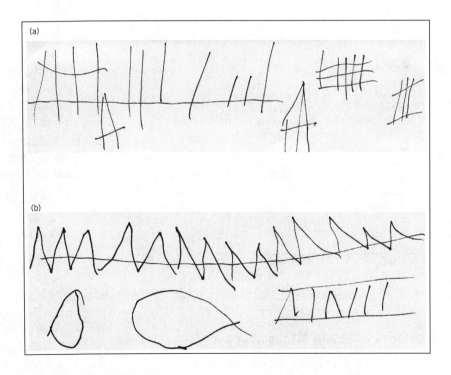

FIGURE 6.4a and b. Two children's guided drawings of fences.

tape the fence into a circle shape. Children can use these in the Block Center with plastic farm animals in pretend play. Another guided drawing activity is to make balloons. Here the teacher demonstrates making circles in different colors all over a page. To make these into balloons, children carefully draw a down line from the bottom of each circle.

Another guided drawing activity is to make mountains and snakes. Here teachers demonstration slants forward and slants down to make inverted V shapes for mountains and curved lines for snakes. It is important to keep in mind that while teachers demonstrate good formations using letter formation talk, most children make approximations of these movements and actually explore making other shapes and lines during the activity (as shown in Figures 6.4a and 6.4b). After children have been introduced to all the letter formation lines, teachers can use a slightly more complex form of guided drawing where they use lines and shapes to draw to a story. The teacher tells a story and makes lines and shapes on her paper which the children imitate. These guided drawings usually have three lines of marks and shapes that are produced left to right across the page to help children practice left-to-right orientation. For example, the teacher might make up a story of riding a school bus one day. She begins telling the children, "The bus drives and stops, drives and stops, drives and stops" (for each drive, the teacher draws a horizontal across line and for each stop makes a dot). Then the teacher can return sweep to the next line and say, "Now we are passing tall grass [drawing short down lines], and now tall trees [drawing long down lines]. Now we go over three bumps [making three hump shaped lines]." Then the teacher can return sweep to the next line and say, "Oh it is starting to rain [making several small circles], it is raining hard now [making larger circle shapes]. Turn on the windshield wipers [drawing two slant lines]. Here is the school. We are happy [drawing a person with a smile]."

After several weeks of guided drawing, most children, even those with few drawing experiences, know how to make lines that look like downs, acrosses, slants, curves forward, circles back, and little lines. Children can use this familiarity with drawing lines and shapes as they practice writing their names in imitation of a printed model. Children can learn to write everyone's beginning letter. Teachers can demonstrate how to write a beginning letter using letter formation talk, and children can imitate. Again, letter approximations are expected. As children gain experience with drawing and with writing beginning letters and their own names, the attendance activity in the morning routine evolves. Children come into the classroom and locate their name cards. These now serve as models for their writing their names on blank cards, which they then place in their name pockets.

ALPHABET LETTER KNOWLEDGE

An early avenue to alphabet knowledge is learning to sing the ABC song.

Singing the ABC Song and Matching Letters

Young children easily learn the ABC song along with many other songs and chants used frequently in morning, cleanup, and transitional routines in preschools. Learning the

ABC song does help children learn to say the unique names of alphabet letters. Children learn that many things, for example, different kinds of dogs, have unique names; so do alphabet letters. However, to go beyond merely learning 26 unique letter names, children learn to match the letter names that they sing to letter shapes that they see. Teachers can make ABC letter-matching mats for children to use as they sing the song during small-group activities. The letters are printed in lines to coincide with the phrasing of the ABC song: *ABCD* on one line, *EFG* on the next, and so on with *HIJK*, *LMNOP*, *QRS*, *TUV*, *WX*, and *YZ*. Young children cannot sing and match all the letters at one time, so, for example, teachers at first expect children to match only the letters *A*, *B*, *C*, and *D* as they sing, only sweeping their fingers across the other letters. Next children are expected to match correctly as they say two lines of letters—*A*, *B*, *C*, *D*, *E*, *F*, and *G*, and so on, until they can sing slowly and match one to one all 26 letters. Teachers need to monitor children and help them adjust their pointing so they are matching one to one. Later, the letter-matching mats can be placed in centers so teachers and assistants can help individual children who need practice with correct matching and return sweeping to start the next line.

Recognizing and Writing Upper-Case Letters

Early emergent readers and writers only begin the long journey of learning to name each letter of the alphabet. Alphabet knowledge is multifaceted, and the journey usually begins with the capital letters. Children must learn to recognize the shape of each letter, distinguish it from other letters with similar shapes (distinguishing, for example, *M* and *W*, *N* and *Z*, *A* and *H*), name the letter, and write it. We usually teach more than one letter at a time so that children must distinguish among several letters. We usually teach three letters that are easy to write (e.g., letters with downs and acrosses) in early lessons and progress to more complex letters as children acquire more letter knowledge. We demonstrate writing the letter using letter formation talk (see Figure 6.3) to highlight its features. For example, *T* is down and across at the top, *L* is down and across at the bottom, *E* is down and across 1, across 2 across 3. We name the letters, say the formation talk, demonstrate writing as we say the talk, and name the letter again. Children name the letter and practice writing it. We always comment about the letter's being a first letter in someone's name (and in most classrooms many upper-case letters are first letters for some child). Once children have named and practiced writing the letters several times, we introduce letter name games. Three familiar games are sort letters, wiggle worm, and memory match (McGee & Dail, 2010). For all games, the letters are printed on long strips of paper with the letter situated at the top in order to help children always orient the letter right side up. See Figure 6.5 for an example of letters printed on the orientation paper strips. In letter sort, children are given the letters, for example, *T*, *L*, and *E* printed in three different fonts. Children sort the letters into a pile of three *T*'s, a pile of three *L*'s, and a pile of three *E*'s; then they glue the letters of each pile onto a sheet of construction paper. For wiggle worm, we glue several letters on tongue depressors, for example, several *T*'s, *L*'s, and *E*'s. We also glue pictures of worms on several tongue depressors. All the tongue depressors are placed picture or letter side down in a cup. Each child picks a tongue depressor and shows it to the other children. If a child's tongue depressor has a

FIGURE 6.5. Letters printed on orientation papers.

letter, he or she says the letter name; if it has a worm, he or she wiggles like a worm. For memory match, we glue four *T*'s, four *L*'s and four *E*'s on index cards. We place the cards letter side down in a pocket chart. Children go to the pocket chart, pick two cards, and flip them over so that the letter is displayed. If the letters match, the child keeps the pair of cards. If the letters don't match, the cards are returned letter side down to the pocket chart. Then the next child picks two cards.

Many children produce letter reversals. These are expected in the writing of preschoolers and kindergartners. Commenting about them or correcting them usually is not helpful; children often ignore such input. The more children write and see the writing of others (watching the handwriting process when others write and reading texts of all kinds, especially in shared reading or big books), the more conventional and legible their handwriting will become. When children notice their letters are reversed, teachers can provide help for getting the letter started in the right direction. Only occasionally do idiosyncrasies that interfere with legibility persist into the elementary school years; only in such cases and at that time is direct remedial handwriting instruction appropriate.

Shared Writing: Extending Oral Comprehension and Vocabulary, Demonstrating Concepts about Print, and Providing Practice with Alphabet Letters in Text

In Chapter 3 we described shared writing activities in which the teacher prepares an activity, children engage in the activity, they talk about it, and finally the teacher helps them write something about it. For early emergent readers and writers the most effective shared writing texts are short, rarely with more than a dozen words. Shared writing can also be used after an interactive read-aloud to extend children's oral comprehension and vocabulary learning from the story or informational book that was read. For example, after reading *Do Like a Duck Does!*, teachers could ask the higher-level question, "Why did Mother Duck take the fox to the mud and to the pond?" Young children usually can recall what the fox and baby ducks did at those locations (eat bugs and swim), but often they cannot say why Mother Duck put the fox in situations where he'd be expected to do those things (his not liking to eat bugs and inability to swim demonstrated that he was *not* the duck he was pretending to be). During small group, teachers can revisit this familiar book by having children recount the story using the pictures. This provides ample opportunities for using vocabulary such as *protect, guard, duckling, claws, waddle, strut, creep, sneak up close, muck, scum,* and *slink away*. Next, the teacher can begin a shared writing chart titled "Things Fox did not like to do"; we recommend teachers begin shared writing with the title already written. Then children discuss the things the fox didn't like doing. The teacher writes the list saying, "Many of you said the fox does not like to eat bugs. Let me write *eat bugs*."

Shared writing can have many formats including Venn diagrams, timelines, graphs, webs, or lists. Figure 6.6 presents examples of a variety of shared writing formats based

FIGURE 6.6. Formats for shared writing based on *Knuffle Bunny* (Willems, 2004).

on a read-aloud of the book *Knuffle Bunny* (Willems, 2004). In addition to these formats, the teacher might help children compose a sentence about the book: "Trixie got upset because Knuffle Bunny was lost in the washer."

Shared writing provides many opportunities to develop concepts about print. During shared writing, effective teachers make deliberate comments about left and right and top and bottom. They point to the top left of the chart paper and say, "All right, I'm going to start writing here where I'm pointing. Put your eyes up here where I'll write the first word. Watch while I make the first letter" and "Look, before I start the next word, I'm going to move my marker over and leave a good word space." And, "I don't have space to write the next word so I am going to sweep down to the next line. Get your eyes ready to sweep across to the next line, right here."

Reading a big book provides further opportunities to extend concepts about print. Teachers can point out that they begin reading on "this page" (pointing to the left-hand page). After reading the right-hand page, teachers can comment, "I'll turn the page and keep on reading."

After shared writing, teachers use an activity called "step-up" to help children locate and match alphabet letters in texts. Teachers can use magnetic letters as models, such as using the capital letters *T, K,* and *B* or lower-case letters *w, l,* and *t.* Teachers show and name the model magnetic letter (with children chiming in) and have one child step up to the chart and point to the letter, circle it with a marker, or put a sticky circle around the letter. Another effective step-up activity for children in this developmental phase is to have them locate letters that appear more than one time. Teachers can point to an *e,* for example, and have children step up and find another *e.* Children can step up to the chart until all the letter *e*s have been located. Another step up activity is for the teacher to bracket a word by putting a finger before the word and after the word. The teachers says, "I'm going to show just one word. Watch, I'll put a finger here right before the word and here after the word." Now children can step up and bracket a word. Some children will need guidance because they may not notice word spaces. Because not all children will have a turn in a whole-class group to step up and locate a letter or bracket a word, the teacher places the chart and magnetic letters on a table for use during center time. By stopping at the chart during center time and inviting children in the early emergent reading and writing phase to locate letters, practice writing letters, locate repeated letters, and bracket words, teachers are able to provide a few minutes of one-on-one guidance and feedback to individual children.

Another activity after shared writing of a sentence is to cut up the sentence into words. Teachers copy the sentence onto a sentence strip and demonstrate cutting at the spaces between words. They then reassemble the words onto a pocket chart, carefully demonstrating that they are placing the words from left to right and using a return sweep. They comment on where to begin the sentence with the first word, where to put the next word, and so on. They leave very large, exaggerated spaces between the words in order to draw attention to this feature of print. Next they point to each word and reread the sentence, inviting children to reread along. Teachers can make extra word cards for children to match those in the pocket chart. Some teachers start with only the first and last word. After children match the word, they say whether it was the first word or last word. After sentence-matching activities, children are usually invited to draw a picture about the sentence or the book they read. Then children are invited to write about their drawing.

BEGINNINGS OF PHONOLOGICAL AWARENESS

Most children begin the journey to full phonological awareness (which will include phonemic awareness) by simply enjoying listening to their parents or others read aloud nursery rhymes and participating in childhood movement games, such as playing "Patty Cake" or "This Little Piggy." Thus, we argue that 3- and 4-year-old early emergent readers and writers should have lots of opportunities to enjoy read-alouds of books with rhyme and alliteration without teachers explicitly teaching what these are. We recommend that whole-class routines include daily singing, reading big books, and reading charts with rhyme and alliteration. Many preschools introduce a new nursery rhyme each week on a pocket chart, and children learn finger and hand movements to accompany the rhyme. Children should be encouraged to join in singing and saying the rhymes or adding words and phrases as teachers read big books.

After several weeks of merely enjoying such songs, books, and charts, teachers can bring back an old favorite for more deliberate teaching. The teacher says, "The song 'A-Hunting We Will Go' has lots of fun words to say; they are called rhyming words. *Fox* and *box* are rhyming words. Listen, f—ox, b—ox. They sound alike. Their last parts are the same in my mouth. F—ox b—ox." From this time forward, teachers can comment at the end of their reading about rhyming words they heard. Some children catch on to this concept quickly. Soon, without even being asked to, they announce rhyming words they have heard and thus help to call classmates' attention to rhymes.

We have already discussed another early phonological activity of clapping syllables in children's names. In a small-group lesson, the teacher uses pictures to extend syllable clapping to names of objects and animals. The teacher uses photographs of animals, foods, household items, appliances, and clothing to elicit children's syllable segmentation by their naming an animal or item and clapping the syllables in the name. Then the students group the items by category. The teacher encourages syllable blending by displaying the pictures in a pocket chart and then pronouncing the name of a pictured animal or household items one syllable at a time. A child shows that he or she knows which pictured animal or item the teacher intended by blending the syllables to pronounce the name normally. Then the child takes the picture from the chart.

Teachers prepare children for later detecting and manipulating phonemes as is required in phonemic awareness by directing "sounds in motion" movement activities during transitions. Children say a phoneme in isolation but articulate it as a sound made by a real-world object, animal, or activity. For example, a grandfather clock's sound mimics the phoneme /t/. Children can hold their arms down in an inverted V shape and swing back and forth while saying, "/t/-/t/-/t/." To introduce the movement, sound, and name, teachers show a picture of a grandfather clock and talk about its movement and sound. Then they demonstrate the movement and say the sound, calling this motion and

Phoneme	Phrase	Motion
Teachers demonstrate the motion, articulate the sound, and say the phrase.		
/k/	"kick it up"	kick up the leg
/m/	"m-m good"	rub tummy
/t/	"tick tock"	swing arm back and forth like arm on grandfather clock
/s/	"ssssssnake!"	use arm to make snakeslike movement
/b/	"bounce it"	dribble pretend basketball
/f/	"fighting cat"	hunch back, make claws with hands
/d/	"drum"	beat a pretend kettle drum
/p/	"spitting pits"	spit pretend watermelon seeds into hand
/g/	"gulp gulp"	hold hand up like gulping a drink
/h/	"HOT"	pant and wipe sweat off forehead
/j/	"jackhammer"	hold pretend bouncing jackhammer in two hands
/r/	"rip it"	rip a pretend paper into two pieces

FIGURE 6.7. Sounds in motion.

sound "tick tock." Next, children practice "tick tock." Another sound in motion imitates cats humping up their backs and putting out their claws while making and holding the sound /f/ for a few seconds. This is called "fighting cat." Figure 6.7 presents several sounds in motion movements and sounds and their names, including "kick it," "m-m good," "bounce it," and "spitting pits." During a transition, the teacher says a child's name and the name of a sound in motion (e.g., "tick tock"). Then the child demonstrates the motion and sound and gets in line.

CHAPTER SUMMARY

In this chapter we provided examples of deliberate and systematic instruction that extends children's learning as young emergent readers and writers. We provided activities that are embedded in read-alouds, shared reading, and shared writing activities. We also provided examples of separate, more explicit instructional activities, including name games, guided drawing, and writing beginning letters, which introduce alphabet learning. Singing the ABC song and learning to point to letters one to one while singing is another introduction to the alphabet. Alphabet writing and games extend children's learning of capital letters. Shared reading and writing provide many opportunities for teachers to demonstrate a variety of concepts about print and extend children's oral comprehension and vocabulary. Step up and cutting up sentences are activities that further support children's development of concepts about print and alphabet knowledge. Children begin learning phonological awareness as teachers expose them to many songs, poems, chants, and books containing alliteration and rhyme. Later teachers draw deliberate attention to rhyme. Children are introduced to segmenting and blending syllables by clapping syllables in their names and playing syllable games with other vocabulary.

CHAPTER 7

Small-Group Differentiated Instructional Activities for Later Emergent Readers and Writers

In this chapter we describe instructional activities that are designed to later (older) emergent readers and writers in the Awareness and Exploration phase of literacy development. We describe research-based instructional activities across a broad array of literacy learning, including name writing, alphabet knowledge, phonemic awareness, and concepts about print. We also suggest a few instructional activities to accelerate oral comprehension, vocabulary development, and text writing, although much of this can be accomplished through whole-class and center activities described in Chapters 2 and 3. Acquisition of the alphabetic principle usually signals the end of this phase of learning. Thus, we describe how children begin to learn to associate sounds in orally spoken words with letters. We describe how this occurs using unconventional sound–letter matches and how teachers support this learning during shared writing.

CONSIDERING WHAT LATER EMERGENT READERS AND WRITERS KNOW AND CAN DO

In later emergent reading and writing, children show considerable conventional knowledge, but they still read and write in many unconventional ways. Table 7.1 presents the characteristics of the beginnings of this period of the Awareness and Exploration phase and suggests instructional activities. In addition, the table presents expected outcomes of several weeks or months of instruction. Children in this phase of development may range from 3 to 5 years old. Three- and 4-year-olds in this phase are on target and likely progressing on the literacy continuum without difficulty. Five-year-olds who are within this stage as they enter kindergarten may be slightly behind some of their peers, yet they have a strong foundation to make expected progress. Late preschoolers and early kindergartners in this phase need many experiences across all domains of literacy knowledge in whole-class, small-group, and center activities where they can interact with teachers one on one. With good teaching and adequate opportunities to engage in a wide variety of literacy experiences in effective preschool and early kindergarten programs, these children should move quickly through this phase. Children who remain in this phase after 3 months or more of adequate learning opportunities in a rich kindergarten classroom raise concern and require closer observation. After performing careful observation and perhaps assessment and analysis, teachers may decide to initiate supplemental small-group instruction for such children who seem "stuck" in this phase of development. Children who at the end of kindergarten have not reached the end of this phase require additional supplemental small-group instruction. Children who do not move beyond this phase of development by the end of kindergarten are at risk for struggling to learn to read and write.

Table 7.1 shows that a watershed accomplishment at the end of this phase of development is children's acquisition of the alphabetic principle. With sufficient conventional knowledge of the alphabet, the beginnings of phonemic awareness, and strong concepts about print (especially directionality and one-to-one matching), children are able to capitalize on the sound–letter information available in alphabet books and in teacher talk during shared reading and writing.

NAME WRITING AND ALPHABET LEARNING

Preschoolers and kindergartners who are in the later emergent reading and writing phase already have much alphabet knowledge. They have learned to recognize and attempt to write their names and can do so with a few readable letters. They can identify and write initial letters of their names and can write and recognize a few other capital letters, often those in classmates' names. In the later emergent literacy phase, they will learn to recognize and write more of the capital letters and begin learning the lower-case letters. We emphasize that we do not suggest teaching the alphabet through any particular handwriting method, nor through using trace-and-copy worksheets. Although in Chapter 6 we described using consistent letter formation talk to describe letter-writing strokes and we recommend that teachers demonstrate those strokes, the goal is not exact copying. Instead, children need to experiment with and *discover* the features of letters. They gradually master the visual–motor and fine-motor control needed to form all upper- and lower-case letters of the alphabet (McGee & Richgels, 1989). For many children, sufficient opportunities to learn about letter features occur in the contexts of writing their names, observing their teachers write, and engaging in pretend reading and writing during dramatic play (see Chapter 2).

Using the Sign-In Procedure and Writing Names Game Activity

Children's name writing continues to be an important component of literacy development through the late emergent reading and writing phase. Teachers may begin to use the *sign-in procedure*, which also involves having children write their names as a daily attendance activity (Harste, Burke, & Woodward, 1983). This sign-in procedure is slightly altered from the attendance routine we discussed using with early emergent

TABLE 7.1. Characteristics of Later Emergent Readers and Writers at the Onset and End of This Period of Development, with Recommended Instructional Activities

Later emergent readers and writers	Characteristics at onset of this period	Instructional activities	Outcomes of teaching; characteristics at end of this period
Oral comprehension and vocabulary	Make comments and answer questions about books read aloud; acquire vocabulary from books; attempt telling about illustrations	Interactive read-alouds; drama and retelling; book acting during center time (see Chapter 3)	Do minimal retellings with a few details of easy narratives and informational books; acquire and use vocabulary from read-alouds
Name writing	Write first name with letter-like forms and some legible letters	Sign in; name-writing game	Write first name with many legible letters, a few reversals and/or omissions
Concepts about print	Demonstrate book-handling and some directionality concepts	Shared reading of poems with repeated words and many high-frequency words; fingerpoint reading on pocket chart of short nursery rhymes and songs, with matching words, masking words, locating words using fingerpoint reading; What Can You Show Us? activity	Demonstrate directionality; move from tracking with sweeps or taps to attempting one-to-one matching during fingerpoint reading of familiar, patterned text
Alphabet knowledge	Identify a few alphabet letters; use motor skills to control lines used in letter writing and drawing	Direct instruction in upper- and lower-case recognition and writing with games and puzzles; shared writing with Write Ons; reading alphabet and letter books with games; environmental print walls; shared reading of alphabet charts	Recognize many alphabet letters; write some to many letters in legible form

Phonological and phonemic awareness	Learn nursery rhymes and respond to rhythm and rhyme	Shared writing with teacher demonstrations of rhyming words and segmenting and hearing first sounds and spelling words; 3-2-1 scaffolding of segmenting beginning phoneme	Know many nursery rhymes; may identify and produce rhyming words; segment a few beginning phonemes
Alphabetic principle: invented spelling	Demonstrate no understanding of the alphabetic principle; write with random letter strings	Shared writing with the teacher inviting children to hear beginning sounds and select a letter to spell that sound	Invent a few spellings with one highly salient sound spelled (showing emergence of the alphabetic principle)
Phonics: decoding	May know no consonant sound–letter correspondences	3-2-1 scaffolding of segmenting beginning phoneme with consonant letters added to the activity	Know a few consonant sound–letter correspondences
Text complexity and level: comprehension	May have no experience attending to, remembering, and chanting the words of songs or poems printed on charts	Shared reading and writing of familiar poems and songs	Read with support (remember and chant along with a group) familiar poems or songs on shared writing charts
Text writing	Make a representational drawing of person (tadpole) with few details; may use scribbles or mock letters in writing	Drawing activities to accompany book read-alouds, shared writing and reading, and other classrooms activities (see Chapter 3)	Make representational drawing of person (tadpole or with body) with a few details; may write with scribbles, mock letters, or random letters; may attempt to spell a label or word with one sound–letter correspondence

readers and writers. Teachers prepare a sheet of paper on which four or five children sign in. As the children enter the classroom, they locate their sign-in sheet and sign in. Figure 2.5 in Chapter 2 presents a sign-in sheet used in a prekindergarten classroom. The teacher in this classroom used different colors for the sign-in sheets, and they were placed in special locations in the classroom. As the children entered the classroom, they put away their belongings and then went to their sign-in sheet and wrote their names. Over time, most children's name writing begins to appear more conventional, and the letters became more readable, especially as children engage in games that involve name writing.

In the Writing Names Game (Cunningham, 2000), all children attempt to write their classmates' names. Each day a child's name is selected, and the teacher prepares a writing name game sheet (the same name sheet as is shown in Figure 6.2a) by writing the selected child's name at the top and at the bottom of the sheet, with each letter of the bottom copy enclosed in a box. Each child in a small group receives a copy of the name game sheet. The children (rather than the teacher) cut out the boxed letters while they and their teacher name the letters and talk about their features. The children scramble the cut-out letters and then arrange them to match the name printed at the top of the game sheet. They place the letters from left to right to spell the name as the teacher calls the letters. After reassembling the name several times, the teacher can play "show me" games ("Show me the capital *E* . . . Show me the *d*"). Next, the children glue the letters in order from left to right on the game sheet. Then on a large chart, the teacher demonstrates writing the selected child's name. The teacher demonstrates writing each letter, using letter formation talk for the initial capital letter. The children follow their teacher's example, writing each letter on their sheets. They are encouraged to write the letters left to right across the page as many times as they wish. The papers are gathered up and stapled together, and the named child gets to take the resulting name book home.

Figure 7.1 presents one preschool child's attempts at writing Eldric's name. This 4-year-old has a range of letter-writing abilities; her writing demonstrates linearity and

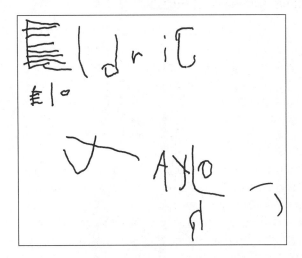

FIGURE 7.1. Jaylen writes Eldric's name.

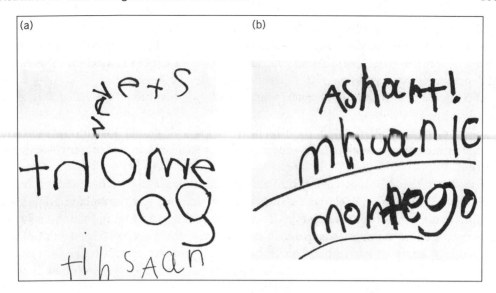

FIGURE 7.2a and b. Two children's attempts at copying names.

directionality as well as correct formation of several letters. Many children continue name writing during center time. Teachers can encourage children to use clipboards on which they might copy classmates' names printed on their cubbies. Or they might copy as many name cards available in the Letter and Word Center as they find interesting. Figure 7.2 presents two children's attempts to write names of other children in the classroom. One child demonstrates strong directionality, while the other child has copied every letter but without consistent left-to-right directionality, and in fact, more often writes right to left.

Alphabet Instruction, Games, and Puzzles

Direct upper- and lower-case alphabet instruction continues for children in the later emergent reading and writing phase. Children know several upper-case letters and may know a few lower-case letters. Now teachers use for lower-case letters the same instruction we described in Chapter 6 for upper-case letters. The same games of sorting, memory match, and wiggle worm can be played with lower-case letters. They begin with the letters that have the same or nearly the same formation in both upper and lower cases: *c, j, k, o, p, s, t, u, v, w, x* and *z*. They teach the upper- and lower-case letters together: *A* and *a*, *B* and *b*, and so on.

To extend alphabet learning, teachers can plan for alphabet activities in a Letter and Word Center or at the Writing Center. For the Letter and Word Center, teachers can construct many kinds of alphabet puzzles. One we recommend is writing a series of letters on a sheet and having children match letter tiles or plastic letters to each of the letters on the sheet. We recommend that the letters spell significant words, such as classmates' names or words related to theme study. Teachers or aides are nearby to give guidance when children select commonly confused letters (Schickedanz & Collins, 2013).

Teachers place alphabet charts in the Writing Center. These are large charts with 26 squares on which all of the alphabet letters are printed in upper and lower case along with a picture for each letter. Teachers can make a copy of the alphabet chart to use as a shared reading experience.

Write On

Write On is a follow-up to shared writing. The first part of shared writing involves an experience, or a book read aloud. For example, after sharing many nonfiction books and talking about the information they provide on bird nests, teachers engage children in recall of the information to extend their oral comprehension and vocabulary. They help children recall that a cup nest is built with sticks to provide support and with grass and fluff to provide warmth and insulation. Birds drop the building materials into a pile and then sit on them. They turn around and around in a circular motion to make the round, cup-shaped nest. Then teachers help children compose the shared writing chart shown in Figure 7.3. First, teachers write the title: "To make a cup nest," and the subtitles "Birds use," and "Birds move." Then they invite children to fill in the phrases.

Now that they have attended to meaning, teachers and children can focus on the print during Write On. Children come to the chart on which the shared writing is written and point to, identify, and write an alphabet letter; point to two words that are the same and write the word; or find a word that has, for example, three letters and write the word. Some teachers have children use one color of marker to circle all of the same alphabet letters or words. When completed, the Write On chart can be hung in the Writing Center for further writing during center time (Figure 2.6 in Chapter 2 presents an example of a preschool Write On chart). Children may also want to draw a picture

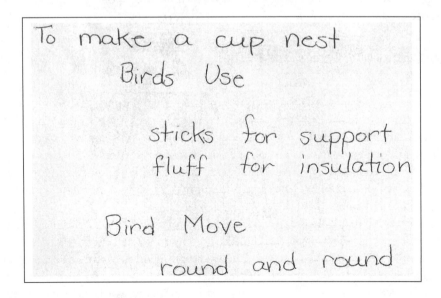

FIGURE 7.3. Shared writing about making cup nests.

for the shared writing chart and to add it to the Write On. Or teachers may reread the shared writing chart on another day and engage children again in talking about how birds make nests. Then they may invite children to draw a picture and to write about nest making. Teachers would expect that later emergent readers and writers might copy words or use random letters. By the end of this phase, teachers may guide some children's spelling of *bird* or *nest* using *B* or *N*.

For another kind of Write On, teachers simply write the upper- and lower-case forms of a letter on a shared writing chart and invite children during center time to cut from newspapers or magazines words that have that letter and glue them to the chart. Children may also add to the chart by writing the target letter, copying words, or practicing writing anything on the chart. Figure 7.4 presents a Write On chart for the letter *M*.

Alphabet Books

Reading alphabet books provides many opportunities for children to learn the names of alphabet letters and hear the phonemes associated with them. As teachers read alphabet books, children chime in saying the letter names. They develop a sense of the entire

FIGURE 7.4. Alphabet Write On and letter cutting for *M*.

sequence of alphabet names, A to Z. Listening to and participating in the reading of the texts of alphabet books does not necessarily teach children the phonemes associated with letters; nonetheless, they receive valuable exposure to the initial sounds of the words featured for each letter in an alphabet book. Alphabet books that provide the best exposure for this are those in which each alphabet letter is prominently printed in isolation, and each page includes only a few familiar objects and printed words. Pictures of unfamiliar animals or foods are not particularly helpful in allowing children to discover the relationship between letters and phonemes (for example, on an O page one child continually called an opossum a mouse, and so he read, "O is for mouse" (Yaden, Smolkin, & Conlon, 1989). Appropriate alphabet books have simple texts like "A is for apple" or "M is for mouse." As teachers read these books, they can make more prominent the connection between the alphabet letter name and its phoneme. After reading the text, teachers can say, for example, "M spells mmm in mmm-mouse" (adapted from Murray, Stahl, & Ivey, 1996, p. 311).

Unlike an alphabet book, which treats the entire alphabet, A to Z, a letter book treats a single letter, an entire book for the letter A, and another for the letter B, and so on. These books are generally only a few pages long and have colorful photographs or illustrations. Each page of a letter book presents one object, its label, and the featured letter. At the end of some letter books is an alliterative poem or riddle featuring a sound associated with the letter.

After teachers read alphabet and letter books, they place the books in the Letter and Word Center. Teachers cut pictures from extra copies of the book and laminate them to use in alphabet matching games. Children can match the pictures to pages in the alphabet book. Alternatively, teachers can prepare alphabet letters created with many different fonts for children to match to pages in an alphabet book.

Alphabet books and letter books inspire the collecting of words that beginning with the same letter; such collections lead eventually to writing alphabet books. Teachers read several alphabet books and, with shared writing, compose lists of words that begin with letters of interest. They invite children to bring in environmental print items from home (such as empty food boxes or snack wrappers, etc.), and teachers help children construct an alphabet wall of environmental print. Children can glue environmental print items on large chart paper divided into 26 squares, each labeled with an alphabet letter. Teachers also make large alphabet charts to use frequently for shared reading. These charts have 26 squares, one for each letter in upper- and lower-case forms, with one picture selected from clip art. For shared reading, children read either the environmental print wall or the alphabet chart. The teachers point to and the children name the letter and the picture or environmental print items.

A Final Word about Alphabet Learning

Most of what is important about alphabet letter learning takes us beyond just the letters themselves. In fact, the print-processing skills (alphabet knowledge, concepts about print, and phonemic awareness) that we describe in this chapter are intertwined during development. At first children may think that letters by themselves have an almost magical power to communicate. They write random strings of letters that they intend to convey a message. However, these letter strings have nothing to do with spelling because their letters bear no relationship to the sounds in the words they are intended to spell. Eventually, children do generate theories about how to combine letters in some systematic relation to sounds they hear in words. This conscious use of sound–letter correspondences coincides with the beginning of invented spelling. However, children usually do not achieve an understanding of the alphabetic principle until near the end of the later emergent reading and writing period. We will discuss more about this after we first describe later emergent readers' and writers' phonological and phonemic awareness.

PHONOLOGICAL AND PHONEMIC AWARENESS

Phonological awareness is highly complex and requires children to attend consciously to the sounds in words in addition to their meanings. Early emergent readers and writers have much experience, albeit unconscious, with the sounds and rhythms of oral language. They have learned and can say and sing nursery rhymes, songs, and poems with alliteration (words with the same beginning letter/phoneme) and rhyme. Children in this early period of development have begun to acquire some phonological awareness. In Chapter 6 we described having children engage in clapping syllables in their names and other words and even having teachers pronounce the first phoneme in children's names as part of transition activities. However, we cannot assume that experiences with nursery rhymes and clapping syllables are enough to develop the beginnings of awareness of phonemes. Beginning to appreciate the alphabetic principle involves being able to hear at least one individual phoneme within spoken words.

We know from research that phonemic awareness training is unwarranted until children can recognize at least a few alphabet letters (Johnston, Anderson, & Holligan, 1996; Stahl & Murray, 1994). Because later emergent readers and writers do know some alphabet letters and have had many playful language experiences with alliteration and rhyme, they are poised to begin acquiring the ability to isolate initial phonemes in words.

Continued Phonological Instruction during Shared Reading

In Chapter 6 we recommended that once children have experience with many nursery rhymes and other poems with rhyme, teachers introduce the concept of rhyming words by calling attention to rhyming words in a familiar book or poem. Teachers can continue this same kind of "sound talk" with later emergent readers and writers. For example, after reading teachers can comment that they noticed several rhyming words. For example with *Fred, bed,* and *shed,* the teacher might say, "Yes, all those words rhyme. *Fred—bed—shed.*" Dr. Seuss books are especially effective. During a reading of *The Cat in the Hat* (Dr. Seuss, 1957) the following exchange occurred between the teacher and Sara:

TEACHER: Okay, listen for the rhyming words when I read this time. [Reading] The sun did not shine. It was too wet to *play*. So we sat in the house all that cold, cold, wet *day*.

SARA: Cold, cold.

TEACHER: We repeated the word "cold" but listen again for rhyming words, those words that sound like music together [repeats reading, stressing and pausing before rhyming words].

SARA: Play, day. (Ukrainetz, Cooney, Dyer, Kysar, & Harris, 2000, p. 10)

Books used to develop phonological awareness can be placed in a specially developed Sound Center. Teachers can place audiotapes or access to iTunes and copies of the books for children's listening and make picture cards for matching games. Observing children as they play with the materials in the Sound Center gives teachers an opportunity to assess how well children have grasped concepts being demonstrated in small-group lessons.

Introducing Phonemic Awareness and Sound–Letter Matches during Shared Reading

Shared writing offers many opportunities for teachers to demonstrate slowly saying words, emphasizing phonemes, and matching letters with those phonemes. Effective teachers know that with most 4-year-olds, it is enough to demonstrate saying and hearing only a few initial sounds in words but that with most kindergartners they can take the next step of demonstrating invented spelling based on sound–letter matching. Such decisions are based on teachers' knowledge of children's current levels of phonemic awareness.

For example, a teacher might write the day's schedule, saying, "I'm going to write *Music* here so that you know we have music class today. I hear *mmm* at the beginning of *Music*. When I just start to say *Music*, I say *mmm*. Do you hear the *mmm*, like in our friend Maria's name, and like in our calendar word *Monday*? *Mmmaria*. *Mmmonday*. *Mmmusic*. Maria uses an *M* to write her name, don't you, Maria? And I see an *M* here at the beginning of *Monday*. So I'm going to start writing *Music* with the letter *M*." This teacher's sound talk relates the phoneme /m/ to words the children know (one of their classmates' names and the name of a day of the week). The teacher draws attention to the printed letter in those words, demonstrating for children a strategy they might use in their own writing, and she uses that letter to spell the new word *Music*. Notice that the teacher did not begin by asking children to name the letter that corresponds to the phoneme. Instead, she demonstrated thinking about and discovering links between letters in words they know and sounds in words they want to write.

Conceptual Development, Not Skill Practice

The best instruction in phonological awareness is thoughtful and based on careful observation of what children can do. Effective teachers realize that phonological awareness is an orientation toward language acquired through exposure and experience, not a skill developed through drill and practice (Adams, 2001). Consider Justin and Duran, two beginning kindergartners. When assessed by his teacher prior to school entry using a rhyming word assessment like that presented in Appendix B, Justin could not match pictures using rhyme or beginning phonemes. In fact, when shown some of the pictures (e.g., rain) he began singing the "Itsy Bitsy Spider" song and matched a picture of a sun to the picture of rain. In his prekindergarten assessment, Duran stated that he had never heard of rhyming words. His teacher followed the directions on the assessment, but she could tell Duran was unsure of the concept. Still, he matched four out of eight rhyming pairs. However, the teacher noticed that Duran attempted a sound strategy: he elongated the words just as she had demonstrated. She was curious about whether Duran would be able to improve his performance with rhyming words. Two weeks into the school year she readministered the rhyming word assessment, and Duran matched all eight of the rhyming pairs.

What is the difference between Justin and Duran? Prior to kindergarten Justin likely had not developed any *metalinguistic* awareness, whereas Duran had. Metalinguistic awareness includes any paying attention to a word beyond its meaning. It involves, for example, paying attention to the length of a word, its letters, and its sounds. Duran had some metalinguistic awareness, as demonstrated by his elongating sounds in words. What he lacked was specific appreciation of what constitutes rhyming; once he acquired that appreciation, he quickly mastered rhyming word matching. Justin, on the other hand, clearly focused only on word meanings. He needs many experiences that draw his attention also to the visual and sound properties of words. His teacher might begin with conscious attention to syllables, which are very easy to detect. Justin might acquire the beginnings of metalinguistic awareness as he learns to clap out a word's syllables. This will provide the foundation for his later learning about rhyming words and beginning phonemes.

Because phonological and phonemic awareness have been the focus of so much attention, teachers may be pressured to adopt a phonemic awareness training program that research has demonstrated to be effective. The best such programs are short. Research suggests that a total of from 8 to 18 hours of instruction overall is plenty of time for children to develop phonological awareness. And their lessons are short. They provide game-like, small-group activities that take as few as 10 minutes.

3-2-1 Scaffolding for Learning to Segment a Beginning Phoneme

Children who know several alphabet letters and can clap syllables are ready to begin learning how to segment a beginning phoneme from a spoken word. (It is not necessary that children know rhyming words before beginning to learn to segment phonemes.) Further, if children have participated as early emergent readers and writers in sounds in motion activities, they already are oriented toward sounds in spoken words. For sounds in motion, teachers call out a phrase or word to elicit a movement and pronunciation of a phoneme. For example, teachers call out "Kick it up," and children pretend to kick a ball and say "/k/." Or teachers call out "Tick tock," and children pretend to be a grandfather clock (swinging their arms) and saying "/t/."

The technique of 3-2-1 scaffolding was developed to help children gradually learn what to listen for when their teachers ask them to say the beginning sound of a word (McGee & Ukrainetz, 2009). It is a useful technique for children who in shared writing are not catching on to sounds and sound–letter matches. At first, when teachers ask children to say the beginning sound of a word, they have no idea what to do. In fact, many teachers can recall amusing incidents of children saying, for example, that the first sound of *dog* is "woof" or the first sound of *bus* is "rrrrr." They have difficulty separating the spoken word from its real-life referent. Actual dogs make sounds like "woof" when they bark, and buses make sounds like "rrrr" as they drive down the road. Another mistaken response to being asked for the initial sound of a word is merely to repeat the word. Some children shrug their shoulders or cleverly wait for another child to answer this tricky, unfathomable question. Here we present a series of scaffolds to lead children toward success in saying initial phonemes of words. At first we provide intense (level 3) scaffolding, with three or more hints; then moderate (level 2) scaffolding, with two hints; and finally minimal (level 1) scaffolding, with one hint, before providing no help at all.

Level 3 scaffolding consists of three hints: pointing to the position of the mouth or using fingers to draw attention to the position of the lips and teeth, repeatedly saying the initial phoneme or elongating it, and modeling and then asking for pronunciation of the phoneme. For example, for the word *mud,* teachers pinch their fingers together near their lips (as the lips are pressed together when saying /m/) and say, "watch my lips." Next, they elongate the initial sound when saying the word, "mmmmmud." And finally they say, "The first sound is /m/. You say /m/." After the child has repeated /m/, they confirm, "Yes, mmmmmud; /m/ is the first sound." Notice that level 3 scaffolding ensures that a child gives the correct response without guessing. Teachers continue to give words with the same initial phoneme, using level 3 scaffolding, until they sense a child can do the task with level 2 scaffolding: using finger movements and pointing to the mouth, elongating or repeating the phoneme at the beginning of the word, and then asking the child to produce the phoneme without the teacher's modeling it. Now children are expected to hear and segment the phoneme. If children cannot do so, then teachers can return to level 3 scaffolding simply by offering the third hint ("The first sound is ____. You say ____.").

When children are successful with level 2 scaffolding, teachers move to level 1 by providing only the hint of elongating or repeating the initial phoneme in the target word: "What is the first sound in *mmmmmoon*?" Soon children can do the task with no scaffolding: "What is the first sound in *moon*?" Some children need level 3 scaffolding, but not all. Teachers should be sensitive to the amount of scaffolding that children need to be successful and gradually reduce scaffolding. Table 7.2 summarizes 3-2-1 scaffolding and provides two example words.

Once children can say just a few initial phonemes, they seem to have acquired the concept of phoneme segmentation. Researchers have found that children who respond successfully to scaffolding for as few as six phonemes are then able to segment phonemes for which they have received no scaffolding (Byrne & Fielding-Barnsley, 1991). We recommend scaffolding segmentation of high-utility consonant phonemes and digraphs, beginning with continuants. Continuants are phonemes that can be elongated

TABLE 7.2. Summary of 3-2-1 Scaffolding for Teaching Segmenting Beginning Sound, Using the Words *Sun* **and** *Time* **as Examples**

Scaffold	Level of support	Supports provided	Example: *Sun*	Example: *Time*
Scaffold: 3 hints	Heavy	1. Fingers imitate mouth and teeth position or action, point to part of mouth or place of articulation, or show letter shape. 2. Elongate or pop sound repeatedly in word. 3. Say the phoneme and elicit it from child.	"What is the first sound in *sun*?" Make an *S* shape in front of mouth repeatedly as /s/ is elongated. "ssssssssssun." "/s/ is the first sound in *sun*. You say /s/."	"What is the first sound in *time*?" Flick out first finger from bottom lip each time /t/ is articulated. "t-t-t-t-ime." "/t/ is the first sound in *time*. You say /t/."
Scaffold: 2 hints	Moderate	1. Fingers imitate mouth and teeth position or action, point to part of mouth or place of articulation, or show letter shape. 2. Elongate or pop sound repeatedly in word.	"What is the first sound in *sun*?" Make an *S* shape in front of mouth repeatedly as /s/ is elongated. "ssssssssssun."	"What is the first sound in *time*?" Flick out first finger from bottom lip each time /t/ is articulated. "t-t-t-t-ime."
Scaffold: 1 hint	Minimum	1. Elongate or pop sound repeatedly in word.	"What is the first sound in *sun*?" "ssssssssssun."	"What is the first sound in *time*?" "t-t-t-t-ime."
No hints	None		"What is the first sound in *sun*?"	"What is the first sound in *time*?"

TABLE 7.3. Continuant and Stop Consonant Phonemes.

Continuant consonant phonemes	Stop consonant phonemes
/f/, /l/, /m/, /n/, /r/, /s/, /v/, /z/, /sh/, /th/ (as in *thing*), /TH/ (as in *this*), and /zh/ (as in the middle of *treasure*).	/b/ /c/ /d/ /g/ /h/ /j/ /k/ /p/ /t/ /w/ /y/

for several seconds, as at the beginning of *mmmmmud*; these include /f/, /l/, /m/, /n/, /r/, /s/, /v/, /z/, /sh/, /th/ (as in *thing*), /TH/ (as in *this*), and /zh/ (as in the middle of *treasure*). In contrast, stop consonants are pronounced with a burst of air, so they cannot be sustained or elongated. When emphasizing initial stop consonants, teachers pop the phonemes repeatedly, for example, for the word *top*, saying "t-t-t-top." Table 7.3 lists the consonant phonemes that are continuants and stops. Most teachers begin scaffolding segmentation by focusing on just two different phonemes, often /m/ and /s/. Then they move on to /f/, /n/, /l, and /v/. Words that begin with stops can be taught next or intermixed after some continuants have been learned.

CONCEPTS ABOUT PRINT

Early emergent readers and writers begin learning concepts about print as they acquire understandings about directionality. They can match words to a sentence placed in a pocket chart, locate words on a shared writing chart, and bracket words with teacher support. As later emergent readers and writers, they begin to learn about the one-to-one match between spoken and written words during fingerpoint reading activities.

Shared Reading and Writing with Later Emergent Readers and Writers

There are some simple methods for directing children's attention to the forms of written language. When teachers display a text, for example, a poem printed on chart paper or placed in a pocket chart, they can use color to highlight the organization of the text and repeated words. A kindergarten teacher we know writes the lines of a displayed text in two alternating colors so that it is easier for children to focus on one line at a time and to know which line to look at when she or classmates talk about a particular letter, word, or line of the poem (Richgels, Poremba, & McGee, 1996). Later emergent readers and writers notice more details about texts, for example, the same word appearing frequently in a poem, a recipe, or a page of a big book.

After examining the poem in Figure 7.5 displayed in a shared writing chart, students will usually notice the repetition of the word *Running*. "There it is again!" they will say. If they do not, the teacher may point to its first appearance and say, "Where else do you see this word?" or "How many other times do you see this word?" or "Do you see any other words in more than one place?"

Sometimes children find particular letters or words especially interesting or significant. Often these are letters in the children's names ("That's mine") or words such

> **Running**
>
> Running in the rain.
> Running through the snow.
> Running on the beach.
> Rrrrr-rrrr-rrrr!
> That's how I like to go.
> Running up and down.
> Running all around.
> Running in and out.
> Rrrrr-rrrr-rrrr!
> That's the way I sound
> When I'm on the go.
> Running!

FIGURE 7.5. Running poem.

as *Mom, Dad,* or *love.* They easily find and remark about these letters and words in a displayed text. Effective teachers celebrate these discoveries and make these connections explicit in order to reinforce the discoverer's learning and to prompt classmates' learning.

What Can You Show Us?

Stepping up to a chart, pointing out letters or words, and commenting on them is part of the What Can You Show Us? activity (Richgels, Poremba, & McGee, 1996). Teachers use What Can You Show Us? before leading children in a shared reading of an enlarged text on chart paper. Suppose a teacher were going to use What Can You Show Us? with the poem "Running" shown in Figure 7.5. Before reading the poem to the children, the teacher invites them to step up to the chart and show something they notice. They may point to alphabet letters that are in their names, repeated letters, repeated words, and perhaps words they know (such as *go* or *like*). Only after many children have had an opportunity to step up and show what they know does the teacher read aloud the poem, pointing to the words as she slowly reads.

What Can You Show Us? may continue over several days of return readings of the same poem. Each day children first step up to tell what they know; as the days pass, they remember and can locate more words. Their talk shows increased literacy knowledge as they have more such experiences with the same printed text. After three or four days, many children have memorized the poem. The teacher may put a copy of the poem in the Book Center and encourage children to fingerpoint read it during center time.

Fingerpoint Reading

Fingerpoint reading is used to help older preschoolers and kindergartners learn directionality, to track print word by word, and, eventually, to recognize some sight words. Fingerpoint reading follows an interactive read-aloud of a big book or an enlarged chart. While children do enjoy tracking the print found in both big books and on charts, we recommend that teachers use pocket charts for fingerpoint reading. The text of big books is not always large enough for groups of children to see the words adequately, the word spaces may not be prominent enough, or the text may be too long for the kind of memorization work children need to do in fingerpoint reading. Even charts of poems may be too long for preschoolers, but may be appropriate for kindergartners who have had more practice with fingerpoint reading.

The first step in fingerpoint reading is to familiarize children with the story or poem. Good books are always presented in interactive read-alouds so that their meanings are thoroughly explored. The initial reading of the text is followed by several shared readings in which children chime in and say any repeated words or dialogue. If teachers use a big book or enlarged poem on chart paper, they point across the lines of text with a hand or a pointer as the children recite.

Next teachers select a portion of the text (usually 10–15 words in length) to use in fingerpoint reading. The selected text should be easily recognized and understood; therefore, many teachers select the first sentence or a sentence that is repeated. Shorter texts allow for quick memorization and focusing of attention on the print, rather than spending time learning to say the text words exactly. Teachers copy the text on sentence strips using larger-than-normal word spaces. For example, one teacher used the text from the *The Three Little Kittens* tale and reproduced it in three lines:

> Three little kittens
> they lost their mittens
> and they began to cry.

Teachers make an additional copy of each of the words in the text for matching activities. They also construct *word frames* in a variety of sizes (see Figure 7.6). These are cut from tag board and have openings through which individual words can be seen.

To introduce the pocket chart text, teachers read it aloud to children, pointing to each word on the pocket chart. (We do not recommend that teachers use long pointers during fingerpoint reading because younger children have a difficult time holding and controlling the pointer to isolate words one by one. Instead, teachers can use shorter sticks, pencils, 12-inch rulers, or specially made fingers cut from construction paper and taped to a plastic drinking straw.) Teachers and children read and reread the pocket chart, pointing to each word one at a time. In order to develop print concepts, children must have the text memorized so that as they are saying a word, the teacher can help them point to that word. As all the children recite the text, individual children are invited to fingerpoint, and teachers help them stay on track.

There are many activities for drawing attention to print. Teachers select activities depending on the knowledge and experience of the children. Teachers can have children

FIGURE 7.6. Word frames.

match words written on cards to words in the text. They can demonstrate checking whether two words match by comparing the letters in each word from left to right. Then teachers can frame a word and have children select from among three word cards the word that is framed. Teachers can hold up a word card and invite children to identify it by fingerpoint rereading until they reach that word. They can challenge children to find a word that has just two alphabet letters, three letters, and so on. They can ask children to find words that begin with a target alphabet letter or match words from the fingerpoint reading text to words in the big book or in the chart-paper text.

Teachers place the fingerpoint reading pocket chart, pointer, word cards, and frames in a center for children to use independently. This may be a special Pocket Chart Center or the Letter and Word Center. Observing children as they independently fingerpoint read and locate words provides teachers with insights about children's literacy development and suggests next steps for instruction. As children become familiar with fingerpoint reading, teachers select longer texts with several high-frequency words,

CHAPTER SUMMARY

In this chapter we described the behaviors and knowledge that teachers can expect from later emergent readers and writers. We described a variety of instructional activities what are designed to address the specific needs of such children. We discussed using the sign-in activity and engaging children in name-writing games in which they attempt to write all their friends' names through teacher modeling. By the end of this phase, children can write their first names with nearly all readable letters. Alphabet learning is extended in a variety of ways, including continued direct instruction in upper- and lower-case letter recognition, writing, games, and puzzles. We also recommended using alphabet books and letter books; these bring a new aspect of alphabet learning, connecting with letter sounds. We recommended that teachers have children gather environmental print objects and use them to make an alphabet wall. Teachers continue to use shared writing follow-ups, now called Write Ons, for practice writing letters and for copying words. By the end of the later emergent reading and writing phase, children recognize and write many upper- and lower-case letters. During this phase they acquire the beginnings of phonemic awareness as evidenced by initial phoneme segmentation. Children are supported in this by teacher modeling during shared writing and by 3-2-1 scaffolding activities. We introduced the What Can You Show Us? activity, which is used prior to shared reading across several days of reading and enlarged text. Children learn to fingerpoint read short poems and sentences placed in pocket charts. They frame words and fingerpoint to locate words. By the end of this phase, children fingerpoint read with nearly perfect one-to-one, speech-to-print matching. Many of them also acquire the alphabetic principle, the understanding that sounds in spoken words are related systematically to letters in written words. These children begin invented spelling, especially with teacher support during shared writing and individual writing.

CHAPTER 8

Small-Group Differentiated Instructional Activities for Experimenting Readers and Writers

In this chapter, we describe instructional activities that help children move into and through the experimenting reading and writing phase of literacy development. A critical development late in the previous phase or early in this phase is children's discovery of the alphabetic principle. This development is often signaled by children's first invented spellings. Children also demonstrate awareness of the alphabetic principle during fingerpoint reading when they monitor whether the word they are pointing to does, indeed, begin with the letter they would expect based on the initial sound of the word they are saying. One way to think about this development is that children's attention has moved away from alphabet letters per se to what they can do: spell words. Children notice words in the environment and learn a few sight words during fingerpoint reading and other text-reading activities such as What Can You Show Us?, shared reading, and shared writing. Their phonemic awareness becomes more complex and is intertwined with sound–letter knowledge. Eventually, toward the end of this phase of reading, children actually begin reading very simple pattern texts. Table 8.1 presents what experimenting readers and writers know at the onset of this phase of development and the outcomes teachers can expect at the end of the phase, after several months of instruction. This table summarizes the instructional activities introduced in this chapter.

BEYOND NAME WRITING AND ALPHABET KNOWLEDGE: GATHERING AND WRITING WORDS

Recognizing the letters of the alphabet is one of the hallmarks of literacy achievement in preschool and kindergarten, and experimenting readers and writers have progressed very far along in learning to write their names and in recognizing and writing alphabet letters. Usually children only have a few letters left to sort out, often the easily confused lower-case letters *b, d, p,* and *q.* Children may still reverse a few other letters, especially

TABLE 8.1. Characteristics of Experimenting Readers and Writers at the Onset and End of This Phase of Development, with Recommended Instructional Activities

Experimenting readers and writers: almost readers and inventive spellers	Characteristics at onset of this phase	Instructional activities	Outcomes of teaching; characteristics at end of this phase
Oral comprehension and vocabulary	Do minimal retellings with few details of easy narratives and information books; acquire and use vocabulary from read-alouds	Interactive read-alouds; shared writing with independent drawing and writing activities; drama and retelling; book and drama centers	Do somewhat elaborated retellings with more details of narratives and information books; acquire and use Tier Two vocabulary
Name writing	Write first name with many legible letters and a few reversals or omissions	Sign in with first and last name, using model for last name	Write first name with all legible letters; attempt to write last name
Concepts about print	Demonstrate directionality; move from tracking with sweeps or taps to attempting one-to-one matching during fingerpoint reading of familiar, patterned text	Fingerpoint reading of familiar texts; locating words; checking words based on first letters; other monitoring games	Secure one-to-one matching during fingerpoint reading of familiar, patterned texts
Alphabet knowledge	Recognize many alphabet letters; write some to many letters in legible form	Letter guessing games such as mystery letter; matching upper- and lower-case letters; focus on teaching good letter formation strokes on all letters	Recognize most upper- and lower-case letters; write many to most letters in legible form
Phonemic awareness	Know many nursery rhymes; may identify and produce rhyming words; segment a few beginning phonemes	Continue 3-2-1 scaffolding; use beginning phoneme games; extend 3-2-1 scaffolding to segmenting last sound; add onset–rime blending activities to making and breaking rhyming words	Segment most beginning phonemes; segment and blend single phoneme onsets and rimes; identify and generate rhymes; segment ending phonemes

Alphabetic principle: invented spelling	Invent spellings of a few words, each with one sound–letter correspondence of a highly salient sound	Guided invented spelling by practicing stretching out words and hearing sounds; Elkonin sound boxes, including with substitution of beginning consonants of familiar rhyming words; dictated sentences	Invent spellings with at least one letter–sound match and later with boundary spellings; spell new words by substituting consonants of familiar rhyming words
Phonics: decoding	Know a few consonant sound–letter correspondences	Add letter–sound instruction to 3-2-1 scaffolding and teach high-utility consonants; picture sorts to categorize by beginning letter–sounds; direct teaching of making and breaking rhyming word families by breaking off a consonant, retaining the rime, and adding a new consonant	Know most consonant sound–letter correspondences; read new words by substituting consonants of familiar rhyming words
Sight vocabulary	Recognize no, or only a few, words by sight	Direct teaching of a few high-frequency words from little books	Recognize 15–30 high-frequency sight words
Text complexity and level: comprehension	Read with support (remember and chant with a group) words to a song or poem written on a chart	Guided reading of little books at levels 1–3/4 (A–C)	Read with accuracy and understanding easy, preprimer texts with teacher support and consistent use of one-to-one matching
Text writing	Make a representational drawing of person (tadpole or body) with a few details; write with mock letters, copied words, or letter strings; may attempt to spell a label or word with one sound–letter correspondence	Drawing and writing activities with read-alouds and other curriculum activities	Make representational drawing of person with body and some details; write words, phrases, or simple sentences with invented spellings

when they are concentrating on hearing and recording sounds during writing, and this should not be cause for concern unless it persists to the end of first grade. Most experimenters are eager to learn to spell their last names and given a model learn to do so quickly and easily. Because experimenters know so much about the alphabet, routine whole-class activities provide ample opportunity for practicing writing for functional purposes. Kindergarten teachers who have many experimenting readers and writers can begin these routines early in the school year, or whenever many children in their classes reach this stage of literacy development. For children who need extra support, such as those just entering this phase late in kindergarten, teachers might provide these activities in small groups with much teacher demonstration and feedback.

Extended Sign-In

Teachers can capitalize on experimenting readers' and writers' extensive knowledge of alphabet letters and interest in words by extending the sign-in procedure to gathering interesting words. Now teachers give each child a clipboard with a sign-in sheet like the one shown in Figure 8.1. The sheet has room for the child to write his or her name (Tara J. in Figure 8.1) and to write other words and text. Children are invited to walk around the classroom and gather words and text from books, the calendar, and other displays. Tara's extended sign-in writing reflects the prominent display of color words in her classroom. She also wrote information that she found on a shared writing chart

FIGURE 8.1. Tara's sign-in sheet.

on which the teacher, Mrs. Poremba, had written "Bear Facts" earlier in the week. This display was created as part of an extensive thematic unit which this teacher used at the beginning of the kindergarten year.

Tara was able to find much to write about on her sign-in sheet because she was so familiar with the text posted around the classroom. Her teacher, Mrs. Poremba, taught extensive units and each day added new words and texts related to the current unit on a variety of classroom displays. As part of the bear unit, the teacher read factual and fictional books about bears. She also planned an activity where children would research facts about bears and she would write these as a shared writing experience. This activity resulted in the shared writing of the Bear Facts poster from which Tara copied for her sign-in activity. As a part of the theme, Mrs. Poremba also planned What Can You Show Us? activities with big books about bears and with a Brown Bear Bread recipe, interactive reading of many big books, making Brown Bear Bread from the recipe and eating it at snack time, reading and comparing of several versions of the Three Bears story, reading of other bear storybooks, and having a teddy bear picnic. Thus, use of themes with repeated exposure to similar content and vocabulary along with use of routine literacy activities helped all the kindergartners in this classroom find many familiar words. The big books that were read as part of the theme were repetitive, pattern texts, and many of the children also read little versions of these books as guided reading activities (explained later in this chapter).

Another Word-Gathering Activity

Another routine that Mrs. Poremba used at the beginning of each day was Words for Today. She posted a sheet of paper titled "More Weather Words" near the weather report chart. As part of the morning routine children would identify the weather. The words *sunny, cloudy, windy, rainy,* and *snowy* were posted on the weather chart for children to use. Now Mrs. Poremba wanted the children to suggest other words besides these familiar ones to add to the weather words chart. At the beginning of the year, the students performed comfortably within the routine by supplying many of the same words day after day and allowing Mrs. Poremba to do the writing and reading work. She would slowly say the word a child suggested, then articulate the first sound and say the letter that spells that sound, demonstrating use of using phonemic awareness and knowledge of letter–sounds for the purpose of spelling. For example, on the very day that Mrs. Poremba introduced More Weather Words, Tara suggested *wet*, and that became a favorite word for weeks. Thus, Mrs. Poremba had frequent opportunities to comment that it was a short word and to demonstrate the correspondence between its sounds and its spelling. When another child suggested *wet* on the 4th day of doing More Weather Words, Mrs. Poremba said, "Www-et. We've been using that word a lot lately too. *Www-et.* Watch me carefully as I write that word. This is a word we've been using a lot. *Wwww—ehhh-t*" (Richgels, 2003).

On the next school day, when Steven suggested *wet*, Mrs. Poremba said, "*Wet.* We have that word up here a lot on our graph, don't we? *Wwwet.* Starts with a *W.* It's a small word. Watch me write that. *W-e-t.* Look at how small, only three letters in *wet.* It's a small word." Mrs. Poremba's and her students' talk about *wet* was not only about sounds and letters and the length of the word. They also talked about meanings. Of course, *wet* was meaningful as a weather word during a rainy time of the fall, but the meaning talk went beyond that. On the same day that Tara first suggested *wet*, Eric suggested a synonym, *damp*.

"But what does *damp* mean?" asked Mrs. Poremba.

"*Damp* means wet," answered another kindergartner.

"Not real wet," commented Steven.

"That's a very good way of telling us what damp means. I like that idea." Then Mrs. Poremba said the first sound and then the whole word: "*D-damp*."

"*D*," said several kindergartners.

Later in the year when most students were experimenters and several children had moved into the more advanced phase of first-grade-level reading and writing, the students took over the role of recorder, so that one of the two helpers of the day led the class through the routine and Mrs. Poremba sat on the side to provide help only when requested (and even then, she often turned the request back on the students).

One day in May, not all the suggestions for Words for Today were even single words. With the whole class's help and using a variety of strategies including copying, sounding out, using sight word knowledge, and looking words up in a picture dictionary, Ian wrote three classmates' suggestions, the first a word, the second a phrase, and the third a complete sentence: *breeze* (BeZA, with a backwards Z), *Tri-City Soccer* (tRy SIty SACR), and *The world is our home* (the WORld Is OUR HOMe) (Richgels, 2003).

A Word about Handwriting

We have suggested that teachers not use a particular method of handwriting or use repeated copying of words and letters on worksheets, and instead have recommended that teachers demonstrate appropriate use of letter strokes and call attention to these using letter formation talk (see Figure 6.3). Most children imitate the teachers and eventually learn to form readable letters easily. When children begin to invent spellings and attempt to write texts, their attention first must focus on listening to sounds and then writing letters to go with those sounds. Less attention should be directed to what the letter looks like, and children should be able to form the letter they have selected for the spelling efficiently, that is fairly quickly with little conscious attention. Some children, unfortunately, develop strange ways of forming letters that interfere with efficient letter writing and result in less readable letter formations.

For example, at the end of kindergarten Dylan had just begun to invent spellings. However, he resisted writing even when supported one on one by the teacher. He knew all the alphabet letters (except confusing *b, d, p,* and *q*), and he could name the sounds associated with 12 of 16 high-utility consonants. He easily segmented the initial phonemes of words, and in fact could segment short consonant–vowel–consonant (CVC) words into all three phonemes. Yet, his teacher was very concerned about his unwillingness to write even though he seemed to have all the foundational knowledge in place: very good phonemic awareness, high alphabet knowledge, and good sound–letter correspondence knowledge. Watching Dylan copy words during the sign-in procedure gave his teacher some additional information. She noticed that Dylan wrote many letters using a bottom-to-top stroke rather than the expected top-to-bottom stroke. Figure 8.2 presents eight lower-case letters and the strokes that Dylan used to make them. When he wrote lower-case *f*, *h*, *p*, and *r*, his first stroke was up rather than down. When he wrote lower-case *e*, his first stroke was up and over to the right instead of the slight-up-and-over-to-the-left expected stroke, and he sometimes used two strokes and sometimes three strokes (forming first the top and then the bottom of the letter). Dylan often erased as he wrote on his sign-in sheet and usually wrote much less than the other children. His teacher concluded that Dylan's letter formations were inefficient, so that he usually had to concentrate too much on handwriting. She decided to help him practice writing these letters using the expected strokes in sand poured into a cookie sheet.

She also played the Mystery Letter Game (Schickedanz & Collins, 2013) with Dylan and a few other children. For this, teachers write a secret letter on a scrap of paper and fold it so no one can see. Then they write the first stroke of that letter on a piece of chart paper. Children take turns guessing the mystery letter. Figure 8.3 presents the upper- and lower-case letters grouped by the first stroke in their formations. That is, some letters begin with either a long or short down stroke. Other letters begin with a slight-up-and-over-to-the-left stroke, and some letters begin with a slant down to the right. When children guess a letter that is not the mystery letter, teachers point out what is the same in the guessed letter and the mystery letter, and they tell something the selected letter has that the mystery letter does not. For example, if the mystery letter is *w*, and

FIGURE 8.2. Dylan's letter strokes on eight lower-case letters.

FIGURE 8.3. Upper- and lower-case letters grouped by their first stroke.

a child guesses *v*, the teacher would write *v* and say, "*v* has a slant down and slant up [writing these strokes], but the mystery letter has more than two strokes." Or if a child guesses *x*, the teacher would write *x* and say, "*x* has a slant down, and then a slant back across [writing those strokes], but the mystery letter doesn't have a slant back across." This game draws much attention to letter formation. Children can practice writing the mystery letter and all the guesses.

Many children do not use expected strokes as they write letters; they may use, like Dylan did, up strokes instead of down strokes. This does not necessarily pose a problem if children quickly write readable letters. However, in Dylan's case letter formation was effortful and required attention, often resulting in letters he found unreadable or unsuitable. He erased frequently and displayed frustration. His teacher showed him ways to make letters faster and more easily, and with a little practice and experience playing the mystery letter game, he was writing more quickly and confidently. Soon he began composing longer texts that included invented spellings often having two or three appropriate sound–letter matches.

PHONEMIC AWARENESS AND DEVELOPING THE ALPHABETIC PRINCIPLE

As children have more and more experience with classroom print and environmental print, they build personal repertoires of letters they can name, letters they can write legibly, and words they can read without hesitation (sight words). Even a small repertoire of such knowledge can serve as the foundation for building another kind of knowledge, knowledge of sound–letter correspondences. These repertoires certainly need not include knowledge of and ability to form all the letters of the alphabet. Children can begin to discover the alphabetic principle and to explore how sounds and letters work together in our writing system when they know only a handful of letters and when they can segment initial phonemes in words.

Sound–Letter Correspondence Instruction

The best instruction for helping children discover and use the alphabetic principle is teachers' demonstrations during writing and their feedback to individual children's attempts at writing (recall Mrs. Poremba's sounding out and spelling during Words for Today). Effective teachers of sound–letter correspondences know what they are teaching. That is, before they teach phonemic awareness, they know what a phoneme is, and before they teach sound–letter correspondences, they know the ins and outs of *phonics* better than their students ever will need to know them (see Appendix A for more information about phonics and phonemes). Phonics is far more complex than simply learning one phoneme associated with one letter. For example, some letters (such as the letter *c*) correspond with more than one sound (consider *candy* and *city*). Some sounds correspond with no single letter (such as the sound at the beginning of *shake*). Effective teachers of sound–letter correspondences find out what their students know and build on that (see assessments in Appendix B). They find out by providing abundant opportunities for children to write and then watching what they do, participating in what they do, and conversing with them about what they do. They model and talk about what they want their students to learn. Finally, they provide meaningful opportunities for students to learn and apply what they learn, usually in shared writing and also increasingly in fingerpoint reading (see our discussion later in this chapter).

Effective kindergarten teachers use frequent assessment to make sure the children are making progress in learning to recognize alphabet letter names and to associate phonemes with them, especially the consonant letters. This can happen informally when teachers place materials in a Letter and Word Center for children's use. When indicated, teachers can provide small groups of children with additional practice in identifying letters and associating sounds with them. The teacher can first explicitly teach the sound associated with two letters, then play short sound–letter correspondence games with children. Usually, sound–letter practice includes and builds on phonemic awareness practice. That is, sound–letter instruction usually begins when children can already reliably segment five or six different initial phonemes. Instruction focuses on letters that correspond to two of those phonemes. We begin with continuants, that is, phonemes whose pronunciations can be sustained for several seconds (see Figure 7.6).

Teachers usually begin with the letters *m* and *s* because these are usually also the first phonemes children learn to segment as a part of 3-2-1 scaffolding (see Chapter 7). They use a pocket chart, the letters *m* and *s* written on cards, and picture cards of words that begin with those letters (e.g., *moon, mask, mop, milk, man,* and *sun, soap, sink, socks, six*). First teachers have children practice initial phoneme segmentation, which they should be able to do easily. Then they introduce the new part of the lesson with a direct explanation and a demonstration: "The word *moon* starts with /m/, and that sound is spelled with the letter *m* (placing the letter card with *m* in the pocket chart and the picture of the moon under the *m*). When I say *m*, I can hear /m/: /e•m/. Now, let me find a picture of something else that is spelled with *m*; it will also start with /m/. *Mop* begins with /m/ and is spelled *m* [placing the picture of the mop under the picture of the moon]." Then teachers turn from demonstration to supporting children's performance of the task: "Now we can do one together. The word *milk* begins with what sound? What letter spells the sound /m/? Good the letter *m* [placing the picture in the *m* column]. Let's try another. What sound does *man* start with? What letter spells that sound?" Then teachers demonstrate and support children's practice with the second letter, *s*. After both sound–letter correspondences have been introduced and children have had supported practice, teachers scramble the pictures and have individual children decide whether a picture goes with *m* or *s* and place it in the pocket chart. Once children are introduced to a sound–letter correspondence, teachers can engage them in playing games such as sorting pictures, fishing for pictures and saying the letter, or playing memory match where pictures must be matched with letters.

We suggest teaching two sound–letter correspondences at a time until the two are known, which usually takes about two or three lessons, and teaching letters in roughly this order: *m, s, f, n, l, v, r, z, t, b,* hard *c/k,* hard *g, h, p, d, w, j.* Letters are repeated frequently in games.

From Shared to Interactive Writing

As we discussed in Chapter 7, shared writing offers many opportunities for teachers to demonstrate slowly saying words, emphasizing phonemes, and matching letters with those phonemes. Effective teachers recognize when it is sufficient to demonstrate how to spell only a few words and then only their first sounds (with 4-year-olds, for example) and when it is useful to demonstrate how to spell several words, with sound–letter matching of beginning and ending phonemes, and perhaps also middle phoneme (with some kindergartners). These decisions will be based on their knowledge of children's current levels of phonemic awareness, sound–letter correspondence knowledge, and ability to orchestrate these during spelling.

Experimenters can benefit from a challenging form of shared writing in which children write portions of the message with the teacher's help. This is called *interactive writing* or *shared pen writing*. Once the topic and purpose of writing are established, the first step in interactive writing is to negotiate a sentence. The teacher and children make suggestions about what a sentence might say. The teacher helps children keep the exact words of the sentence in mind by slowly repeating the sentence and holding up a finger (from left to right) for each word in the sentence as they say it. Then children repeat the sentence as the teacher again holds up a finger for each word. Some teachers draw blank horizontal lines on chart paper from left to right to show where each word of the sentence will be written. The lines help children keep track of the message and its words as they are writing. When the children have the sentence clearly in mind, the second step is to recall a word and slowly stretch out its pronunciation. Next, the teacher shares the pen and selects a student to write letters associated with the sounds in the word. The teacher helps this child articulate the first sound and write a letter. After the first letter is written, the teacher may decide to write the remainder of the word him- or herself because of its length or the complexity of its spelling, or children may contribute other letters to the word's spelling. Next, the teacher restates the sentence, pointing to the words that have been written, and then helps children recall which word comes next. Then that word's pronunciation is elongated, and another child is selected to share the pen and write one or more of its letters.

The spelling on an interactive writing chart is usually conventional because the chart is intended to be read and reread by the children or by others (for example, when it is placed in the hallway for other children, teachers, and parents to read). This is one reason for the teacher's writing the difficult parts of the words and sharing the pen only for writing relatively easy phonemes. However, teachers may decide not to help children spell the words conventionally. Instead, they may demonstrate by writing words with a few letters and emphasizing that those letters do capture sounds in the word. The decision of whether the words are to be spelled conventionally or with invented spellings should be based on the purpose and use of the writing. It should also be clear to children whether they are using grown-up spellings so that others can read it or "kid spellings" so that children can do all the writing. Figure 8.4 presents a kindergartner's response to *The Grouchy Lady Bug* (Carle, 1996) using the technique of composing a message, counting the words and drawing a line for each word, and then listening to the phonemes in each word to produce a spelling.

Because of the complexity of sharing a pen with several children, reading and rereading the sentence, and taking time to stretch out the sounds of words, interactive writing usually produces only a single-sentence text. Small-group or even one-on-one instruction is best for this activity so that every child has a chance to participate. In addition, small groups can be selected so that children with similar needs (such as listening to the ends of words, or learning to hear initial phonemes) are addressed in the lesson.

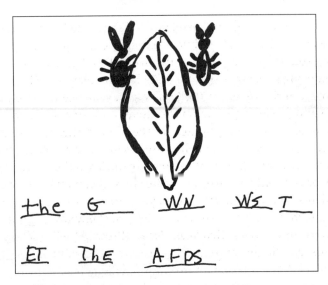

the G   WN   WE T

ET The   AFDS

FIGURE 8.4. Response to *The Grouchy Lady Bug* (Carle, 1996): "The grouchy one wants to eat the aphids."

Supporting Children's Early Attempts at Invented Spelling

Teachers are always pleased to see children make the transition from writing with random letter strings to writing with letters that are systematically related to the phonemes in a word. Although we do not want to overemphasize the importance of being able to invent spellings (especially for preschoolers and beginning-of-the-year kindergartners), first invented spellings are a milestone in every child's literacy development. Some children achieve this without adult support and before they enter kindergarten. Other children, even after several months of demonstrations in shared writing and small-group lessons in phonemic awareness and sound–letter correspondences, need an adult's guidance to begin inventing spellings.

Not all children need to be encouraged to engage in invented spelling. However, if a teacher observes, for example, that a young writer uses one letter per word and that the letter usually corresponds with a sound in the letter's name, then she might provide feedback about the effectiveness of this strategy to the student: "I see you wrote *fun* with this *f*. That works; I can hear *fff* in *fffun* and *fff* in *efff*." Later, when that same writer asks how to write *roller coaster*, the teacher can say, "Wow, that's a hard one! Let's see, what sounds do you hear in *roller coaster, rrrroller coaster*?" The student may identify the *rrr* sound and choose the letter *r*, and the teacher may with similar talk help the student to hear the long *o* sound and choose the letter *o*. The teacher may encourage even more segmenting and spelling—"What else do you hear in *rollllller coaster*?" If the student then answers, "*Rrr* again" and says, "That's all," then the teacher accepts and celebrates *ror* as a spelling of *roller coaster*. "Yes! I can read that: 'Roller coaster!' Can you read your whole story to me?" Such an interaction, short though it is, can help a writer move from spelling with just one letter to hearing more than one sound and spelling with more letters per word.

Difficulty inventing spellings independently can be related to the messages children want to write. Some children seem to know that it is OK to write only a word or two. For them, hearing sounds in those one or two words is relatively easy. Other children have trouble composing a message that they can keep in memory. Their long sentences change as they try to write them. In the jumble of a sentence in which words change over time, many young writers give up on the attempt to listen to sounds in words. It is as if the words will not sit still long enough for the writer to hear any sounds in them.

There are three ways teachers can help with this message problem. One is by having children draw a picture of anything that interests them. Then the teacher helps the child select just a few words or only one word to write about that picture. Another way teachers can help students compose shorter messages is to select writing prompts that call for only one-word responses. This can happen in *guided invented spelling* activities. For example, the pattern in the book *Goodnight Moon* (Brown, 1947) includes the phrases "goodnight, kittens; goodnight, mittens." The pattern of "goodnight, _____" is a good prompt for helping children attempt an invented spelling. Teachers can read the book, establish the pattern, and prepare a *Goodnight Moon* response booklet with the word *goodnight* written on each page. Then they can demonstrate how to think up words to write in the "goodnight" pattern. As a group, children can remember phrases from the book or make up their own responses ("goodnight, lamp; goodnight, shoes; goodnight, bed"). Then teachers can demonstrate saying the words slowly, listening for sounds, and selecting letters to use to spell those sounds—thus guiding children's invented spelling.

The third way that teachers can help children keep their messages firmly in mind as they write is to use the *magic line* (adapted from Feldgus & Cardonick, 1999). As children compose their sentences, they write a magic line for each word (as teachers have demonstrated in interactive writing). Then children go back to the first word, say it slowly, and write on the line the letters they hear in that word. If they cannot hear any sounds, then the magic line will say the word. For many children, the magic line frees them to attempt writing because they know that when all else fails, the line can do the work! Figure 8.5 presents a kindergartner's journal response. She composed a message consisting of one letter string (*ci* to spell *he*), an empty magic line (for *eats*), an invented spelling (*cs* for *cookies*), and a placeholder—a letter without any sound–letter relationship (*L* for *now*). This child's use of the magic line is another example of a problem-solving strategy. Instead of teaching this child to use, for example, the letter *h* to spell *he* and the letters *e* or *t* to spell *eats*, her teacher taught her to use what she did know to solve the problem of composing a message and spelling its words. With the magic line, Natasha was able to signal her entire message and spell at least one word, *cookies*, with

FIGURE 8.5. Kindergartner's journal entry: "He eats cookies now."

its initial and final sounds. Effective teachers teach problem-solving strategies that allow children to complete a task with greater success with each successive attempt.

Spelling and Reading New Rhyming Words: Developing the Ability to Segment and Blend Onset and Rime

Because experimenters are interested in words, already have acquired some phonemic awareness, and are learning consonant–letter correspondences, they are poised to learn to spell and read words in familiar word families. We know that 37 word families comprise hundreds of different words (the -*at* family includes words such as *bat, cat, fat, hat, mat, rat, sat, vat, chat, brat, drat, flat, gnat, slat, splat,* and many more). Each word in a word family consists of the same rime (-*at*) with different onsets (every letter coming before the vowel in the rime: *s, sl,* or *spl* in the words *sat, slat,* and *splat*).

To teach children how to read and spell word-family words, we use a magnetic board and magnetic letters. We start with the -*at* family, using pictures of a cat, bat, and hat. We usually start with the picture of a cat and *cat* spelled with magnetic letters. We say, "Today I am going to teach you the -*at* family. *Cat* is in the -*at* family. *Cat* has two parts. Watch me: (sliding the letter *c* over to the left) /k/, (sliding the letters *a* and *t* together over to touch the *c*) /a•t/, (underlining the whole word with a finger) *cat*. Watch me do it again." We repeat the word, always underlining the entire word, pulling off the first letter and saying its sound, then the rime and saying it, and finally saying the entire word, underlining it with a finger. When we begin this instruction, many children have difficulty retaining the rime (that is, saying just the –*at* part). We practice with *cat, bat,* and *hat,* always segmenting the first sound, saying the rime, and underlining and saying the entire word. The next day, we make explicit that we can take off the first letter and replace it with another to make a new word. We might make the new words *sat, rat,* and *mat.* We continue to emphasize retaining and saying the -*at* part of the word. Then we introduce a new family: -*ig,* with *big, dig, fig, jig,* and *pig.*

Segmenting Words Into Phonemes

At the beginning of the experimenting phase, many children cannot yet segment a spoken word into all of its phonemes, but they can engage in a game in which their teacher scaffolds such segmentation (McGee & Ukrainetz, 2009). For example, children can "fish" for words using a telescoping pointer with a magnet at its end. Each "fish" is a picture of a word with two or three phonemes (for example, *toe, bee, ice, tie, bed, man, moon, sun, lip*). Children fish out a picture and the teacher demonstrates saying its phonemes. She holds up her fist and then uncurls a finger one at a time as she says each phoneme (e.g., /t/, /O/). The children imitate this. Teachers can use this as a transition activity, where they segment a word as they uncurl fingers from a fist, and call on a child to repeat the segments and say the word blended together in order to line up.

At the end of the experimenting phase, as children begin to read little books during guided reading at levels above 1 or 2 (see the section on guided reading later in this chapter), they make a shift into what is called first-grade reading and writing. Some children do this in kindergarten; they are ahead of the developmental progression in literacy and can be expected to become good readers and writers in first grade. Helping children to segment words with three phonemes contributes to making this shift. We recommend that teachers carefully consider whether and when children are ready to attend to all the sounds in words such as *sun, sheep, mom,* and *feet.*

An activity that helps stretch children's phonemic awareness and strengthens their understanding of the alphabetic principle is using *sound boxes.* Sound boxes are small squares drawn on a white board or on paper that is affixed to the board. Teachers use sound boxes to show children how to listen to each phoneme in a word and later to match it with an alphabet letter or letters. For example, a teacher might introduce the word to a small group by giving a meaning clue ("When I take off my shoes and socks, you can see my—"). Next, the teacher demonstrates sliding one token into a box for each phoneme in the word ("—*ffff-eeeee-ttttt*"). Then he moves his finger from left to right under the letters in the boxes and reads, "*Ffff-eeeee-ttttt, feet!*" Last, he may read a short, funny poem about feet. The teacher may choose to demonstrate segmenting and blending other words, such as *seat, beat,* or *meet.* As the children in the group say the words, segment them, and push up tokens, the teacher provides feedback and further demonstrations. Children who can easily hear and segment three-phoneme words while sliding tokens into sound boxes might be helped to spell words using *letter boxes.* Letter boxes are sound boxes into which children write letters that spell the sounds (rather than sliding tokens into boxes to represent the sounds). Kindergarten teachers who want to help children use letter boxes can expect them to be quite skilled with consonants, but to need support with vowels. If kindergartners write *f-e-t* in letter boxes to spell *feet,* their teacher can simply say, "That word has two *e*'s."

What is important for this lesson is not the correct spellings of the words (that will come later). Rather, for kindergartners the focus is on segmenting words into each of their phonemes and associating an appropriate letter for each sound. Effective teachers are careful to make sure children actually need this kind of instruction before they provide it. For example, if a child spells *pickle* as *pekl,* the teacher will recognize the very sophisticated phonemic awareness and sound–letter knowledge demonstrated by that spelling. He will know that this child does not need phonemic awareness teaching, although another child, who spells *pickle* and every other word she wants to write with a random string of letters, does need such teaching.

CONCEPTS ABOUT PRINT

Because experimenters are familiar with fingerpoint reading, teachers can plan fingerpoint reading lessons with longer texts than are used in earlier phases and texts that include several high-frequency words, some words from familiar word families, and some words with known sound–letter correspondence at their beginnings and ends. The poem "Running" (see Figure 7.5 in Chapter 7) is a perfect choice for children who have had experience with fingerpoint reading, have developed many concepts about print, and are beginning to learn sound–letter correspondences. It provides opportunities to learn the high frequency words *in, the, on, I, to,* and *go.* Teachers can teach the sound–letter correspondence /r/–*r* and perhaps contrast it to /s/–*s.*

Teachers will prepare this text by writing each word on a card and placing it in the pocket chart. They can expect experimenters to be fairly accurate with their tracking, perhaps needing help only when they misjudge two- or three-syllable words, such as *running*. Teachers can take advantage of experimenters' growing knowledge of letters and sounds as well. They can cover up several words in the text with blank word cards. As children reread the familiar text, they predict which word is under the word cover and guess the beginning letter of that word (e.g., for the words *rain, snow, beach*). Teachers pull off the cover and confirm children's guesses. Another activity that helps children use sound–letter correspondences during reading is to make the text into a cloze activity. Here, several word cards are removed from the text leaving blank, cloze spaces. The removed cards are placed in the pocket chart below the poem. Again, children reread to figure out which words belong in the cloze spaces and then use sound–letter correspondences to select the target word cards from those that were taken out of the text and placed below the poem.

Teachers can draw even more attention to the print in the text by having children build new words using one or two familiar rhyming words from poem. For example, children can find the word *way*, and teachers can write it on a white board. Then teachers can say, "This word is *way*, but what if I wanted to read the word *day*. How would I have to change this word to make it *day*?" Children could use their own white boards to write several other words, including *bay, hay, may, pay*, and *say*. Later, children will enjoy playing with these materials during center time. Having white boards, the pocket chart poem, and cover-up cards encourages children to reread the chart and to write their own words.

An Exemplary Teacher: Shared Reading in Preparation for Guided Reading

Rather than only reading aloud complex books that stretch comprehension and support vocabulary expansion (which teachers will continue to do for read-alouds and content study), we suggest that teachers also select big books that have repeated phrases similar to those in texts that children will encounter as they begin to read on their own. Mrs. Poremba is an exemplary kindergarten teacher who reads a variety of texts to meet her different purposes for teaching. She skillfully intertwines concept development and vocabulary teaching with teaching about print and how it works.

Recall Mrs. Poremba's theme unit about bears, which we introduced at the beginning of this chapter. As part of that unit she shared *Bears, Bears, Everywhere* (Connelly, 1988). Each page of this text is a predictable rhyme that uses a pattern beginning always with "Bears, bears, everywhere" and ending always with "Bears _____ _____." The blanks are filled with activities such as climbing stairs, chasing hares, riding mares, eating pears, and paying fares. One page has bears in pairs, another has bears in lairs. These unusual words require much discussion. For example, bears in pairs causes some confusion.

"I wonder what it means—'bears in pairs?'" Mrs. Poremba asks.

Jason knows. "Two together make a pair."

Mrs. Poremba responds, "Oh, there are two together. So this isn't the kind of pear that you buy at the store and eat, like a fruit. This is a different way to use the word *pair*.

Jason said that a pair is when two things are together. Look at your shoes. Like a pair of socks."

The children try out this idea. They shout their examples, and Mrs. Poremba repeats many of them: "Pair of shoes!" "Pair of earrings!" "Pair of shoelaces!" "Pair of eyes!" "Ears!" "Pair of arms!" "A pair of legs!"

Several pages later there are bears eating pears. "Look at what they're eating here," directs Mrs. Poremba.

Several kindergartners answer, "Pears!"

"Now that's a new way to use the word *pear*," observes Mrs. Poremba. "Here's the pear that's a fruit, and back here—" Mrs. Poremba stops to find the "Bears in pairs" page.

"—is a pair of people," finishes Jason.

"—a pair that means two together," finishes Mrs. Poremba.

Mrs. Poremba directs the reading of this page, " 'Bears—' "

Again, several kindergartners join this familiar part, " '—bears, everywhere. Bears—' "

"What are they doing?" asks Mrs. Poremba.

"Eating," answer some kindergartners.

" '—eat pears,' " say Mrs. Poremba and some of the kindergartners, finishing the sentence.

Mrs. Poremba demonstrates how easily talk about sounds and letters can be included in shared reading when teachers read books interactively, when they read *with* their students instead of *to* their students, and when they build conversation into their book reading. For example, on the second page of the book, Mrs. Poremba uses the repeated *B* words to teach about an aspect of form. She directs the kindergartners' attention to the first words on the page, the same words as in the book's title:

"I wanted to show you something here. Do you see that *B* in the beginning of *Bears*? Well, look at this one." Mrs. Poremba points to the lower-case *b* at the beginning of the second word, *bears*.

" 'Bears, bears everywhere,' " reads Deborah.

"But look at this *bear*. Look at this *B*."

"Lower-case," notes Eric D. This is true, and, of course, it is unlike the upper-case beginning of the second word in the title on the book's cover.

"It's a lower-case *B*."

"Mmm hmm," confirms Mrs. Poremba.

Mrs. Poremba turns the page. "Look at the bears—"

" 'Bears, bears—' " begins one kindergartner, and several others join in, " '—everywhere.' "

Another lesson about form presents itself on the very next page, this time about the importance of letter order in writing. The bears on this page are on chairs.

"—sitting in chairs," suggests one kindergartner.

No! suggests another kindergartner.

"What's this word?" asks Mrs. Poremba, pointing to *on*.

Two more kindergartners voice their suggestions: *"And." "No."*

"Look at this word," repeats Mrs. Poremba.

"No," repeats another child.

"*Zero!*" shouts Zack.

"Does anybody know what *O-N* spells?"

"*No*," answer several children.

"*On!*" shouts one child.

"Let me show you," says Mrs. Poremba, and she picks up a small erasable board and a marker.

She directs the children's attention to her erasable board writing: "Here is how you spell *no*."

"*N-O*," notes Tara.

"How do you spell it?" continues Mrs. Poremba. "With *n* first and then—"

Eric D. exclaims, "Oh I get it! I get it. The *O* has to be on that side and the *N*'s on that side."

"Yes," explains Mrs. Poremba, "when the *O* is first and the *N* is second, that's the word *on*."

"Oh!" says one kindergartner.

Several kindergartners exclaim: "*On!*" "*On.*" "*On.*" " '*On* chairs!' " "It's '*On chairs*'!" " '*On chairs*'!"

"So it's 'Bears—' " says Mrs. Poremba.

" '—on chairs,' " read Mrs. Poremba and several students together.

Mrs. Poremba makes explicit a connection between this reading and her students' writing: "Some of you have been writing *on* in your sign-in sheets." (See Tara's sign-in sheet in Figure 8.1 where she has written both the words *no* and *on*.)

Guided Reading

A few children may demonstrate levels of reading and writing knowledge that indicate they can benefit from guided reading instruction. Most kindergartners will not reach this level of literacy knowledge, but some will. Table 8.2 presents a list of indicators of

---

TABLE 8.2. Literacy Behaviors That Indicate the Onset of Early Reading

The child . . .
1. Recognizes nearly all alphabet letters fluently.
2. Demonstrates phonological awareness by tapping syllables, producing rhyming words, sorting words by beginning phoneme, isolating beginning phonemes, and blending single-consonant onsets with rimes.
3. Demonstrates knowledge of consonant letter–sound relationships.
4. Spells words with boundary phonemes included on some words.
5. During fingerpoint reading, memorizes text and tracks print with nearly one-on-one correspondence.
6. Corrects tracking during fingerpoint reading using concept of word and letter–sound checking.
7. Attempts independent reading of familiar text using memorization, fingerpoint reading, known words, and letter–sound cross-checking.
8. Retells important events from stories and main details from informational text with some literary and technical vocabulary.

---

the onset of early reading, indicating that children can benefit from conventional reading instruction usually provided in guided reading. Teachers may use books that have been leveled according to difficulty to facilitate selecting appropriately easy texts for beginning conventional reading instruction. There are several book-leveling systems. One, associated with Reading Recovery, levels books from 1 to 20, with levels 1–3 considered kindergarten; 4–16, first grade; and 17–20, second grade. Irene Fountas and Gay Su Pinnell (1996) use alphabet letters to indicate levels, with A–C considered kindergarten level, D–I/J considered first grade, and J–M second grade (adapted from Schulman & Payne, 2000, p. 175). Many commercial companies also publish leveled books with their first level of text usually the primer level.

We expect that several kindergartners in a classroom will reach the level of literacy achievement where they can benefit from guided reading instruction. Some will quickly accomplish this after having entered kindergarten already in the experimenting phase of reading and writing. Others will do so in spring of kindergarten. Books used in early guided reading (at levels 1–3 or A–C) are highly predictable; they are patterned books with many repeated words in predictable sentence patterns. Rather than have children memorize the text first, teachers provide a strong introduction to a book and then expect that children will read it on their own.

At level 1 or A, the text of most leveled books appears on one page and the illustration on the opposite. The two are very closely related. From two to five words are included on each page, in a phrase or sentence on one line of text. The words are printed in a large font with very large spaces between words. The pattern of the text is repeated, with only one word changing per page. For example, a book titled *Playing at the Park* might have an establishing shot (a picture of an entire playground at a park, including a parking lot with a car in it, a swing set, a slide, a sandbox, a hill in the background, and a little girl climbing up the slide). The book might be structured like this:

Page 1: I am swinging.	Page 2: (picture of the girl on the swing set)
Page 3: I am digging.	Page 4: (picture of the girl digging in the sandbox)
Page 4: I am sliding.	Page 5: (picture of the girl sliding down the slide)
Page 6: I am running.	Page 7: (picture of the girl running up the hill)
Page 8: I am rolling.	Page 9: (picture of the girl rolling down the hill)
Page 9: I am going home.	Page 10: (picture of the girl in the car with her mother)

Children will be expected to read this text by using the pictures, listening to their teacher share the pattern of the sentences during a book introduction, matching words one to one, and perhaps using the sight word *I* and learning the new sight word *am*. Teachers introduce the book to the children by (1) telling them what the book or story is about in general, (2) introducing any tricky concepts or vocabulary, if needed, (3) sharing the sentence pattern or repetitive pattern in the text, and (4) visually introducing one or two new words to be used and learned in this text. Book introductions are not picture walks: teachers do not show or talk about every page in the book.

The book introduction begins using the title page, and the teacher gives the overall theme of the story: "In this story a little girl is playing at a park, have you ever gone to a park? What do you like to do at a park?" For a small group of children, the teacher would listen to a few children tell about their experiences at a park.

The book introduction usually continues on the first page of the text: "This little girl is saying, 'I am swinging.' Do you see her, where is she? She says, 'I am swinging.' You say that. She will say 'I am' on every page." The teacher might next introduce the new word *am*. "The word *am* is in this story. Let me show it to you. Here it says *am* [pointing to the word on the page and making sure each child in the group is pointing to the word in his or her own book]. You say it slowly and check it." (Children slide their fingers under the word and say the word slowly.) Now the teacher may show one more page that has the pattern "I am _____" and have the children guess what the child is doing. The teacher would have the children repeat the phrase "I am _____." Finally, the teacher would turn to the last page where the pattern is interrupted. "On this page the little girl is going somewhere. Where do you think she is going? Would she be going home? Let's read this book and find out." All the children turn back to the beginning and begin reading quietly aloud using their fingers to track the text. Teachers listen in to one child at a time read a page or two.

After reading, the teacher would initiate a short discussion about the story: "What would be your favorite thing to do at the park?" Then she may praise good problem solving. One child might have read "I am tumbling" for "I am rolling" but self-corrected. In this case the teacher would praise looking at the first letter and confirming that what was read has to look right (have the expected first letter in the text). After reading, the teacher might reinforce sight word learning. The children might be given white boards and asked to locate the word *am* and tell what the first letter is and how many letters are in the word. They would cover the word in the text and write it on their white boards and then check it. Each child would write the word several times. The teacher would make a note to be sure to check the next time this group meets whether the children can spell *am* from memory.

All the children would read this book the following day. The teacher might watch one child read the entire text, doing so with a different child each day of the week, and take running records (see Chapter 4) so that every 2 weeks the teacher has a running record for each child. Now the book should be easily read by everyone in the group, and can be a book placed in each child's independent reading basket for reading during independent book browsing or as a part of work station or center activities (see Chapter 2).

Little books on levels C or D (levels 3 through 6) usually have less repetition and call for additional sight word knowledge. They are longer, with 50 to 75 words and three to four lines of text per page. These books continue to have strong picture support. However, children must be able to coordinate using the pictures to anticipate text they will read, remembering words and language structures introduced in the book introduction, recognizing sight words on the run as they read unfamiliar text, and using sound–letter knowledge to guide what they anticipate the text will say and monitor what they do read. Children who manage this level of text reading have entered the phase of first-grade-level reading and writing.

CHAPTER SUMMARY

In this chapter we have described ways teachers can embed instruction that supports children's development of phonemic awareness and the alphabetic principle as a part of whole-class routines, such as Words for Today. We described an extended sign-in procedure in which children copy words of interest from classroom displays. We provided an example of a complex letter-learning game that draws attention to expected letter strokes: the Mystery Letter Game. We discussed how teachers can use shared reading of poems and books to draw attention to rhyme and even to demonstrate how to segment words into phonemes. Teachers can capitalize on shared writing to demonstrate segmenting words, hearing sounds, and selecting letters to spell those sounds. Thus, shared writing demonstrations can be crafted to help children discover more about sound–letter correspondences and the alphabetic principle. Teachers can also extend children's understandings of these concepts when they help children write. When needed, teachers can provide more explicit instruction about sound–letter correspondences and help children learn to read and spell new words in familiar rhyming families. Finally, when children can orchestrate a sufficient amount of literacy knowledge, they begin to finger-point read longer texts, participate in shared reading of predictable texts, and eventually begin guided reading of little, leveled books. They will begin learning sight words for reading and writing. These are the expected literacy milestones for the end of kindergarten. These achievements prepare children for successful reading and writing in first grade.

CHAPTER 9

Differentiated Instruction in Action

This chapter describes how teachers can organize and deliver differentiated instruction in prevention and intervention programs for prekindergarten and kindergarten children. First we present Eric's case and discuss the intervention program his preschool teacher created for him and three other children. Then we describe a kindergarten classroom and how the teacher in this classroom planned differentiated instruction for all children. The kindergarten context described in this chapter includes planned themes and units and greater attention than in preschool to developing alphabet knowledge, phonemic awareness, and understandings of sound–letter correspondences, along with helping all children begin to write compositions with strong invented spellings and to read easy, little books with some sight words. We describe one case-study student, Sarah, and how her instruction progressed across time. While she began kindergarten with levels of concepts and skills that suggested she was at risk, her instructional program allowed her to reach end-of-year kindergarten benchmarks. The intervention activities that we describe in the chapter have been tailored to meet the needs of specific children, but we are careful to detail how teachers can use assessment information to pinpoint needs and align them with instruction for any child. The interventions we describe were delivered by classroom teachers; however, intervention specialists can use the same approaches to tailor instruction that they provide.

ERIC AND PRESCHOOL INTERVENTION PROGRAMS

Recall from Chapter 5 that Eric was assessed in January of his preschool year. At that time, he attempted to write his name with three symbols and recognized four uppercase letters. His drawing was nonrepresentational although it included a circle, dots, and lines, and he attempted to write using mock cursive. He produced a short retelling using the illustrations from *Owl Moon* (Yolen, 1987).

How and When to Make Decisions about Providing Intervention Instruction

Eric's teacher, Ms. Warren, used her initial assessments in January to decide whether individual children needed intervention instruction. Most children in her classroom began preschool without any conventional knowledge of literacy. She used the first part of the year to provide them an opportunity to learn how to write their names, to begin learning alphabet letter names, and to discover concepts about print. By January, she believed that only a few children would need intervention instruction—those that seemed to be lagging behind their classmates. Her small-group intervention would be in addition to the instruction her children normally received in half-class heterogeneous groups (she normally taught one half of the class while her assistant taught the other half). She used a typical five-step model to make decisions about which children might need further intervention instruction and what the aim of that instruction might be (Tilly, 2008).

The first step in making intervention decisions is to decide whether individual children have problems. Teachers ask whether a child is making adequate progress or is lagging significantly behind his or her peers. The answer usually comes from screening assessments. These usually have benchmarks against which to measure children's performances when determining whether they are on target or are at risk. Those children whose results suggest they are at risk are the target group for intervention.

The second step in making intervention decisions is to determine what might be causing a child's problem. Teachers ask why a child is not making progress in an area of literacy development. The causes can vary, including, but not limited to, their not having sufficient background or foundational knowledge or skill, their not having sufficient practice or opportunity to get individual feedback, and their not attending sufficiently to instruction.

The third step in making intervention decisions is to consider what ought to be taught and how. Teachers must decide how to group children, how many children to include in the group, and how frequently to provide intervention.

Similarly the fourth step is to adjust and make modifications in instruction and group membership on an ongoing basis based on student response to instruction. Most teachers tailor instruction to small-group needs and make decisions about how to adjust instruction based on children's responses. We do not recommend intervention programs that require following in lockstep a sequence of instruction in a particular area of literacy development regardless of how well children perform as the intervention proceeds.

The final step in the intervention decision process is to assess the progress of the child's learning after some instruction. Progress monitoring tools can be simple teacher-made assessments (such as determining whether a child has learned to recognize letters taught by naming them or writing them) or standardized progress monitoring tools such as the Individual Growth and Development Indicators for Infants and Toddlers (*IGDI*; Greenwood et al., 2008).

After giving all her preschoolers the screening measures in January, Ms. Warren decided to provide an additional daily lesson for Eric and three other children. None of the children in this group recognized more than six alphabet letters, and none could write a readable signature, although two children were making at least the initial letters of their names in readable form. These children displayed little conventional knowledge about literacy although they all enjoyed whole-class read-alouds, participated in nursery rhyme choral readings and retellings, and used adequate spoken language as they interacted with their peers and friends during center activities and in outside play. Only one of the children frequently selected literacy activities as a first choice in center time, usually wanting to go to the Writing Center, where she enjoyed using the materials but rarely attempted or pretended to write a message without teacher support and prompting. The other three children did not visit the Book Center or the Writing Center without teacher invitations. Ms. Warren concluded that these children preferred more active learning games and activities.

Checking on Foundations to Make Decisions about the Content of the Intervention

From her initial assessment of the four target children, Ms. Warren decided that for them two areas of development to address were recognizing and writing their own names and identifying and writing alphabet letters. The children also struggled to develop concepts about print and displayed no conventional phonological awareness. Next, Ms. Warren carefully considered what might be the cause of these children's lack of progress. In order to learn more about what the children could do, she quickly assessed their knowledge of letter strokes. Children who have a strong understanding of letter strokes (how to make, for example, vertical lines) have heightened awareness of features that distinguish one letter from another. Ms. Warren assessed the four children's awareness of letter strokes (which she had taught previously in guided drawing and other writing activities). She asked children to write "a down" and observed whether the children wrote a vertical line from top to bottom. She assessed what they did when asked to write "across," "slant," "up and around," and "curve forward"—all the foundational strokes used to form letters. She found that the children were not sure what these strokes were without a demonstration from her. She knew that without more control over these basic letter-making strokes, children would continue to struggle learning to write their names and to distinguish among letters.

Finally, she wondered whether these children could sing the alphabet song. Knowing the alphabet song by itself is not equivalent to identifying letters, but it does indicate whether children have the letter names in their spoken vocabularies. Two children in this group had difficulty singing the entire song. Now that Ms. Warren had an idea of the children's difficulties and their possible causes, she was ready to make decisions about the nature of the instruction she would provide. She concluded that these children needed foundational work in learning letter features, how to make letter strokes, and how to match letters to their names while singing the alphabet song. The context for this work would be the children's name writing.

Delivering the Intervention

Ms. Warren decided to initiate a new theme for her daily read-alouds with the entire class, a theme that would support her small-group intervention work with the four target children. She decided to read several books about the importance of a child's name and how names are part of making friends and getting along in a new situation. Figure 9.1 lists the name books that she read aloud to the entire class, using her usual three-day reading routine: "push-in" demonstrations of how to think, "pull-out" questions that call on children's thinking, and reconstruction prompts that ask children to "tell what is happening here" (see Chapter 3). Doing the read-alouds with the entire class would draw everyone's attention to how important names are. Ms. Warren would be able to refer to whole-class talk about names during the later small-group intervention work.

Ms. Warren decided that the first few weeks of the intervention instruction would have three components: singing the alphabet song and matching letters, name recognition games and puzzles, and guided drawing to focus on letter strokes followed by free drawing about the name books. Singing the alphabet song the first week would involve singing slowly while the teacher pointed to each upper-case letter printed on a large poster (the letters were grouped in lines to match the phrasing of the song). After singing and matching all the letters, children practiced singing again to a particular letter (usually the first letter of one of the children's names). For example, when it was Eric's turn, everyone would sing and be challenged to stop just after they sang *E*. On Whitney's turn, everyone had to sing all the way to *W*. When the children became more adept at the singing, they received small alphabet mats that replicated the large alphabet poster. They then used these for pointing and matching letters themselves while singing. This became a quick and easy warm-up activity for each lesson.

The second component of the intervention was name work. First, children selected their own names from names written on cards displayed in a pocket chart. After the first week, the number of names displayed on the pocket chart was doubled so that every child had to select from other names that began with their same first letter (Eric had to make sure not to select Ethel, and later Evan, and—most challenging—Erin). After selecting their name cards, they matched magnetic letters to the letters on the cards. Later, they used the magnetic letters to write their names without reference to the name cards. They always practiced writing their names on small chalkboards, and the teacher helped each child each day. They also practiced writing the initial letters of their group mates' names. Then the names were placed back in the pocket chart and each child practiced reading all four names. Children counted the number of letters in a particular name and stepped up to the chart to point to letters that were the same (other name activities are found in Chapters 6 and 7).

Chrysanthemum by Kevin Henkes

Corduroy by Don Freeman

My Name Is Yoon by Helen Recorvits

The Name Jar by Yangsook Choi

Tikki Tikki Tembo by Arlene Mosel

FIGURE 9.1. List of name books read aloud in whole-class group.

Finally, children engaged in the third component of the intervention: guided and free drawing (see Chapter 6). In guided drawing Ms. Warren at first focused on children's using down and across strokes. She gradually increased to using all letter strokes. On other days children drew pictures about the name book of the day and talked with the other children and the teacher about their pictures.

Changing the Intervention over Time

Ms. Warren used informal progress monitoring assessments throughout the intervention. When children could easily select their names even from among confusing alternatives and could sing the alphabet song with nearly perfect matching, she no longer began each day with the alphabet song or with name selection. Instead children signed in by writing their name on a blank card and putting it in the pocket chart. A child of the day read all of these names. Now Ms. Warren introduced three or four upper-case letters to be learned for the week. She began with *T, E,* and *F,* and then taught the other letters with downs and overs: *L, H,* and *I.* Now instead of guided drawing, after introducing the letters and showing the children how to write them, Ms. Warren played numerous letter games with the group (see Chapters 6 and 7). One of the favorites was the "parking lot game" (Scanlon, Anderson, & Sweeney, 2010). Each child had a small toy car and a mat to serve as a parking lot, with parking spaces labeled with letters (see Figure 9.2). All four parking lot mats displayed the same letters, but in different parking spaces. Ms. Warren called out a letter, and the children had to park their car on that letter. She used a set of cards with the letters printed on them to allow children to self-check. Later a child was selected to read the letters. Children also cut letters from magazines and newspapers and glued them to posters.

Ms. Warren helped children compose shared writing charts at least twice a week. The topics of this writing related to other classroom activities or books she read aloud to the whole class. One day the children recalled and named the characters from *The Little Red Hen* (*Makes a Pizza*) (Sturges, 1999). Shared writing allowed her to demonstrate left-to-right and top-to-bottom directionality and between-word spaces. After reading the chart with Ms. Warren, the children stepped up to the chart to demonstrate concepts about letters and words. They counted letters in words and located letters they knew. For example, after Ms. Warren wrote the words *Little Red Hen, Dog, Duck,* and *Cat* on

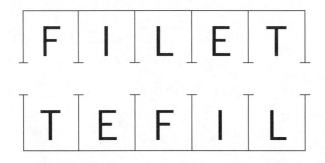

FIGURE 9.2. The alphabet parking lot game board.

the shared writing chart, the children located the letters *L, R, H, D*, and *C* and practiced writing them. Over the next 6 weeks, Ms. Warren taught the most frequently used upper-case letters (leaving out *Q, U, V, X*, and *Y*) and assessed children's naming and writing the letters she had taught. Everyone named at least 15 letters.

Now the lessons changed again to focus on learning lower-case letters. Ms. Warren began using 3-2-1 scaffolding to teach initial phoneme segmentation (see Chapter 7). The intervention lessons continued to connect with books read aloud to the whole class, and they continued to provide meaningful shared-writing contexts for finding letters and listening to sounds in words. By the end of the year, Ms. Warren met with the intervention group only twice a week instead of daily. In brief lessons she composed a sentence on a sentence strip, cut it into words, and placed the words in the pocket chart. Children began fingerpoint reading the sentence. They were given their own copy of the sentence to cut into words, reassemble, and illustrate. She also introduced guided invented spelling, where she demonstrated how to say words slowly and hear a sound she could spell with a letter.

Eric and his three classmates in the small-group intervention ended their prekindergarten year knowing most alphabet letters and writing their names with readable letters. Only one child could not segment the first sound in words, although he had learned the sounds associated with several consonant letters. The other children not only could segment first sounds, but also were nearly perfect fingerpoint readers. With Ms. Warren's support, Eric could invent spellings with at least one letter. In fact, in the end-of-year assessment, the four children in this group outperformed a few other children who had not been identified in January as at risk.

SARAH AND SMALL-GROUP PREVENTION INSTRUCTION IN KINDERGARTEN

The process of identifying children at risk and making decisions about instruction is similar in kindergarten to what we have described for preschool. However, in kindergarten there is greater need to provide differentiated instruction for all children. As in preschool, the process begins with screening assessments. In Chapter 5 we examined the results of screening assessments given to three kindergarten children: Sarah, Marceli, and Jacob. These three children were in the same classroom and represent the range of learners most kindergarten teachers can expect. Their teacher, Mrs. Meier, used several screening assessments to make decisions about how to group children for instruction and which instructional strategies she would use for differentiated instruction. The first step she used in making decisions about differentiated small-group instruction was to use screening assessment results to create a class profile.

Building a Class Profile

Mrs. Meier gives several sets of screening assessments. The first includes name writing, identification of upper-case letters, concepts about print, and retelling. Based on the results of this first set of screening assessments, some children are given part or all of a second set that consists of fingerpoint reading and lower-case letter identification. If children know eight or more concepts about print, they are also given the fingerpoint reading assessment. If children know 10 or more upper-case alphabet letters, they are given the lower-case alphabet letter assessment. These cutoff scores are based on Mrs. Meier's experience: If children know some concepts about print, they might be fingerpoint readers. If they know some upper-case letters, they are likely to know some lower-case letters. Based on the results of this second set of screening assessments, children may be given a third set of assessments, which include writing alphabet letters, segmenting initial phonemes, and producing sounds of consonant letters. That is, if children know 15 or more alphabet letters (upper- and lower-case combined), Mrs. Meier will administer the third set of assessments. She reasons that children who know several alphabet letters will also know how to write letters. Finally, Mrs. Meier decides which children will take a fourth, invented spelling assessment. She has found that children who can segment initial phonemes of at least two words and can say the sounds associated with at least two consonant letters are likely to invent spellings and thus will provide useful information in the developmental spelling assessment.

Later in the year, if children can spell at least one consonant sound in every word of the developmental spelling assessment, they are given a final set of assessments that includes rhyme, onset–rime segmentation, word reading, word writing, and segmenting phonemes of two- and three-phoneme words. This stepwise decision making about assessments reduces the amount of time each child is assessed. Some children receive only the first set of assessments, while other children receive two, three, four, or even five sets.

The results of Mrs. Meier's screening assessment of her entire class of 21 kindergartners are presented in Figure 9.3. She orders children on the class profile from the child with the highest upper-case alphabet identification score to the child with the lowest. A blank cell indicates that a child was not given an assessment.

Using this class profile, Mrs. Meier identified four groups of children at similar levels of development. These groups are separated in Figure 9.3 by heavy black lines. At the bottom of the class profile are five children who have very little conventional literacy knowledge. They can identify only a few alphabet letters and have some concepts about print. Mrs. Meier considers them early emergent readers and writers. Next are seven children Mrs. Meier considers later emergent readers and writers. They know some alphabet letters and concepts about print, but they cannot yet fingerpoint read. She identified four children as early in the phase of experimenting reading and writing. They can identify many alphabet letters, write some letters, fingerpoint read, and produce sounds for a few consonant letters. At the top of the class profile are five children who are experimenting readers and writers. They can identify and write most letters, fingerpoint read, segment several initial phonemes, produce sounds for many consonants, and produce invented spellings that use some expected consonant letters.

Mrs. Meier knows that some of her students will move from one group to another during the year, and she prefers to start the year with as small an early emergent group as possible. She placed Doug and Anna in the later emergent reading and writing group although they have much the same knowledge as the early emergent reading and writing group. She will carefully observe how all children respond to her instruction and will

Names	Retell	Concepts About Print, 20	Fingerpoint, 12 (Use if CAP ≥8)	ABC, 26	abc, 26 (Use if ABC, ≥10)	abc—write, 26 (Use if ABC + abc ≥15)	Segmenting beginning phonemes, 16 (Use if ABC + abc ≥15)	Consonant letter sounds, 17 (Use if ABC + abc ≥15)	Rhyme, 10	Onset–rime, 10	Word reading, 20	Word writing	Spelling (Use if seg. beg. phs. ≥2 and cons. ltr. snds. ≥2)	Segmenting phonemes, 10
Leonard	MF	20	12	26	23	20	10	15					15	
Jacob	ES	15	7	25	23	22	8	5					8	
Gina	EM	19	10	25	21	16	10	13					13	
Lena	MS	17	7	20	17	14	8	10					7	
Jeffery	ES	15	7	19	15	14	6	8					6	
Marceli	ES	11	6	18	15	14	0	0						
Guadalupe	ES	12	5	15	10	7	0	2					0	
Do Thi	ES	10	4	12	8	10	0	5					2	
Antonin	ES	9	3	12	7	6	0	4					0	
Maria	MF	11	0	11	3									
Myzar	MF	12	0	11	3									
Abdelrahman	MF	7		10	4									
Fifi	MF	8	0	10	4									
Sally	MS	8	0	10	3									
Doug	MS	7		9										
Ana	MF	7		9										
Pedro	MF	7		7										
Seth	MS	3		4										
Sarah	MF	9	0	3										
Alicia	MF	3		2										
Leon	MF	4		0										

FIGURE 9.3. Class profile.

Retell: MF, minimum with few details; MS, minimum with some details; ES, elaborated with some details; EM, elaborated with many details.

consult with the reading specialist to coordinate intervention instruction. She will be careful to provide extra support to Doug and Anna in order to make sure that they can learn in the later emergent reader and writer group, but if they have difficulty, she will move them to the early emergent group.

Mrs. Meier knows that small-group, differentiated literacy instruction will not begin until October. She uses August and September to assess children and familiarize them with daily kindergarten routines and the work stations where they will work independently while she teaches small groups. Beginning in October, her daily schedule will include a 20-minute lesson for three of the four small groups. She will teach two groups daily, her classroom assistant will teach one small group daily, and the reading specialist who comes to the classroom 3 days a week will teach the fourth group. The

7:45	Book browsing, sign-in/question of the day, lunch sign-up				
8:00	Greeting, calendar, words for the day, morning message, What Can You Show Us?				
8:30	Daily literacy work stations and small group literacy lessons				
Week 1	**M**	**T**	**W**	**Th**	**F**
8:45					
Teacher	Group e	Group e	Group e	Group e	Group e
Assistant	Group a	Group a	Group a	Group a	Group a
9:10					
Teacher	Group i	Group i	Group i	Group i	Group i
Reading specialist	Group o		Group o		Group o
Week 2	**M**	**T**	**W**	**Th**	**F**
8:45					
Teacher	Group e	Group e	Group e	Group e	Group e
Assistant	Group o	Group o	Group o	Group o	Group o
9:10					
Teacher	Group i	Group i	Group i	Group i	Group i
Reading specialist	Group a		Group a		Group a
9:45	Literature theme read-aloud				
10:15	Specials (M and Th PE, T art, W computer lab, F library)				
11:00	Literature theme activities (writing workshop beginning in February)				
11:30	Lunch and recess				
12:30	Math and table-top math activities and games				
1:15	Science or social studies theme read-alouds and activities				
2:00	Work stations, classroom computers, independent reading, listening center (small-group intervention lessons)				
2:30	Daily summary of the day				
2:45	Dismissal				

FIGURE 9.4. Mrs. Meier's daily schedule.

small-group schedule changes every other week. While the classroom teacher always teaches the early and later emergent reading groups, the reading specialist and assistant trade off teaching the early experimenting and experimenting reading groups. Figure 9.4 shows the entire daily schedule.

Year-Long Planning: Whole-Class Literature Study, Science, and Social Studies

Mrs. Meier begins laying out plans for the year by identifying two themes per month: themes for whole-class read-aloud of literature and themes for social studies and science content study. She uses her school system's curriculum guides and state standards to plan for these themes. For example, in November her literature study and read-alouds will focus on "talking beasts" from folklore (*Goldilocks and the Three Bears*, *Three Billy Goats Gruff*, etc.), and her science theme will be force and motion. In January, her literature study and read-alouds will explore fantasy and especially the home–away–home structure of many stories. The social studies theme will be geography and maps (see Figure 9.5).

Mrs. Meier plans in themes or units to provide children with deeper and richer concepts about science and social studies and to increase their knowledge about literature. The Common Core English Language Arts Standards (National Governors Association Center for Best Practices & Council of Chief State School Officers, 2010) mandate that teachers select and group books for children in ways that build breadth within a theme and across grade levels. Teachers help children read closely by paying attention to what the text says and what the illustrations show. Their goal is to build deep understandings of key ideas and themes in stories and key ideas and concepts in informational books. Mrs. Meier uses 3 days of repeated reading aloud to help her children attend closely to texts and illustrations.

Small-Group Differentiated Instruction

Her class profile changes from year to year, but Mrs. Meier always has children like this year's Sarah and Jacob (see Figure 9.3), who seem to know very little about reading and writing, and other children who are nearly reading and already spelling. Thus, she knows she must quickly begin small-group differentiated instruction, meeting children at their current level of knowledge and helping them to move ahead as quickly as they can. In general her small-group instruction has three components, each increasing in complexity and difficulty as the children progress. The first component is reading short texts with children or supporting children's reading them on their own. The second component is teaching what Mrs. Meier calls literacy skills, such as alphabet letter recognition, phonemic awareness, and eventually decoding and spelling of words. The third component is supporting children's writing.

These three components of small-group instruction are research based. For example, a study found that kindergartners who were taught with all three of these components learned more than those who received only the literacy skills component (Craig, 2006). The experimental group experienced all three components in the course of a

Yearly Planning Guide	August/ September	October	November	December
Whole class: Literature theme	Friends and Family	Poetry	Talking Beasts: Folklore	What a Character: Character Traits and Motivation
Whole class: Science or social studies theme	Social Studies: Starting school, Money	Science Processes: Observing Fall Changes	Physical Science: Force and Motion	Earth Science: Rocks
Group e: early emergent literacy learners		Shared reading, writing, retelling of nursery rhymes (print concepts, vocabulary); *name games*; *alphabet song*; **guided drawing, drawing and writing**	Shared reading, writing, retelling of big-book versions of favorite folktales (print concepts and vocabulary); *ABC instruction* **with writing; drawing and writing**	Shared reading, writing, retelling of big-book versions of favorite characters (print concepts and vocabulary); *ABC instruction* **with writing**; *3-2-1 scaffolding of segmenting beginning phonemes*; **drawing and writing**
Group i: later emergent literacy learners		Shared reading, writing, retelling of big-book nursery rhymes (print concepts, vocabulary); *alphabet song*; *ABC instruction* **with writing; drawing and writing**	Shared reading, writing, retelling of big-book versions of favorite folktale versions (print concepts and vocabulary); *ABC instruction* **with writing**; *3-2-1 scaffolding of segmenting beginning phonemes*; **drawing and writing**	Fingerpoint reading of a sentence (word cutting and matching); *ABC instruction* **with writing**; *3-2-1 scaffolding of segmenting beginning phonemes with consonant sound–letter instruction*; **drawing and writing**
Group a: early experimenting learners		Fingerpoint reading of 1–2 sentences (word cutting and matching); *ABC/abc instruction* **with writing**; *3-2-1 scaffolding of segmenting beginning phonemes*; **drawing and writing**	Fingerpoint reading of nursery rhymes (locating words and letters); *ABC/abc instruction* **with writing**; *3-2-1 scaffolding of segmenting beginning phonemes with consonant sound–letter instruction*; **drawing and writing**	Guided reading of little sight word books; *learning sight words*; *finish up alphabet instruction*; **writing** *and reading familiar rhyming words and consonant sound–letter instruction*; *onset–rime segmenting and blending*; **drawing and writing**
Group o: experimenting learners		Fingerpoint reading of nursery rhymes; learning sight words; **writing** *and reading familiar rhyming words and consonant sound–letter instruction*; onset–rime segmenting and blending; **drawing and writing**	Guided reading of little sight word books; *sight word learning*; *segmenting 2- and 3-continuant phoneme words using sound boxes*; **interactive writing and guided invented spelling with feedback**	Guided reading of level 1 books; sight word learning; *segmenting 3-continuant and noncontinuant phoneme words using sound boxes*; **dictation and feedback to invented spelling**

FIGURE 9.5. Yearly planning guide for small-group differentiated instruction.

180

January	February	March	April	May
Fantasy: Home, Away, Home Again	Realistic fiction: Bravery	Fiction and Nonfiction: Animals	Fiction and Nonfiction: Good Eats	Small but Mighty
Social Studies: Geography and Maps	Social Studies: Symbols of USA	Science, Living Things: Animals	Science, Living Things: Plants	Science, Living Things: Insects
Fingerpoint reading of sentence (word cutting/matching; locating words/letters); *abc instruction* **and writing**; *3-2-1 scaffolding of segmenting beginning phonemes with sound–letter instruction*; **drawing and writing**	Fingerpoint reading of 2 sentences; *sight word learning; mystery letter and alphabet finish-up;* **writing** *and reading familiar rhyming words; onset–rime segmenting and blending;* **drawing and writing**	Guided reading of little sight word books; *sight word learning; segmenting 2- and 3-continuant phoneme words using sound boxes;* **interactive writing and guided invented spelling with feedback**	Guided reading of level 1 books; *sight word learning; segmenting 3-continuant and non-continuant phoneme words using sound boxes;* **daily dictation with feedback to invented spelling**	Guided reading of level 2 books; *sight word learning; reading and spelling BME letter boxes with new short-vowel families;* **interactive writing of compositions and reading back writing**
Fingerpoint reading of 2 sentences; *sight word learning; mystery letter and alphabet finish-up;* **writing** *and reading familiar word families; onset–rime segmenting and blending;* **drawing and writing**	Guided reading of little sight word books; *sight word learning; segmenting 2- and 3-continuant phoneme words using sound boxes;* **interactive writing and guided invented spelling with feedback**	Guided reading of level 1 books; *sight word learning; segmenting 3-continuant and non-continuant phoneme words using sound boxes;* **daily dictation with feedback to invented spelling**	Guided reading of level 2 books; *sight word learning; reading and spelling BME letter boxes with new short-vowel families;* **interactive writing of compositions and reading back writing**	Guided reading of level 3 books; *sight word learning; spelling and reading CVC words focusing on short-vowel learning; substituting BME letter boxes;* **writing compositions and reading back writing**
Guided reading of little sight word books and level 1 books; *sight word learning; segmenting 2- and 3-continuant phoneme words using sound boxes;* **interactive writing and guided invented spelling with feedback**	Guided reading of level 1 and 2 books; *sight word learning; segmenting and spelling 3-continuant and non-continuant phoneme words using sound and letter boxes;* **dictation with feedback to invented spelling**	Guided reading of level 3 books; *sight word learning; spelling and reading BME letter boxes with new short-vowel families;* **interactive writing of compositions and reading back writing**	Guided reading of level 4 books; *sight word learning; spelling and reading CVC words focusing on short vowel learning; substituting BME letter boxes;* **writing compositions and reading back writing**	Guided reading of level 5 books; *sight word learning; instruction in blends and digraphs; CCVC and CVCC letter boxes;* **interactive writing responses to reading activities**
Guided reading of level 2 books; *sight word learning; spelling and reading BME letter boxes with new short-vowel families;* **interactive writing of compositions and reading back writing**	Guided reading of level 3 books; *sight word learning; spelling and reading CVC words focusing on short-vowel learning; substituting BME letter boxes;* **writing compositions and reading back writing**	Guided reading of level 4 and 5 books; *sight word learning; instruction in blends and digraphs; CVCC and CVCC letter boxes;* **interactive writing of response to reading**	Guided reading level 6 and 7 and extended independent reading for fluency; *long-vowel-silent-e instruction;* **writing responses to reading activities**	Guided reading level 8 and 9 and extended independent reading for fluency: *other long vowel spellings;* **writing responses to reading activities**

Key: Text reading, *literacy skills,* **writing**.

week, though not all each day. In contrast, the control group did not have experiences with texts and did not write. Rather, their small-group literacy instruction was a series of systematic, direct-instruction lessons in the alphabet, phonemic awareness, and decoding. Other researchers have found that even preschoolers benefit from literacy skills instruction when it is based on a text that teachers have read aloud (Ziolkowski & Goldstein, 2008). In particular, several researchers have found that children's attempts at invented spelling during writing were a critical factor in learning phonemic awareness and decoding (Ouellette & Senechal, 2008; Rieben, Ntamakiliro, Gonthier, & Fayol, 2005). Thus, daily writing with teacher feedback provides a critical component of daily literacy instruction.

An Example of Small-Group Differentiated Instruction for Early Emergent Readers and Writers

While Mrs. Meier's small-group lessons include text reading with and by children, literacy skill instruction, and writing, all three components might not occur daily. Her students, however, experience all three components many times in the course of a week. The children in Sarah's early emergent group began in October with shared text reading of nursery rhymes coupled with shared writing and retelling. Mrs. Meier wrote short nursery rhymes. Daily, she read these to the children, and they read them in chorus. Mrs. Meier usually introduced two nursery rhymes per week. After reading a rhyme, she led step-up activities to increase print knowledge, including print direction, names of letters, concept of letter, and concept of word (Zucker et al., 2009). For example, she invited children to step up to the chart to find a letter matching a magnetic letter she had displayed, to find two identical letters, or to count the number of words in a line of text. When several nursery rhymes were familiar, Mrs. Meier identified one or two rhyming word pairs. For example, she said, "*Muffet–Tuffet* rhyme. You say them: *Muffet–Tuffet*." She sometimes wrote a shared writing chart listing four rhyming words. Children acted out the rhyme and attempted to say it without teacher help. Children also reread nursery rhymes from previous weeks.

This group's literacy skills lessons during October focused on name recognition and writing and singing the alphabet song with letter matching. (This component of the lessons was very similar to what Eric received in the preschool intervention we described earlier in this chapter.) The writing component included guided and free drawing. Mrs. Meier was careful to use guided drawing to introduce and reinforce letter strokes. Then children were free to draw about a topic related to the nursery rhyme or the class's read-aloud book of the day. Guided and free drawing usually occurred two or three times a week. During free drawing time, Mrs. Meier often wrote about her own drawing and encouraged her students to write about their drawings, but with the realization that these children's writing would not reflect knowledge of the alphabetic principle. Many children chose to practice writing letters. Figure 9.5 includes a summary of the text reading, literacy skills work, and writing activities of Sarah's early emergent group in October.

Figure 9.5 also shows how the instruction for early emergent learners shifts across the year. Mrs. Meier plans instruction by both the week and the month. Her instruction shifts as her learners' accomplishments and needs change. Thus, in November Sarah and the others in her group are now engaged in shared reading of big-book versions of favorite folktales. Notice that the literature study theme for this month during whole-class read-alouds is of "talking beasts" in folktales. In previous years Mrs. Meier noticed that the early emergent group made better gains when they experienced the same books and characters throughout the school day. So she tries to coordinate her whole-class read-aloud books with the shared reading texts she uses in small-group lessons with this group. Figure 9.6 presents a list of books read aloud during literature study with the whole class and the big-book version of the same story used during shared reading for early emergent learners. Now in November text reading includes shared reading by the teacher and choral reading by the children. At least twice a week, Mrs. Meiers invites children to participate in What Can You Show Us? (Richgels, Poremba, & McGee, 1998) before reading the text. Mrs. Meier continues to teach print knowledge as she reads these big books aloud, commenting on which page is read first, pointing out the title page, and using a pointer to demonstrate reading from left to right. She comments on where to start reading and where to go next, with a return sweep.

Literacy skills for November include learning to write and recognize upper-case alphabet letters. Mrs. Meier begins, just as Eric's teacher did, with letters with down and across strokes: *T, L,* and *E.* The writing component focuses on daily alphabet letter writing.

Text Reading with and by Children

Across a year's time the nature of text reading with and by children changes considerably for each group of children (see Figure 9.5). The easiest text reading is the teacher's reading with the children during shared reading and writing. The teacher takes the lead, but most texts used in shared reading have repetitive phrases so that children can

Story	Whole-class version by . . .	Small-group version by . . .
Little Red Hen	Paul Galdone Jerry Pinkney Philemon Sturges	Byron Barton
Three Billy Goats Gruff	Paul Galdone Janet Stevens Peter Asbjornsen	Ellen Appleby
Three Little Pigs	Paul Galdone Gavin Bishop Steven Kellogg	James Marshall
Goldilocks and the Three Bears	Jan Brett Jim Aylesworth James Marshall	Byron Barton

FIGURE 9.6. "Talking Beast" stories read aloud in whole-class instruction and big books read during small-group instruction.

quickly join in reading those. Shared reading of texts is followed by shared writing, step-up (to identify letters or concepts about print), or What Can You Show Us? Most shared reading texts lend themselves to dramatizing or retelling the story with simple props. Thus, shared reading is very interactive, with both the teacher and children participating.

Brown Bear Bread: Shared Reading Interactions in Action

Mrs. Poremba is a kindergarten teacher expert at encouraging children's active learning and thinking. Her shared readings are very interactive. One day when we observed, she prepared a shared reading chart of a recipe for Brown Bear Bread (see Figure 9.7). Her interactions with her kindergartners are examples of how to situate learning about print in a purposeful literacy-based activity, in this case, cooking from a recipe. She had already read many versions of the Three Bears story, and children had researched facts about bears.

She introduces the shared reading chart by saying, "I'd like you to look up at the easel, and I need some ideas for what is going on here."

Ian responds, "About the Three Bears."

Several children repeat this suggestion. Mrs. Poremba calls on Jason to explain.

"Because of the bowls and spoons," Jason says, repeating his and Ian's and Freddy's speculation when they had visited the easel before the group convened, with the recipe already on display there.

As Mrs. Poremba calls on Ian for another idea, Jason adds, "And the bear at the top." And so Ian says, "Actually, Jason already said it."

"You noticed the bear at the top," Mrs. Poremba acknowledges. "So something about bears. Kaitlynn."

"There's a 3 on there, and that means the Three Bears," explains Kaitlynn.

"Ahh. Jeff?"

"There's the table," says Jeff about a picture of a pan.

"You noticed a table. *Maybe* that's a table, and maybe it's something else."

At his turn, Zack says, "Um. There's a spoon. And there's a bear up there."

Mrs. Poremba gives a hint: "I wonder what we would use things like bowls and spoons—"

"Porridge!" shouts Freddy, repeating another notion from his and Ian's and Jason's earlier conversation at the easel.

Other kindergartners repeat this hypothesis, and other Three Bears notions are offered.

"There's three spoons," observes Eric D.

"Three spoons and three bowls," adds another kindergartner.

"So we think it's something about eating," concludes Mrs. Poremba.

Freddy repeats his porridge suggestion.

"Possibly porridge," says Mrs. Poremba. "Maybe it would help you if I read something to you."

"Yeah!" respond the kindergartners together.

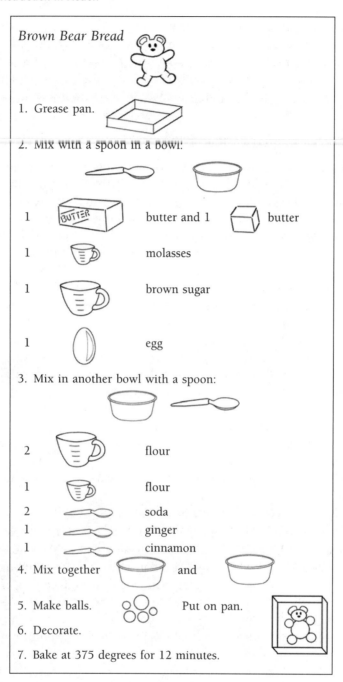

Brown Bear Bread

1. Grease pan.

2. Mix with a spoon in a bowl:

   1 BUTTER butter and 1 butter

   1 molasses

   1 brown sugar

   1 egg

3. Mix in another bowl with a spoon:

   2 flour

   1 flour
   2 soda
   1 ginger
   1 cinnamon

4. Mix together   and

5. Make balls.   Put on pan.

6. Decorate.

7. Bake at 375 degrees for 12 minutes.

FIGURE 9.7. The Brown Bear Bread recipe.

"Where should I—what should I read?"

Two kindergartners show they know that letters have something to do with what Mrs. Poremba will read. "P-g!" suggests one, perhaps thinking that Mrs. Poremba will read the word *porridge*.

"B-B-B-B-" says Kaitlynn, looking at all the *B* words in Brown Bear Bread.

"If we wanted to find out what this was about, where would we have to look?" repeats Mrs. Poremba. "What part of this? At the bottom, or—"

"Top!" say several kindergartners.

"At the top? Let's try the top," responds Mrs. Poremba. "Up here it says, 'Brown Bear Bread.'"

"Brown Bear Bread?" repeats Tara G., not sure what that means.

"We're making bread!" declares Eric D.

"A song!" suggests another kindergartner.

"It could be a song," responds Mrs. Poremba. "Eric had a different idea. What did you think, Eric?"

"We can make bread."

"Maybe this would tell us how to make bread. What would we call it if you're going to make something at home, and you look at something that's written down that tells you how to make something, what is it called?"

"A recipe!" answers one kindergartner.

"It's called a recipe. Actually that is exactly what this is! . . . This is a recipe, and today we're going to make some—" Mrs. Poremba points again to the title at the top of the poster paper—"'Brown Bear Bread.'"

Mrs. Poremba directs the children to stand and stretch and then wash their hands.

The children stand and move about, one of them reading, "It says, 'Brown Bear Bread!'"

More Complex Text Reading with and by Children

As children become more aware of the directionality of print, text reading in small groups shifts from shared reading to fingerpoint reading. In fingerpoint reading a child memorizes a small bit of text and then reads it while learning to point to its words with one-to-one speech-to-print matching. Mrs. Meier introduces fingerpoint reading by selecting only one or two sentences (10 to 14 words total) from a poem, song, or book and writing them on sentence strips on a pocket chart. As children make progress, Mrs. Meier uses longer texts of up to six lines of text. At the end of fingerpoint reading instruction, children have acquired a few key sight words and can nearly always point accurately. High-frequency words located often by finger pointing are candidates to become sight words. Children practice writing these words first by copying and then without looking at them first. Sight words are placed on an alphabetic word wall or word chart.

Finally text reading shifts to reading by the children in guided reading. Mrs. Meier has many copies of what she calls sight word little books that she prints off the Internet. These books have two to four words of text on one page and introduce one or two sight words such as *the, see, look, is, am, go, I,* and, *can.* These little books are for practicing left-to-right directionality and learning some sight words. Some children easily learn sight words from repeated reading of predictable books in which a particular word may appear several times. Most children need more guidance in learning how to look at and remember words. To teach a sight word, teachers have children locate it in a text and identify its first letter. Then the teacher writes the word on a chalkboard or whiteboard for children to copy. Then children are asked to write the word without looking. After checking spelling and if necessary correcting it, children write the word two or three more times. Another way to help children develop sight words is to use word framing. The teacher creates two small masks approximately 1 inch by 3 inches. The teacher frames the word by placing the masks to its left and its right and asks children to read it.

After reading 10 or 12 little books and learning 10 to 15 sight words, Mrs. Meier's students begin using leveled books. She has eight copies of many little books at levels 1 and 2, and fewer copies of books at level 3 and beyond. With appropriate support, children who begin kindergarten as early emergent readers and writers, like the children in Sarah's group, finish the year reading level 2 books. This is considerable progress and is expected achievement for kindergartners in most school districts. Children can easily read these little books by using a few sight words and information in the pictures. Nonetheless, reading them requires one-to-one, speech-to-print matching; consistent left-to-right tracking with return sweeps; and checking that what the reader says is consistent with the text, making use of at least initial letters of words.

Some children end the year reading level 3 texts. Still other kindergartners at year end are able to read texts at level 5 and higher. This level of accomplishment is considered above grade level. Mrs. Meier continues to provide guided reading instruction in small groups for these children. However, later in the school year she may only meet with these children two or three times a week. When children reach levels 6 and above, she introduces two or three new books each week and guides children through their first readings of these new texts. She continues to help children learn sight words. She introduces such reading strategies as looking at the endings of words, for example noticing *-ing, -ed,* and *-s,* and pointing at words with a left-to-right movement when self-checking what one has just read, especially if that seems not to make sense. She introduces reading in phrases, telling children that we read groups of words together. She places a pencil or a mask at the end of a phrase and has children read up to it, putting the words together. She quickly moves the pencil or mask to the end of the next phrase so that children's eyes move across the words in phrases. These children have boxes of books for independent reading. These are books that they have recently read in guided reading. Children read these books to themselves and to a partner daily.

Literacy Skills Instruction

Across the year, literacy skills taught in differentiated instruction change considerably as children gain more conventional understandings. As shown in Figure 9.5, Sarah's group of early emergent readers and writers began in October with the goal of recognizing and writing their names and singing the alphabet song along with matching letters.

In November, their goal is to learn upper-case alphabet letters and then begin learning initial phoneme segmentation, helped by Mrs. Meier's 3-2-1 scaffolding. In December they continue practicing initial phoneme segmentation and begin instruction about consonant letter–sounds. They learn the letter that spells the segmented initial sound. Mrs. Meier uses many segmenting activities such as fishing for pictures then segmenting the sound, matching pictures with the same first sound, and sorting pictures into groups according to a letter. Next, children begin learning to name and write the lower-case letters as they continue learning more letter–sounds. By February the children are learning to divide familiar words such as *cat, sad, map, pig, lip, dot, nut, sun,* and *hen* into onsets and rimes. They use magnetic letters on a board and separately pronounce the onset and rime as they divide a word. Then they learn to substitute a new consonant in place of an onset to spell and read new words that rhyme with the originals, such as *bat, mad, big, sip, got, run,* and *pen.* Mrs. Meier makes word family houses (a file folder with its top cut in a roof shape). On the folder children write members of the word family, for example, *dip, lip, nip, rip, tip,* and *zip* for the *-ip* family).

In March children are ready to learn to segment all the phonemes in two- and three-phoneme words. Mrs. Meier begins with two-phoneme words. She uses the story of *Jack and the Beanstalk* to introduce the words *fee, fie, fo,* and *fum.* Then she teaches the "fist up" game to segment *fee, fi,* and *fo.* She holds up her fist and slowly says a word. As she says each sound in the word, she puts a finger up. Then she does the same with such words as *lay, lie, low, moo, me, no, say, sew, sigh,* and *see.* These words all begin with continuant consonants. She always talks first about what a word means and uses it in a sentence. She keeps a list handy to remind herself what words to practice.

After several days of guided practice with Fists Up, Mrs. Meier introduces sound boxes (McCarthy, 2008). For each child, she draws two boxes, each approximately 2″ by 2″, side by side on sturdy tag board. Each child receives two round plastic markers. Mrs. Meier shows children how to say a word slowly, but still naturally, and how to move a marker into a box for each phoneme, using the left box first and the right box second. She leads the children as they practice slowly saying the word and hearing the phonemes before having them use the markers. When children can coordinate moving the two markers with saying the two phonemes, Mrs. Meier introduces three-phoneme words, again choosing words that begin with continuant consonant sounds, such as *feet, fish, five, leaf, lip, map, mop, moon, nose, nail, rat, rake, road, rope, sock, soap,* and *sun.* Children begin segmenting these words using three sound boxes and three markers. However, Mrs. Meier also begins putting out the magnetic letters *f, l, m, n, r,* and *s.* When the children hear in the initial position the sound made by one of these letters, they put that letter in the leftmost box.

In April children use sound boxes with words that begin with stop consonants, such as *bed, bike, book, bug, cat, cake, coat, cup, dog, duck, gate, goat, hip, hose, hut, jam, kiss, pan, pig, pot, time, tape, tub, wave, wig,* and *wet.* After practicing with only markers, Mrs. Meier again challenges children to put a letter in the first box when they know what letter spells a word's initial sound.

Finally, in May children begin learning short vowel families having the rimes *-at, -ap, -an, -ig, -ip, -it, -op, -ot, -ug, -un, -ed,* and *-et.* They use Beginning, Middle, End (BME) letter boxes. First children practice saying and segmenting words in the *-at* family: *bat,* *cat, fat, hat, mat, rat,* and *sat.* They are given the letters *b, c, f, h, m, r, s, a,* and *t.* Mrs. Meier demonstrates saying a word slowly, selecting the three letters for the three sounds, and placing them left to right in the letter boxes to spell the word. The children discover that the second and subsequent words in a word family use the same letters in the middle and end boxes as the first word did. Next children practice with the *-ap* family and then the *-an* family. Finally, they are challenged to spell words in the three families mixed together, so that only the middle box's letter remains the same. Children move to learning the short-*i* families. More challenging is to mix the short-*a* and short-*i* family words together so that for a new word, all three—beginning, middle, and end—boxes might have a different letter. Children continue learning many short vowel families so that the potential for changing the letter in the middle box increases. This amount of variation is the cornerstone of conventional spelling and decoding (Blachman, Ball, Black, & Tangel, 2000; Manyak, 2008).

This activity reinforces a sophisticated end-of-year literacy skill for children who began kindergarten as early emergent readers and writers, with the fewest conventional literacy skills of any group. Children in other groups learn more advanced literacy skills as they develop more and more conventional understandings of written language. For example, the experimenting readers and writers who began the year with the most conventional knowledge learned in October to segment the onset and rime of familiar rhyming words and substitute consonants to spell and read new words. This was not taught to Sarah's group until February. The most advanced group worked with BME letter boxes in January and by February used them to spell and read short-vowel words not usually encountered as members of word families, such as *web.* When teaching spelling of the words, Mrs. Meier says them, and the children slowly segment them and write a letter for each sound in the letter boxes. To teach reading the words, Mrs. Meier presents a written word in letter boxes, and the children say its sounds and slowly blend them to make a correct pronunciation.

In March the most advanced group learned about consonant blends and digraphs and used four-box letter boxes to spell and read words with these features. In April they were introduced to long-vowel words spelled with the silent *e,* and in May they learned to spell and read words with other long-vowel spellings. They ended the year with foundational reading skills expected of first graders and even some skills expected in second grade, according to the *Common Core State Standards for English Language Arts and Literacy in History/Social Studies, Science, and Technical Subjects* (National Governors Association Center for Best Practices & Council of Chief State School Officers, 2010). Figure 9.8 presents a list of the Common Core Reading Foundational Reading Standards that kindergartners are expected to master. Notice that even the group of children in our example, who began the year with the least conventional knowledge received instruction that accelerated their learning so they ended the year meeting the kindergarten foundational reading standards.

Writing (and Storytelling) by Children

Children write several times each week, and their writing activities increase in complexity as they become aware of the alphabetic principle and gain knowledge about

Print Concepts
- Follow words from left to right, top to bottom, and page by page
- Recognize that spoken words are represented in written language by specific sequences of letters
- Understand that words are separated by spaces in print
- Recognize and name all upper- and lower-case letters of the alphabet

Phonological Awareness
- Recognize and produce rhyming words
- Count, pronounce, blend, and segment syllables in spoken words
- Blend and segment onsets and rimes of single-syllable spoken words
- Isolate and pronounce the initial consonant, medial vowel, and final consonant phonemes in three-phoneme, CVC words
- Add or substitute individual phonemes in simple, one-syllable words to make new words

Phonics and Word Recognition
- Demonstrate basic knowledge of one-to-one sound–letter correspondences by producing the primary sound or many of the most frequent sounds for each consonant
- Associate the long and short sounds with common spellings (graphemes) for the five major vowels
- Read common high-frequency words by sight (e.g., *the, of, to, you, she, my, is, are, do, does*)
- Distinguish between similarly spelled words by identifying the sounds of the letters that differ

FIGURE 9.8. Common Core English Language Arts kindergarten reading standards: foundational skills.

spelling features and patterns. Sarah's group of early emergent readers and writers, for example, begins the year with guided drawing activities, followed by drawing and writing. They are expected to draw a picture that is related to a story they have listened to in whole-class literature study or an information book read aloud as part of a science or social studies theme. As children learn to recognize alphabet letters, they also learn to write them. Early in the year, they practice writing letters nearly daily. When they learn to segment onsets and rimes in familiar rhyming words, they also practice spelling new words.

Mrs. Meier occasionally engages children in storytelling activities instead of drawing and writing. She brings to a small group a storybook that she has recently read to the whole class. The children take turns telling about the book and its story (Middendorf, 2008). Mrs. Meier begins by giving the book to a child and asking him or her to show the book's cover, say its title, and tell the story's problem. The next child opens the book to the title page and again repeats the title. The next children display successive double-spread pages of the story and tell what is happening in the story on those pages. Mrs. Meier expands and clarifies for the children.

She has found that having children hold the book themselves during retelling allows them a closer look at the illustrations and usually sparks conversations about important elements that might be missed when viewing the book during whole-class read-alouds. Children notice changes in font size and color. They notice when words take on shapes or when environmental print is used in the illustrations. For example, there are numerous road signs in the forest setting of James Marshall's version of the Goldilocks story. They say "Turn Back," "Very Risky," and "Not a Good Idea." Mrs. Meier usually does not refer to these signs when reading to the whole class, but does highlight them in small-group activities. Books such as these with highly salient elements of print provide opportunities for teachers to extend both children's awareness of print and their understanding of how print contributes to a book's meaning (Zucker, Ward, & Justice, 2009).

As children develop the alphabetic principle, the nature of writing in small-group instruction changes: the teacher begins guiding invented spelling. Mrs. Meier uses a modification of interactive writing to demonstrate for children how to invent spellings (see March plans for early emergent literacy learners or November plans for experimenting learners in Figure 9.5). On the day she introduced invented spelling as a writing activity with Sarah's group in March, she prepared little books with pictures of animals found on farms: a duck, a pig, a horse, and a dog. She placed larger pictures on four sheets of paper she would use for modified interactive writing. She began by introducing the idea of "kid spelling": "It's the way kids write when they spell by themselves. They say the word slowly, listen for a sound, and then write a letter." She demonstrated with the picture of the duck. She said the word slowly, then said, "I hear /d/, *d*." She wrote a *d*. "Now I'll listen again and see if I hear something else." She said the word slowly again, and then said, "I hear /k/, *k*." She wrote a *k*. "That's kid spelling. That spells *duck*." Then she shows the paper with the picture of the pig and asks, "What do I do first?" Mrs. Meier has everyone practice saying the word slowly. Then she asks, "What do I do now?" Most children call out the first sound /p/, and she invites a child to step up to the paper and write the letter that goes with that sound. They listen again, and another child is invited to spell the next sound that is heard. The children continue saying words slowly and sharing the pen until all four words have been spelled. Then the children receive the little books with the same four pictures and are invited to use kid spelling to write the words. Mrs. Meier observes the children and supports them with prompts to say the word slowly and say the sounds they hear. At the end of the lesson, all the children read their words. Mrs. Meier continues to use modified interactive writing to demonstrate the strategy of saying words slowly, hearing a sound and spelling that sound, and then listening again. When children can do these steps on their own, she discontinues using modified interactive writing and asks children to spell the words on their own. She provides feedback to children on their spellings: "You heard the first sound. Now there is another sound you can hear in that word at the end. See if you can hear it and spell it."

When Mrs. Meier notices that most children are spelling with at least two letters in guided invented spelling, she introduces a slightly more complex form of writing: writing a sentence from dictation. She says the sentence, then says the sentence word by word as the children spell the words using invented spellings or known conventional spellings. When she first uses dictation, she has the children draw a horizontal line for each word as they listen to the sentence the first time. Then as she says a word, they write it on the line. Each day, Mrs. Meier selects at least one spelling from each child to use in helping children gain sophistication in their writing. For example, the sentence for one day in April for Sarah's group was "Max went back to his room and ate his dinner," based on an earlier read-aloud of *Where the Wild Things Are* (Sendak, 1963). One child spelled *to* as *ot*, probably remembering the letters in this word but not their order. Mrs. Meier commented that this spelling had the two letters that spelled that word. Then she had the children listen to the two phonemes in *to* and put the letters *t* and *o* in sound boxes so that they would notice that *o* does not spell the first sound in the word, but that *t* does. Another child spelled *room* as *r*, and Mrs. Meier had the group listen for the ending sound and add it to the spelling. Still another child spelled dinner *dr*, and Mrs. Meier complimented the spelling of the first and last sounds, but asked everyone to listen again and see if they could hear even more sounds in that long word.

When children are adept at inventing spellings as they write from dictation, teachers invite them to write their own compositions and read them to the group. To introduce this kind of writing, Mrs. Meier again uses modified interactive writing. When demonstrating writing a composition, she emphasizes two important ideas: "You think of something to write that is short and stays the same. It is better to write a short sentence that you can remember than a long exciting story that you can't remember and therefore can't write. It has to be short and you have to know it." She demonstrates with a good and bad example: a sentence that all the children can remember and a long, complicated sentence that no two children can remember the same. Then she repeats the short sentence again and writes a line for each word. Then she shares the pen with children as they invent spellings. Children who are ready for this kind of composing know a few conventional spellings in the sample short sentence (usually high-frequency sight words such as *the, to,* and *is*), and they invent spellings of the other words. Then the children, with Mrs. Meier's help, reread the sentence. Mrs. Meier continues to demonstrate for a few days, and then she invites the children to compose a sentence of their own. Each child states his or her sentence for the group and draws a line for each word. Then they all write words on the lines and attempt to read what they wrote.

Not all children write in the most complex form: independent writing in response to a text they have read or heard read aloud. Children can use many forms of writing to respond to something they have read: they might draw and write about the beginning, middle, and end of a story. They might write a retelling of the story. They might write about their favorite part or a favorite character and tell why. Or they might write a book blurb, telling why everyone in the class should read this book. Figure 8.4 (in Chapter 8) presents a response to *The Grouchy Lady Bug* (Carle, 1996). Notice that the writer knew the spelling of the word *the* and spelled most words with two sounds. His most complex spelling was for the word *aphids* where he represented four phonemes.

Monitoring Progress

Mrs. Meier is required to assess her children at the beginning and end of the school year, but she also keeps close watch on children who do not seem to be making adequate progress during the year. At the beginning of the year Pedro, Seth, Sarah, Alicia, and Leon (see Figure 9.3) were considered early emergent readers and writers. Their assessment scores put them in the at-risk category, which Mrs. Meier's school district calls "not on track." For example, Sarah wrote her name in all readable capital letters. She recognized three alphabet letters and knew nine concepts about print. She demonstrated no phonological awareness and only swept her hand across the print when invited to fingerpoint read. She recalled three ideas after listening to *Owl Moon* (Yolens, 1987).

Mrs. Meier's school district requires an intervention plan for all children who, like Sarah, are not considered on track to be grade-level readers by the end of the year.

An intervention plan calls for monitoring assessments as needed. Mrs. Meier works with the intervention specialist in her school to coordinate intervention plans. At the beginning of the year, she and the intervention specialist reviewed Mrs. Meier's differentiated planning for the small group of early emergent readers and writers. They agreed to provide an additional small-group lesson in the afternoon twice weekly while other children were at work stations. The intervention teacher assessed the children in this group just before winter holiday and at the beginning of March and reviewed the results with Mrs. Meier. The monitoring assessments in December demonstrated that all children were making progress, and therefore Mrs. Meier continued the extra small-group lessons.

Sarah's monitoring assessment in March caused some concern. Figure 9.9 presents the results of her September and March assessments. These show she made considerable progress, especially in learning upper-case letters and initial phoneme segmentation. However, Sarah was not consistently matching one to one in fingerpoint reading, could write only two-thirds of alphabet letters legibly, did not yet know all consonant sounds, and had difficulty retaining the rime in the onset–rime assessment. She did attempt to spell two words using one sound–letter match in each spelling. The intervention specialist agreed that Sarah might benefit from one-on-one lessons that she would conduct, focusing on fingerpoint reading, learning to write letters not yet known, and learning the remainder of the consonant sounds through guided practice with invented spelling. Sarah met with the intervention specialist 3 days a week from April until the end of the year and made considerable progress.

September, Kindergarten	March, Kindergarten
Name Writing: All legible letters, upper-case	
Drawing: Representational tadpole with many details, mock letters and real letters, but no alphabetic principle	
Retelling: Three ideas, very minimal with few details	Retelling: Five ideas, some details
Concepts about print: 9/20	Concepts about print: 16/20
Fingerpoint reading: 0/12	Fingerpoint reading: 9/12
Upper-case: Three letters correct (AEO), random naming of other letters (SQHP)	Upper-case: 25/26
	Lower-case: 20/26
	Letter writing: 16/26
	Segment beginning phoneme: 9/16
	Consonant letter–sounds: 11/17
	Segment onset rime: 6/10
	Spelling: Two words (first consonants only)

FIGURE 9.9. Results of Sarah's screening assessment (September) and progress monitoring assessment (March).

CHAPTER SUMMARY

This chapter presented a five-step model for determining intervention and differentiated instruction for individual children. The first step is to do screening assessments and use the results to identify children for small-group intervention with differentiated instruction. The next step is to investigate causes for children's low performance. The third step is to determine the nature of instruction and the size of groups. The fourth step is to adjust instruction based on children's responses. Finally, teachers adjust instruction based on monitoring assessments. Prekindergarten children are not likely to need intervention instruction until it is known how they respond to opportunities to learn. Kindergarten children begin the year with a wide range of conventional knowledge and thus may benefit from small-group differentiated instruction targeted at their current level of development. To determine group needs, kindergarten teachers can give an array of assessments and create a class profile. Small-group instruction has three components, which increase in complexity as children acquire more conventional knowledge and concepts. These are text reading with and by children, literacy skills instruction, and writing by children. Text reading with children includes shared reading and fingerpoint reading. Guided reading instruction begins as children acquire a few sight words and fingerpoint read with nearly perfect speech-to-print matching. Literacy skills include learning the alphabet, acquiring more sophisticated phonemic awareness, and acquiring the alphabetic principle. Some children begin learning about spelling patterns. Children's writing becomes more complex as they acquire the alphabetic principle and use invented spelling and sight words in guided invented spelling, dictation, and composing.

A Primer on Phonics for Teachers

PHONEME PRONUNCIATION KEY

In the following list, the symbol between slashes represents one phoneme—that is, the phoneme whose spelling is underlined in the example word or words that follow the phoneme symbol.

/a/ cat	/I/ height	/r/ rat
/A/ Kate	/j/ Jake	/s/ sat
/ah/ cot	/k/ cake	/sh/ ship
/aw/ caught, awful, fought	/l/ lake	/t/ tip
/b/ bought	/m/ make	/th/ thing
/ch/ chug	/n/ win	/TH/ this
/d/ dug	/ng/ wing	/uh/ cut
/e/ bed	/O/ coat	/U/ cute
/E/ bead	/oi/ boy	/v/ vine
/f/ feed	/oo/ look	/w/ wine
/g/ got	/OO/ flute, shoot	/y/ yes
/h/ hot	/ow/ shout, town	/z/ zoo
/i/ hit	/p/ pat	/zh/ treasure

Notes

- Any phoneme list is dialect sensitive. That is, pronunciations differ from one dialect to another. For example, in some U.S. English dialects, *cot* and *caught* are pronounced the same, both with the middle phoneme /ah/ (rather than saying /aw/ in *caught*).
- There is no "*c* sound"; *c* usually spells /k/ (*cat*) or /s/ (*city*).

Adapted from *Literacy's Beginnings: Supporting Young Readers and Writers, Sixth Edition,* by Lea M. McGee and Donald J. Richgels. Copyright 2012. Printed and electronically reproduced by permission of Pearson Education, Inc., Upper Saddle River, New Jersey.

- There is no "*q* sound"; *qu* usually spells the two sounds /k/ + /w/ (*quick*), but sometimes the one sound /k/ (*plaque*).
- Some phonemes are really combinations of others. The /I/ phoneme is really /ah/ + /E/. The /oi/ phoneme is really /O/ + /E/. The /U/ phoneme is really /y/ + /OO/ (*cute*); notice the difference between the /OO/ in *Luke* and the /y/ + /OO/ in *cute*. The /ch/ phoneme is really /t/ + /sh/.
- There is no "*x* sound"; *x* usually spells the two sounds /k/ + /s/ (*box*) or the one sound /z/ (*xylophone*).
- Our list has only 39 phonemes. Many sources give 44 as the number of English phonemes. Why do we not list 44? We could add /hw/ for those whose dialect of English includes an additional /h/-like sound at the beginning of words spelled with *wh* (those speakers' pronunciation of the beginning of *when* is breathier than their pronunciation of the beginning of *wet*). In addition, some lists of English phonemes include additional sounds for some vowels before /r/. The *r* sound after a vowel often slightly changes the way the vowel is pronounced, but we do not think the difference is enough for nonlinguists to be concerned with. Finally, some lists of English phonemes include the schwa sound (/ə/) for the vowel sound in many unaccented syllables (*about*, *basket*, *rapid*, *cotton*), but the schwa sound is the same as the short *u* sound (/uh/); compare *about* and *cut*.
- When representing more than one phoneme, for example, when showing the phonemes in a whole word, we separate the symbols with a dot (•), just so that the component sounds are clearly distinguishable visually, even though they are blended together when spoken. For example, when representing only the sound at the beginning of the three-phoneme word *shine*, we write /sh/, but when representing the whole word *shine*, we write /sh•I•n/.

SOME BACKGROUND

Phonics, in general, is instruction that helps children to learn the relationships between letters and sounds and to use that knowledge when sounding out or decoding words and in spelling words. First, children are taught to connect phonemes to consonants, then short vowels, digraphs and blends, and finally long vowels. Different phonics programs may teach the sound–letter correspondences in different orders. For example, some programs teach a few consonants and then introduce one or two short vowels so that children can begin blending and spelling words. Regardless of the order in which the letters are introduced, children are usually taught (at least in the beginning of phonics instruction) only one phoneme associated with one letter. This explains why consonants and short vowels are taught first—most consonants and short vowels are highly regular, with each letter generally representing one phoneme. Later, children are taught that some letters (a few consonants and many double-vowel spellings) are related to several different phonemes, and that one phoneme (such as the long *a*) can be related to several spellings (such as in the words *wait*, *pay*, *weigh*, *cake*, and *break*).

Effective teachers of phonics know what a phoneme is. When asked what a phoneme is, teachers most often answer that a phoneme is a sound represented by a letter. However, phonemes have nothing to do with letters. Phonemes are actually the smallest units of sound that matter in a language. In other words, it is the combining and contrasting of phonemes that makes words possible. Consider, for example, the *p* phoneme, the short-*i* phoneme, and the g phoneme. (We write about them this way to make clear we are discussing sounds and not letters.) These three phonemes are combined to make the word *pig*, and the *p* phoneme and the *b* phoneme are contrasted when distinguishing the words *pig* and *big*. The difference in the pronunciations of the *p* sound and the *b* sound is slight. It is only that for the *p* sound we do not use our voice and for *b* sound we do; everything else—how we use our tongue and throat, how we shape our lips, how we part our teeth—is identical. Yet speakers and listeners rely on that very small difference, that contrast; it is all that signals two very different English meanings, an animal that says "oink" versus a dimension of size, the opposite of small.

Another linguistic fact about phonemes that teachers must know is that phonemes are not discrete entities, but rather are categories within which there is much variation. For example, even while it is important in spoken language to be able to perceive the slight difference between the *p* sound and the *b* sound in *pig* and *big*, it is equally important to ignore differences in pronunciations of the *p* sound, for example, in *wrapped* and *rapid*. We do ignore this difference when we teach children about the *p* phoneme as if there is only one, when in fact there is a whole category of them (notice also the real, but ignored difference between the *p* sounds in *spot* and *pot*; to notice this difference, we dangle a piece of paper before our mouths when we say the two words). The following section presents the usual categories of information taught in phonics programs up to and including in second grade. Therefore, much of this information is beyond what preschool and kindergarten teachers actually need. However, in order to keep in mind the larger picture of where children will go in conventional reading and spelling instruction, we present it here.

LETTER–SOUND RELATIONSHIPS

Initial Consonant Spellings (one letter spells one phoneme)		Final Consonant Spellings (one letter usually spells one phoneme although in some instances two letters spell one phoneme*)	
b	boy	b	tub
d	dog	d	mud
f	foot	f	if, stiff*
h	hand	g	pig
j	jelly	k (ck)	stick*
k	king	l	mill*
l	leg	m	swim
m	man	n	van
n	nose	p	map
p	pot	t	hat
r	rope		
t	toe		
v	van		
w	wig		
y	yawn		
z	zebra		

Initial Consonant Blends (two or three letters spell two or three phonemes)		Final Consonant Blends (two letters spell two phonemes)	
br	bride	st	most
cr	crow	sk	mask
dr	drum	ld	sold
fr	frog	mp	jump
gr	green	nd	band
pr	prince	lf	shelf
tr	tree	lt	melt
scr	scream	nt	sent
spr	spray		
str	strong		
bl	blue		
cl	clock		
fl	fly		
gl	glass		
pl	plate		
sl	slow		
spl	splatter		
sc	score		
sm	smart		
sp	sport		
sw	swim		
sk	skirt		
sn	snail		
st	start		
qu	quiet		

Initial Consonant Digraphs (two letters spell one phoneme)		Final Consonant Digraphs (two letters spell one phoneme)	
sh	shoe	sh	dish
ch	chair	ch	peach
wh	white	th	math
th	thumb, this (notice, these are two different phonemes: /th/ and /TH/)	ng	ring

Variant Consonants (consonants that have more than one phoneme associated with them)		Silent Consonants (consonants that are not sounded)	
c	cake, ice	d	judge
g	goat, giant	gh	fight
s	sun, his, sure	w	wrong
x	box, xylophone	b	climb

Short Vowel Sounds (often spelled with one letter)		Long Vowel Sounds (often spelled with two letters)	
/a/	hat	/A/	rain, pay, cake, weigh, prey
/e/	net	/E/	feet, mean, she, chief, happy
/i/	pig	/I/	pipe, might, cry, mild
/ah/	mop	/O/	home, boat, slow, sold, though
/uh/	duck	/U/	cube

Other Vowel Sounds
(not long or short)

/aw/	awful, August
/oi/	boil, boy
/oo/	foot, would
/OO/	boot, blue
/ow/	clown, out

Literacy Assessments

This appendix presents 16 literacy assessments, many of which include a reproducible administration section for the teacher to use with children, and all assessments have directions for administration and scoring. Appendix C (p. 215) is a Literacy Assessment Scoring Record that may be copied for each child, with sections for scoring all of the assessments in the order in which they are found in this appendix. You should have a folder for each child in which to keep his or her assessment tasks and other assessment materials. Be sure to date each assessment.

See Appendix A for a phoneme pronunciation key.

Not all children will be given every assessment in this appendix. Teachers will select assessments based on development levels displayed in classroom activities. Some children will need very few of the assessments because they are at the early phase of awareness and exploration. Other children will need screening assessments so teachers can determine which children might benefit from small-group instruction together. Later, teachers might readminister assessments to monitor children's progress. Some assessments are only suitable for children who are far along the developmental continuum and are almost readers and inventive spellers.

RETELLING CHECKLIST

Locate the Retelling Checklist section of the Literacy Assessment Scoring Record. Read the book *Owl Moon* (Yolen, 1987) aloud to a group of children 3 days in a row. Encourage children to talk about the pictures and their experiences going out in the dark or in the snow. Use a laptop computer with a microphone and install a recording device such as Audacity or Garage Band. Ask each child individually to retell the story (do not show the book) and record the retelling. Prompt the child to retell more by asking him or her to tell what happened at the beginning of the story. Use prompts such as "Do you remember anything that happened before that?" or "Do you remember what they did next?" Listen to the recording and put a check beside the statement on the retelling checklist that most closely matches what the child recalled. If a child recalls additional information *found in the story* but not included on the checklist, add it to the list. Count the number of ideas the child recalled, including those he or she added. Decide if the retelling was very minimal with few details remembered, minimal but with some details, somewhat elaborated with more details, elaborated with many details recalled, or very elaborated with most ideas recalled.

If a child makes no attempt at retelling even with some prompting, open the book and ask the child to tell you about the story as you look at the illustrations. Make note that the book illustrations were used in the retelling activity. Record the attempt at telling about the book and make note of the longest utterance the child makes.

NAME-WRITING ASSESSMENT

Locate the Name-Writing Assessment section of the Literacy Assessment Scoring Record. Ask a child to write his or her name on a blank sheet of paper, then date the paper and write the child's name. Then score it using the name-writing scale. Keep a copy of the name writing in the child's assessment record folder.

CONCEPTS ABOUT PRINT ASSESSMENT

Copy the text for "The Itsy Bitsy Spider" and make a book as shown. Use pictures found on the Internet to correspond to the text.

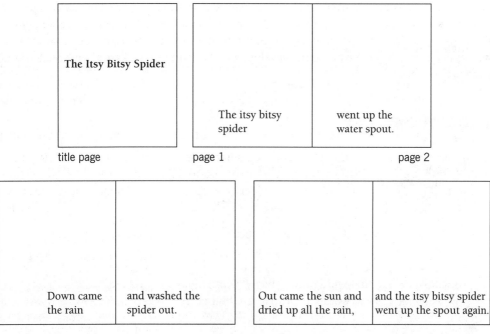

Copy the 20-item list provided below on tag board. Locate the Concepts about Print Assessment section of the Literacy Assessment Scoring Record.

Directions: Read the book to the child. Encourage the child to talk about the pictures and actions of the story. Read the book a second time, pausing to allow the child to say some of the words. Present the book face down and upside down to the child. Say the following:

Book Handling

1. Show me the front of this book.
2. Show me the back.
3. (Turn book over to the front.) Show me the top of this page.
4. Show me the bottom of this page.
5. (Open to pages 1 and 2 and sweep hands across both pages.) Which page do I read first? (Child must point only to left page.)
6. (Sweep hand across left page.) After I read this page, which page do I read next? (Child must point only to the right page.)
7. (Sweep hand across right page.) After I read this page, where do I read next? (Child must turn the page and show the left page.)

Directionality

8. (Turn back to page 1.) Point to exactly where I would start to read. (Child must point to the first word of the sentence in the top line—*The*—and may also sweep across the line after pointing to *The*.)
9. (Point to just the first word *The*.) After I read this word, where do I read next? (Child must point at the second word, *itsy*, and may then sweep across the line of text.)
10. (Sweep finger across the first line of text.) After I read this, where do I read next? (Child must point to the word on second line of text, *spider*.)

Concepts about Letters and Words

11. (For the next questions use two index cards pushed together covering the lines of text. Then slide the two cards apart to display the text. Pulling the two cards apart is called "open me.") Open me and show me just one letter. (Cards must be open so that only one letter can be seen.)
12. (Close the cards so no text is seen.) Open me and show me two letters. (Cards must be open so only two letters are seen.)
13. (Close the cards so no text is seen.) Open me and show me just one word. (Cards must show only one word.)
14. (Close the cards so no text is seen.) Open me and show me two words. (Cards must show only two words.)
15. (Take away the cards.) Count the number of words on this page. (Page 1 has four words.)
16. Show me a capital letter. (Child must point to *T* in *The*.)
17. Show me the letter *s*. (Child must point to *s* in *itsy*, *bitsy*, or *spider*.)
18. Show me the first word on this page. (Child must point to *The*.)
19. Show me the last word on this page. (Child must point to *spider*.)
20. (Show the period on page 1.) What is this? (Child must say "period" or "tells me to stop.")

FINGERPOINT READING ASSESSMENT

Locate the Fingerpoint Reading Assessment section of the Literacy Assessment Scoring Record.

Directions: Say, "I am going to read this story again and point to each word as I read. Then I want you to read with me and you will point." Read the book slowly and point to each word as you read it. Now say, "Now this time you point to the words and say it with me as I read." Say the words slowly and help the child point correctly to each word as you say it. Then say, "This time you will say it and point yourself." Score 1 point for an entire line of text for which the child correctly points to each word while saying it. If needed, you say the poem with the child and score the one-to-one matching.

UPPER-CASE ALPHABET RECOGNITION ASSESSMENT

Copy the administration section below on tag board. Locate the Upper-Case Alphabet Recognition Assessment section of the Literacy Assessment Scoring Record.

Use an index card and unmask one row of letters at a time. Say, "These are alphabet letters. I'm going to see if you know the names of any of these letters." Point at the first letter and wait 5 seconds. If there is no answer, move to the next letter. Mark each correctly named letter on your scoring record sheet with a check and above it write the name of any other letter that has been confused with it (e.g., identifying W as M).

N	J	Y	U
B	R	M	G
H	L	Q	V
I	P	W	A
X	E	K	C
Z	D	F	O
T	S		

LOWER-CASE ALPHABET RECOGNITION ASSESSMENT

Copy the administration section below on tag board. Locate the Lower-Case Alphabet Recognition Assessment section of the Assessment Scoring Record.

Use an index card and unmask only one row of letters at a time. Say, "These are alphabet letters. I'm going to see if you know the names of any of these letters." Point at the first letter and wait 5 seconds. If there is no answer, move to the next letter. Mark each correctly named letter on the scoring record sheet with a check and above it write the name of any other letter that has been confused with it (e.g., saying *m* for *w*).

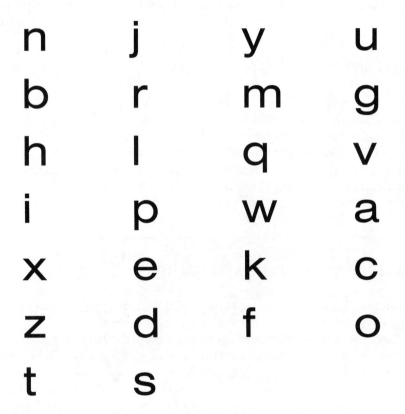

n	j	y	u
b	r	m	g
h	l	q	v
i	p	w	a
x	e	k	c
z	d	f	o
t	s		

ALPHABET LETTER-WRITING ASSESSMENT

Copy the administrative section below on tag board. Use this tag-board page to guide your naming the letters for the child to write, but keep it hidden so the child cannot see the letters. Say, "I am going to ask you to write some letters. You may write the letter any way you can." Give the child a blank sheet of paper and point to where the letters should go (start at top, go down the page, then back up to the top and down again; both sides of the sheet can be used if needed). Locate the Alphabet Letter-Writing Assessment section of the Literacy Assessment Scoring Record. Write notes on this record if needed. Score a letter correct if it has a reasonable resemblance to the expected upper- or lower-case letter. Count reversals as correct except for *p*, *b*, *d*, and *q*.

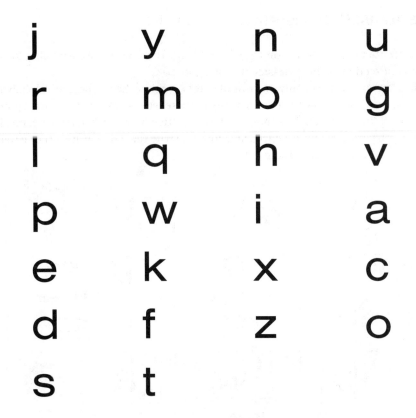

SEGMENTING BEGINNING PHONEME ASSESSMENT

Copy the administration section below on tag board. Locate the Segmenting Beginning Phoneme Assessment section of the Literacy Assessment Scoring Record.

Directions: Say, "I am going to show you a picture of a word. I want you to say only the first sound of the word, a little bit of sound. Like this: This picture is *sun*. You say *sun*. *Sun*. /s/ is the first sound. You say /s/. Now you try one. This is *moon*, you say *moon*. Now say the first sound in *moon*." If child says /m/, say "Yes, that is the first sound. Good." If child says anything else, say, "The first sound of *moon* is /m/. You say /m/." Say each word, have the child repeat the word, then say, "First sound?" Do not elongate sounds in words. Score each phoneme 1 point if the child articulates the phoneme correctly. Total of 16 points.

Demonstration

Practice

1.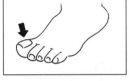

7.

13.

2.

8.

14.

3.

9.

15.

4.

10.

16.

5.

11.

6.

12.

RHYMING ASSESSMENT

Copy the administration section below on tag board. Locate the Rhyming Assessment section of the Literacy Assessment Scoring Record.

Directions: Say, "Here are two rhyming words: *can, fan*. They rhyme. *Can, fan*. You say *can, fan*. Now let's try to find two rhyming words. One of these does not fit: *dog, key, tree*. Which two rhyme?" If the answer is correct, say, "Yes, *key, tree* rhyme." If incorrect, say, "No, *key, tree* rhyme. You say *key, tree*." Next say, "I'll say three words, then you find two that rhyme." Score 1 point for each pair selected, with a possible total of 10 points.

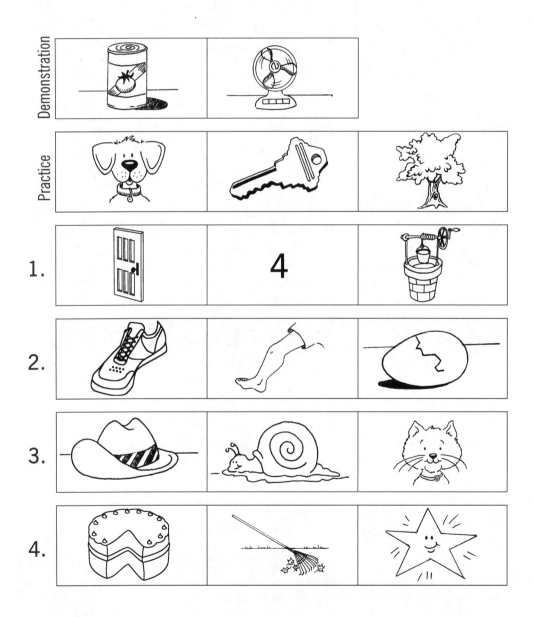

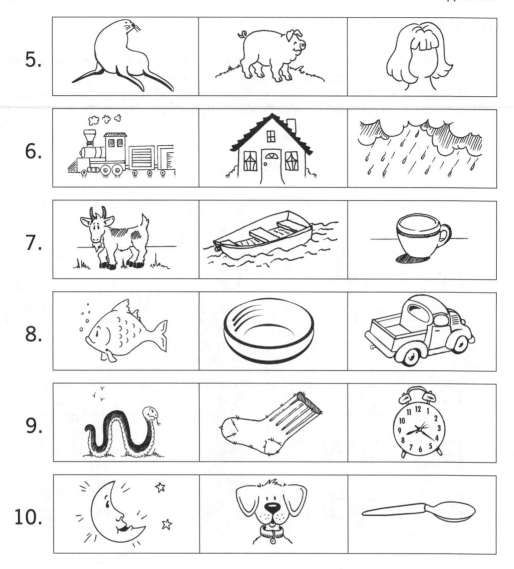

DRAW A PICTURE AND WRITE ABOUT YOURSELF ASSESSMENT

Give the child a blank sheet of paper and markers.

Directions: Say, "I want you to draw a picture of yourself and then write about yourself. What you like to do, your favorite food. Anything you want to tell me about *you*. Write it the way you can. Then I'll ask you to read it to me." After the child has written and drawn, ask the child to read his or her story (record it using a laptop and recording application).

Take note of what the child does when asked to read the text: refuse to read, describe the picture, make up new but related words (usually for invented spellings), use the exact words written (for invented spellings or conventional spellings).

CONSONANT LETTER–SOUND ASSESSMENT

Copy the administration section below on tag board. Locate the Consonant Letter–Sound Assessment section of the Literacy Assessment Scoring Record.

Directions: Say, "Here are some letters. I want you to say the sound each letter spells. Here is the letter s. It spells /s/." Score sounds correctly matched to letters. (Note: *c* can be /k/ or /s/, *g* can be /g/ or /j/.)

Demonstration **s**

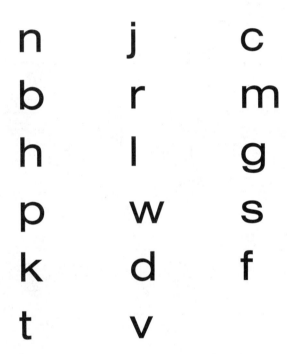

n	j	c
b	r	m
h	l	g
p	w	s
k	d	f
t	v	

SEGMENTING ONSET AND RIME ASSESSMENT

Copy the administration section below on tag board. Locate the Segmenting Onset and Rime Assessment section of the Literacy Assessment Scoring Record.

Directions: Say, "I am going to show you some pictures of words. You will say the words in two parts like this. This is *mop*: /m/, (wait 3 seconds) /o•p/. You say /m/, /o•p/. Remember to wait a bit before saying the second part. Now you try. This is *kite*. Say it in two parts." If the answer is correct (/k/, /I•t/), say, "Yes, *kite* has two parts /k/, /I•t/." If incorrect, give the correct response and have the child repeat the correct response. Repeat with the second practice word, *door* (/d/, /O•r/). Count each word as correct if the child correctly divides the words according to the scoring sheet.

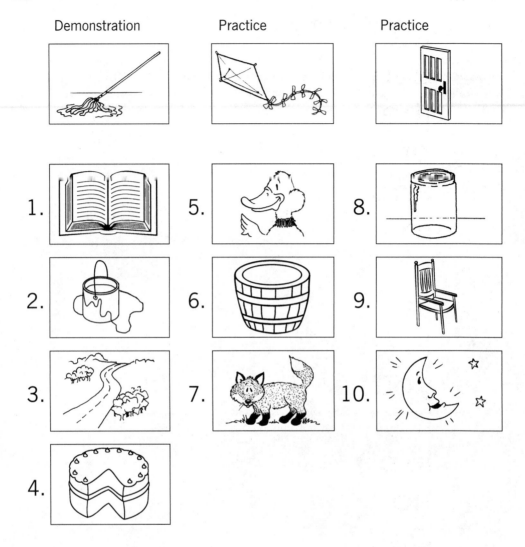

HIGH-FREQUENCY WORD READING ASSESSMENT

Copy the administration section below on tag board. Locate the High-Frequency Word Reading Assessment section of the Literacy Assessment Scoring Record.

Directions: Say, "I am going to show you some words. You may know some of these words. Read them to me if you know them." (For children who are likely to know only a few words, cover the words with an index card and slowly show the words one at a time, encouraging children to read words they know. Score as correct only the words a child reads correctly. For children who are likely to know more of the words, also use an index card, showing words one at a time, but score whether children know each word.)

Mom

can

the

of

and

to

a

in

is

you

it

like

he

Dad

for

on

with

his

no

I

WRITING WORDS ASSESSMENT

Give the child a blank sheet of paper and a marker. Locate the Writing Words Assessment section of the Literacy Assessment Scoring Record.

    Directions: Say, "You are going to write all the words you know how to spell. Start with your name. Spell your name. Now spell all the words you can write. Can you spell *Mom* or *Dad*? *I* or *a*? *Is* or *it*? *He* or *me*? *No* or *yes*? *Dog* or *cat*? *Like* or *see*? *To* or *go*? *With* or *the*? Continue to offer alternatives until 10 minutes are up or the child clearly cannot write more words. Score each word correct only if it is spelled correctly. Write the words spelled correctly on the score sheet.

SPELLING ASSESSMENT

Give the child a blank sheet of paper and a marker. Locate the Spelling Assessment section of the Literacy Assessment Scoring Record. Use the child's spellings to determine which phonemes on the scoring record are spelled conventionally and which unconventionally. Record on the Literacy Assessment Scoring Record.

    Directions: Say, "I am going to say a word and you are going to spell it. If you don't know how to spell the word, say it slowly and write the sounds you hear. Just do your best."

1. bud
2. ham
3. jet
4. fin
5. log
6. note
7. skip
8. train
9. sheep
10. chair

SEGMENTING TWO- AND THREE-PHONEME WORDS ASSESSMENT

Copy the administration section below on tag board. Locate the Segmenting Two- and Three-Phoneme Words Assessment section of the Literacy Assessment Scoring Record.

Directions: For two-phoneme words, say, "I am going to say a word, and you will say its sounds slowly. As I say the sounds, I'll put my finger into the boxes, like this: *tie, /t/, /I/.* As you say each sound, put your finger in each of the boxes. Now you try it. *Ape,* say its sounds, *ape.* If the child is correct say, "Yes, *ape* has two sounds /A/, /p/. Now you try the rest. If the child is not correct, say, "*Ape* has two sounds. Watch me say the sounds and push my finger in the boxes." Repeat the sounds and point to each box as you say the sounds. "Now you try." Have the child repeat the sounds and pointing with you. Score each sound the child says in isolation correctly (words can be scored 0 for no sounds; 1, one sound; or 2, both sounds isolated correctly).

For three-phoneme words, say, "Now we are going to say longer words. I am going to say each word's sounds and point to a box. Like this. *Cup,* /k/ /u/ /p/ (push up fingers into three boxes). Now you try. *Chick.*" If the child is correct, say, "Yes, *chick* has three sounds: /ch/, /i/, /k/. Now you try the next one." If the child is not correct, demonstrate again and have the child practice with your feedback. Score each sound the child says in isolation (words can be scored 0 for no sounds; 1, one sound; 2, two sounds isolated correctly; or 3, all three sounds isolated correctly).

Demonstration			
Practice			
4.			
5.			
6.			
7.			
8.			
9.			
10.			

Literacy Assessment Scoring Record

Child's Name: _____   Date: _____

Retelling Checklist
(oral comprehension and vocabulary)
(emergent, experimenting, conventional)

Pa and I went owling.
That's when you look for owls.
Pa did not call out.
You have to be quiet if you go owling.
Pa stopped at the pine trees.
He called, "Who-who-whoooo,"
the sound of a great horned owl.
We listened.
There was no answer.
We walked on.
I felt cold
You have to make your own heat if you go owling.
We went into the woods.
The woods were dark, black.
You have to be brave if you go owling.
We came to a clearing.
Pa called, "Who-who-whooo."
A sound came through the trees.
Who-who-whoooo.
Pa called back, "Who-who-whooo."
The owls' shadow flew over us.
Pa turned on his flashlight.
We stared at one another.
Then the owl flew back into the forest.
Pa and I walked back home.

(Based on *Owl Moon,* Yolen, 1987)

Additional ideas in the story recalled by child:

Number of ideas recalled _____

Circle: Very minimal with few details,   minimal with some details,
somewhat elaborated with more details,   elaborated with many details,
very elaborated with most ideas recalled

Name-Writing Assessment
(see child's name writing in attached sample)
(emergent)

0   No attempt
1   Uncontrolled scribble
2   Controlled scribble (mock cursive)
3   Individual marks but not letter-like
4   Mock letters or a few real letters with mock letters mixed in
5   Most legible letters (may have one or two reversals or missing letters)
6   All legible letters in first name
7   Legible letters with reduced size and alignment (may include last name)

Comments:

Concepts about Print Assessment
(emergent, experimenting)

1. Front
2. Back
3. Top
4. Bottom
5. Left page
6. Right page
7. Turn to next left page

8. First word top left
9. Second word, first line
10. Return sweep left to
    word on second line

11. One letter
12. Two letters
13. One word
14. Two words
15. Count number of words
    (four)
16. Capital letter *T*
17. Letter *s*
18. First word on page
19. Last word on page
20. Period

Total score _____/20

Fingerpoint Reading Assessment
(emergent, experimenting)

___ The itsy bitsy

___ spider

___ went up the

___ water spout.

___ Down came

___ the rain

___ and washed the

___ spider out.

___ Out came the sun and

___ dried up all the rain.

___ And the itsy bitsy spider

___ went up the spout again.

Total score _____/12

Upper-Case Alphabet Recognition Assessment
(emergent, experimenting)

N	J	Y	U
B	R	M	G
H	L	Q	V
I	P	W	A
X	E	K	C
Z	D	F	O
T	S		

Total score _____/26

Lower-Case Alphabet Recognition Assessment
(emergent, experimenting)

n	j	y	u
b	r	m	g
h	l	q	v
i	p	w	a
x	e	k	c
z	d	f	o
t	s		

Total score _____/26

Alphabet Letter-Writing Assessment
(see child's alphabet writing in attached sample)
(emergent, experimenting)

Total score _____/26   Letters written correctly: _____

Segmenting Beginning Phoneme Assessment
(phonemic awareness)
(emergent, experimenting)

1. toe	7. key	13. horse
2. man	8. dog	14. jar
3. fork	9. goat	15. sock
4. leaf	10. pig	16. web
5. nose	11. rain	
6. bed	12. van	

Total score _____/16

Rhyming Assessment
(phonological awareness)
(emerging, experimenting)

Total score _____/10

Draw a Picture and Write about Yourself Assessment
(see child's work in attached sample)
(emergent, experimenting, conventional)

McGill-Franzen (2006) suggests determining the following (check all that apply):

☐ Nonrepresentational drawing

☐ Representational drawing (tadpole) with meager, several, many details

☐ Representational drawing with body with meager, several, many details

☐ Scribble writing

☐ Mock letter writing

☐ Letters used in writing but no alphabetic principle

☐ Copied words

☐ Invented spellings

☐ Conventional spellings

☐ Word or label

☐ Sentence

☐ More than one sentence, but no sustained, coherent topic

☐ A text with two or more sentences on a sustained, coherent topic

Consonant Sound–Letter Assessment
(phonics)
(experimenting, conventional)

Total score _____ /17   Letters with known sounds: _____

Segmenting Onset and Rime Assessment
(phonemic awareness)
(experimenting, conventional)

Total score _____ /10

1. b-ook	5. d-uck	8. j-ar
2. p-aint	6. t-ub	9. ch-air
3. r-oad	7. f-ox	10. m-oon
4. c-ake		

High-Frequency Word Reading Assessment
(conventional reading)
(experimenting, conventional)

Total score _____ /20   Words read correctly: _____

Writing Words Assessment
(see child's writing in attached sample)
(conventional writing)
(experimenting, conventional)

Total score _____   Words written correctly: _____

Spelling Assessment

(see attached sample)
(phonics)
(experimenting, conventional)
(see Appendix A for phoneme pronounciation key)

Word	Initial consonant	Short vowel	Final consonant	Consonant blend or digraph	Long vowel
hud	/h/	/uh/	/d/		
ham	/h/	/a/	/m/		
jet	/j/	/e/	/t/		
fin	/f/	/i/	/n/		
log	/l/	/aw/ or /o/	/g/		
note	/n/		/t/		/O/
skip		/i/	/p/	/s•k/	
train			/n/	/t•r/	/A/
sheep			/p/	/sh/	/E/
chair			/r/	/ch/	/A/

Letters spelled conventionally: _____

Letters spelled unconventionally: _____

Segmenting Two- and Three-Phoneme Words Assessment

(phonemic awareness)
(conventional)

Total score _____/10

      1. k-ey
      2. sh-oe
      3. i-ce
      4. l-i-p
      5. d-o-g
      6. r-ai-n
      7. f-ee-t
      8. n-o-se
      9. sh-ee-p
    10. c-a-t

Literacy Assessment Scoring Record for Eric

Child's Name: *Eric*   Date: *Jan PK*

Retelling Checklist
(oral comprehension and vocabulary)
(emergent, experimenting, conventional)

Pa and I went owling.	*The walking*
That's when you look for owls.	*owl her*
Pa did not call out.	
You have to be quiet if you go owling.	*walking*
Pa stopped at the pine trees.	
He called, "Who-who-whoooo,"	*who who*
the sound of a great horned owl.	
We listened.	
There was no answer.	
We walked on.	*they walking*
I felt cold	
You have to make your own heat if you go owling.	
We went into the woods.	*walking*
The woods were dark, black.	
You have to be brave if you go owling.	
We came to a clearing.	
Pa called, "Who-who-whooo."	*who who*
A sound came through the trees.	
Who-who-whoooo.	
Pa called back, "Who-who-whooo."	
The owls' shadow flew over us.	*flying*
Pa turned on his flashlight.	
We stared at one another.	
Then the owl flew back into the forest.	
Pa and I walked back home.	*Dad and girl go here to house*

(Based on *Owl Moon,* Yolen, 1987)

Additional ideas in the story recalled by child:

Number of ideas recalled _____ —_____

Circle: Very minimal with few details,   minimal with some details,
somewhat elaborated with more details,   elaborated with many details,
very elaborated with most ideas recalled

used pictures to elicit telling mostly labeled actions/sounds

Name-Writing Assessment
(see child's name writing in attached sample)
(emergent)

0   No attempt
1   Uncontrolled scribble
2   Controlled scribble (mock cursive)
☑   Individual marks but not letter-like   *3 shapes*
4   Mock letters or a few real letters with mock letters mixed in
5   Most legible letters (may have one or two reversals or missing letters)
6   All legible letters in first name
7   Legible letters with reduced size and alignment (may include last name)

Comments:

Concepts about Print Assessment
(emergent, experimenting)

1. Front
2. Back
3. Top
4. Bottom
5. Left page
6. Right page
7. Turn to next left page

8. First word top left
9. Second word, first line
10. Return sweep left to
    word on second line

11. One letter
12. Two letters
13. One word
14. Two words
15. Count number of words
    (four)
16. Capital letter *T*
17. Letter *s*
18. First word on page
19. Last word on page
20. Period

Total score ___7___ /20

Fingerpoint Reading Assessment
(emergent, experimenting)

___ The itsy bitsy
___ spider

__ went up the

__ water spout.

__ Down came

__ the rain

__ and washed the

spider out,

__ Out came the sun and

__ dried up all the rain.

__ And the itsy bitsy spider

__ went up the spout again.

Total score __O__ /12

Upper-Case Alphabet Recognition Assessment
(emergent, experimenting)

N	J	Y	U
B	R	M	G
H	L	Q	V
I	P	W	A ✓
X	E ✓	K	C
Z	D	F	O ✓
T	S ✓		

Total score __4__ /26

Lower-Case Alphabet Recognition Assessment
(emergent, experimenting)

n	j	y	u
b	r	m	g
h	l	q	v
i	p	w	a
x	e	k	c
z	d	f	o
t	s		

Total score __O__ /26

Alphabet Letter-Writing Assessment
(see child's alphabet writing in attached sample)
(emergent, experimenting)

Total score _____ /26   Letters written correctly: _____

Segmenting Beginning Phoneme Assessment
(phonemic awareness)
(emergent, experimenting)

1. toe	7. key	13. horse
2. man	8. dog	14. jar
3. fork	9. goat	15. sock
4. leaf	10. pig	16. web
5. nose	11. rain	
6. bed	12. van	

Total score _____/16

Rhyming Assessment
(phonological awareness)
(emerging, experimenting)

Total score _____/10

Draw a Picture and Write about Yourself Assessment
(see child's work in attached sample)
(emergent, experimenting, conventional)

McGill-Franzen (2006) suggests determining the following (check all that apply):

☑ Nonrepresentational drawing *a circle, lines, dots not organized*

☐ Representational drawing (tadpole) with meager, several, many details

☐ Representational drawing with body with meager, several, many details

☑ Scribble writing *some but overlaps shape of person?*

☐ Mock letter writing

☐ Letters used in writing but no alphabetic principle

☐ Copied words

☐ Invented spellings

☐ Conventional spellings

☐ Word or label

☐ Sentence

☐ More than one sentence, but no sustained, coherent topic

☐ A text with two or more sentences on a sustained, coherent topic

Consonant Sound–Letter Assessment
(phonics)
(experimenting, conventional)

Total score _____/17   Letters with known sounds: _____

Literacy Assessment Scoring Record for Sarah

Child's Name: _Sarah_   Date: _Sept K_

Retelling Checklist
(oral comprehension and vocabulary)
(emergent, experimenting, conventional)

Pa and I went owling.	_They went out_
That's when you look for owls.	
Pa did not call out.	
You have to be quiet if you go owling.	
Pa stopped at the pine trees.	
He called, "Who-who-whoooo,"	
the sound of a great horned owl.	
We listened.	
There was no answer.	
We walked on.	
I felt cold	
You have to make your own heat if you go owling.	
We went into the woods.	
The woods were dark, black.	
You have to be brave if you go owling.	
We came to a clearing.	
Pa called, "Who-who-whooo."	_The called and called_
A sound came through the trees.	
Who-who-whoooo.	
Pa called back, "Who-who-whooo."	
The owls' shadow flew over us.	
Pa turned on his flashlight.	
We stared at one another.	_They saw it_
Then the owl flew back into the forest.	
Pa and I walked back home.	

(Based on _Owl Moon,_ Yolen, 1987)

Additional ideas in the story recalled by child:

Number of ideas recalled _____3_____

Circle: ~~Very minimal with few details~~ minimal with some details,
somewhat elaborated with more details, elaborated with many details,
very elaborated with most ideas recalled

Name-Writing Assessment
(see child's name writing in attached sample)
(emergent)

0 No attempt
1 Uncontrolled scribble
2 Controlled scribble (mock cursive)
3 Individual marks but not letter-like
4 Mock letters or a few real letters with mock letters mixed in
5 Most legible letters (may have one or two reversals or missing letters)
✓ All legible letters in first name
7 Legible letters with reduced size and alignment (may include last name)

Comments: *all caps*

Concepts about Print Assessment
(emergent, experimenting)

1. Fr̶ont
2. B̶ack
3. To̶p
4. B̶ottom
5. L̶eft page
6. Ri̶ght page
7. Turn t̶o next left page

8. First word top left
9. Second word, first line
10. Return sweep left to word on second line

11. One letter
12. Two letters
13. One̶word
14. Two̶words
15. Count number of words (four)
16. Capital letter *T*
17. Letter *s*
18. First word on page
19. Last word on page
20. Period

Total score ___9___ /20

Fingerpoint Reading Assessment
(emergent, experimenting) *I said poem, she couldn't say it perfectly*

___ The itsy bitsy
___ spider
___ went up the

__ water spout.

__ Down came

__ the rain

__ and washed the

__ spider out.

Out came the sun and

__ dried up all the rain.

__ And the itsy bitsy spider

__ went up the spout again.

Total score _____O_____ /12

Upper-Case Alphabet Recognition Assessment
(emergent, experimenting)

N	J	Y	U	
B	R	M	G	*named letters A E O S Q H P*
H	L	Q	V	*randomly*
I	P	W	A ✓	*except A E O*
X	E ✓	K	C	
Z	D	F	O ✓	
T	S			

Total score _____3_____ /26

Lower-Case Alphabet Recognition Assessment
(emergent, experimenting)

named numbers

n	j	y	u
b	r	m	g
h	l	q	v
i	p	w	a
x	e	k	c
z	d	f	o
t	s		

Total score _____ /26

Alphabet Letter-Writing Assessment
(see child's alphabet writing in attached sample)
(emergent, experimenting)

Total score _____O_____ /26   Letters written correctly: _____

                said she could draw

Segmenting Beginning Phoneme Assessment
(phonemic awareness)
(emergent, experimenting)

1. toe	7. key	13. horse
2. man	8. dog	14. jar
3. fork	9. goat	15. sock
4. leaf	10. pig	16. web
5. nose	11. rain	
6. bed	12. van	

Total score _____ /16

Rhyming Assessment
(phonological awareness)
(emerging, experimenting)

Total score _____ /10

Draw a Picture and Write about Yourself Assessment
(see child's work in attached sample)
(emergent, experimenting, conventional)

McGill-Franzen (2006) suggests determining the following (check all that apply):

☐ Nonrepresentational drawing

☑ Representational drawing (tadpole) with meager, several, ✓many details

☐ Representational drawing with body with meager, several, many details

☐ Scribble writing

☑ Mock letter writing

☑ Letters used in writing but no alphabetic principle

☐ Copied words

☐ Invented spellings

☐ Conventional spellings

☐ Word or label

☐ Sentence

☐ More than one sentence, but no sustained, coherent topic

☐ A text with two or more sentences on a sustained, coherent topic

eye brows
earrings
hair
elaborated eyes

Consonant Sound–Letter Assessment
(phonics)
(experimenting, conventional)

Total score _____ /17   Letters with known sounds: _____

Literacy Assessment Scoring Record
~~for Marceli~~

Child's Name: _Marceli_   Date: _Sept K_

Retelling Checklist
(oral comprehension and vocabulary)
(emergent, experimenting, conventional)

Pa and I went owling.	① _Pa & his kid went owling_
That's when you look for owls.	
Pa did not call out.	
You have to be quiet if you go owling.	
Pa stopped at the pine trees.	
He called, "Who-who-whoooo,"	
the sound of a great horned owl.	
We listened.	
There was no answer.	⑤ _They didn't see nothin'_
We walked on.	
I felt cold	
You have to make your own heat if you go owling.	
We went into the woods.	
The woods were dark, black.	
You have to be brave if you go owling.	
We came to a clearing.	
Pa called, "Who-who-whooo."	④ _ooo, that's Dad hooting_
A sound came through the trees.	
Who-who-whoooo.	
Pa called back, "Who-who-whooo."	
The owls' shadow flew over us.	
Pa turned on his flashlight.	⑥ _then they did the flashlight_
We stared at one another.	② _they found the owl_
Then the owl flew back into the forest.	
Pa and I walked back home.	⑦ _They was walking back_

(Based on _Owl Moon,_ Yolen, 1987)

Additional ideas in the story recalled by child: ③ _There was dogs_

Number of ideas recalled _____7_____

Circle: Very minimal with few details,   minimal with some details,
~~somewhat elaborated with more details~~ elaborated with many details,
very elaborated with most ideas recalled
                    notice ideas are not sequenced

Name-Writing Assessment
(see child's name writing in attached sample)
(emergent)

0 No attempt

1 Uncontrolled scribble

2 Controlled scribble (mock cursive)

3 Individual marks but not letter-like

4 Mock letters or a few real letters with mock letters mixed in

5 Most legible letters (may have one or two reversals or missing letters)

☑ All legible letters in first name

7 Legible letters with reduced size and alignment (may include last name)

Comments:

Concepts about Print Assessment
(emergent, experimenting)

1. F**r**ont	8. First wo**r**d top left	11. One letter
2. B**a**ck	9. Second word, first line	12. Two letters
3. T**o**p	10. Return swe**e**p left to	13. One **word**
4. B**o**ttom	word on second line	14. Two **words**
5. **L**eft page		15. Count n**u**mber of words
6. Right page		(four)
7. Turn to next left page		16. Capital letter *T*
		17. Le**t**er *s*
		18. First word on page
		19. Last word on page
		20. Period

Total score   *11*   /20

Fingerpoint Reading Assessment
(emergent, experimenting)

✓ The itsy bitsy

✓ spider

✓ went up the

__ water spout.

✓ Down came

✓ the rain

✓ and washed the

__ spider out.

__ Out came the sun and

__ dried up all the rain.

__ And the itsy bitsy spider

__ went up the spout again.

Total score ____6____ /12

Upper-Case Alphabet Recognition Assessment
(emergent, experimenting)

```
N        I̸ G      I̸       I̸
B        R        M        G
H̸        L        Q̸        V
I̸ L      P̸ B      W̸ H      A
X        E        K        C
Z        D        F        O
T        S
```

Total score ____18____ /26

Lower-Case Alphabet Recognition Assessment
(emergent, experimenting)

```
n        j        I̸       I̸
b        r        m        g̸
h̸        l        q̸ b      v
I̸ g      p̸ b      w̸ m      a
x        e        k̸        c
z        d̸ b      f̸        o
t        s
```

Total score ____15____ /26

Alphabet Letter-Writing Assessment
(see child's alphabet writing in attached sample)
(emergent, experimenting)

Total score ____14____ /26   Letters written correctly: *NrMBLwiaeKcoST*

Segmenting Beginning Phoneme Assessment
(phonemic awareness)
(emergent, experimenting)

1. toe	7. key	13. horse
2. man	8. dog	14. jar
3. fork	9. goat	15. sock
4. leaf	10. pig	16. web
5. nose	11. rain	
6. bed	12. van	

Total score _____/16

Rhyming Assessment
(phonological awareness)
(emerging, experimenting)

Total score _____/10

Draw a Picture and Write about Yourself Assessment
(see child's work in attached sample)
(emergent, experimenting, conventional)

McGill-Franzen (2006) suggests determining the following (check all that apply):

☐ Nonrepresentational drawing

☐ Representational drawing (tadpole) with meager, several, many details

☑ Representational drawing with body with meager, several, many details   *eye lids*
                                                                            toes
☐ Scribble writing

☐ Mock letter writing

☑ Letters used in writing but no alphabetic principle

☐ Copied words

☐ Invented spellings

☐ Conventional spellings

☐ Word or label

☐ Sentence

☐ More than one sentence, but no sustained coherent topic

☐ A text with two or more sentences on a sustained coherent topic

Consonant Sound–Letter Assessment
(phonics)
(experimenting, conventional)   *refused*

Total score _____/17   Letters with known sounds: _____

Literacy Assessment Scoring Record
~~for Jacob~~

Child's Name: _Jacob_   Date: _Sept Kinder_

Retelling Checklist
(oral comprehension and vocabulary)
(emergent, experimenting, conventional)

Pa and I went owling.	_It's about a kid going owling_
That's when you look for owls.	
Pa did not call out.	
You have to be quiet if you go owling.	
Pa stopped at the pine trees.	
He called, "Who-who-whoooo,"	_Dad went ooo_
the sound of a great horned owl.	
We listened.	
There was no answer.	
We walked on.	
I felt cold	
You have to make your own heat if you go owling.	
We went into the woods.	
The woods were dark, black.	
You have to be brave if you go owling.	
We came to a clearing.	
Pa called, "Who-who-whooo."	
A sound came through the trees.	_they heard it_
Who-who-whoooo.	
Pa called back, "Who-who-whooo."	
The owls' shadow flew over us.	
Pa turned on his flashlight.	_they used a flashlight_
We stared at one another.	_and found an owl_
Then the owl flew back into the forest.	
Pa and I walked back home.	_a went home_

(Based on _Owl Moon,_ Yolen, 1987)

Additional ideas in the story recalled by child:

Number of ideas recalled   6

Circle: Very minimal with few details,   minimal with some details,
~~somewhat elaborated with more details,~~ elaborated with many details,
very elaborated with most ideas recalled

Name-Writing Assessment
(see child's name writing in attached sample)
(emergent)

0 No attempt
1 Uncontrolled scribble
2 Controlled scribble (mock cursive)
3 Individual marks but not letter-like
4 Mock letters or a few real letters with mock letters mixed in
5 Most legible letters (may have one or two reversals or missing letters)
6 All legible letters in first name
7 Legible letters with reduced size and alignment (may include last name)

Comments: *mixed upper lower*

Concepts about Print Assessment
(emergent, experimenting)

1. Front
2. Back
3. Top
4. Bottom
5. Left page
6. Right page
7. Turn to next left page

8. First word top left
9. Second word, first line
10. Return sweep left to
    word on second line

11. One letter
12. Two letters
13. One word
14. Two words
15. Count number of words
    (four)
16. Capital letter *T*
17. Letter *s*
18. First word on page
19. Last word on page
20. Period

Total score ___15___ /20

Fingerpoint Reading Assessment
(emergent, experimenting)

✓ The itsy bitsy
✓ spider
✓ went up the

___ water spout.

✓ Down came

✓ the rain

✓ and washed the

✓X ✓ ✓ ✓ spider out. *sc*

___ Out came the sun and

___ dried up all the rain.

___ And the itsy bitsy spider

___ went up the spout again.

Total score ___7___ /12

Upper-Case Alphabet Recognition Assessment
(emergent, experimenting)

N	J	Y	U
B	R	M	G
H	L	*Q*	V
I	P	W	A
X	E	K	C
Z	D	F	O
T	S		

Total score ___25___ /26

Lower-Case Alphabet Recognition Assessment
(emergent, experimenting)

n	j	y	u
b d	r	m	g
h	l	*q* p	v
i	p	w	a
x	e	k	c
z	*d* b	f	o
t	s		

Total score ___23___ /26

Alphabet Letter-Writing Assessment
(see child's alphabet writing in attached sample)
(emergent, experimenting)

Total score ___22___ /26   Letters written correctly: *JNUrMbGlhpwiAeKcDfz*

OS+ (2 reversals: G + Z)

Segmenting Beginning Phoneme Assessment
(phonemic awareness)
(emergent, experimenting)

1. toe	7. key	13. horse
2. man	8. dog	14. jar
3. fork	9. goat	15. sock
4. leaf	10. pig	16. web
5. nose	11. rain	
6. bed	12. van	

Total score ___8___ /16

Rhyming Assessment
(phonological awareness)
(emerging, experimenting)

Total score _____/10

Draw a Picture and Write about Yourself Assessment
(see child's work in attached sample)
(emergent, experimenting, conventional)

McGill-Franzen (2006) suggests determining the following (check all that apply):

☐ Nonrepresentational drawing

☐ Representational drawing (tadpole) with meager, several, many details   *shirt stripes*
                                                                         hands

☑ Representational drawing with body with meager, several, many details   *feet*

☐ Scribble writing   *pants*

☐ Mock letter writing

☐ Letters used in writing but no alphabetic principle

☐ Copied words   *I P N W M F*

☑ Invented spellings   *I'm playing with my friend*

☐ Conventional spellings

☐ Word or label

☑ Sentence

☐ More than one sentence, but no sustained coherent topic

☐ A text with two or more sentences on a sustained coherent topic

Consonant Sound–Letter Assessment
(phonics)
(experimenting, conventional)

Total score ___5___/17   Letters with known sounds: _____

Segmenting Onset and Rime Assessment
(phonemic awareness)
(experimenting, conventional)

Total score _____/10

1. b-ook	5. d-uck	8. j-ar
2. p-aint	6. t-ub	9. ch-air
3. r-oad	7. f-ox	10. m-oon
4. c-ake		

High-Frequency Word Reading Assessment
(conventional reading)
(experimenting, conventional)

Total score _____/20   Words read correctly: _____

Writing Words Assessment
(see child's writing in attached sample)
(conventional writing)
(experimenting, conventional)

Total score _____   Words written correctly: _____

Spelling Assessment
(see attached sample)
(phonics)
(experimenting, conventional)
(see Appendix A for phoneme pronounciation key)

Word	Initial consonant	Short vowel	Final consonant	Consonant blend or digraph	Long vowel
bud	/b/ ✓	/uh/	/d/		
ham	/h/	/a/	/m/ ✓		
jet	/j/	/e/	/t/ ✓		
fin	/f/ ✓	/i/	/n/		
log	/l/ ✓	/aw/ or /o/	/g/		
note	/n/ ✓		/t/	✓	/O/
skip		/i/	/p/	/s•k/	
train			/n/	/t•r/	/A/
sheep			/p/ ✓	/sh/	/E/
chair			/r/	/ch/	/A/

Letters spelled conventionally: _____8_____

Letters spelled unconventionally: _____

References

Adams, M. (1990). *Beginning to read*. Cambridge, MA: MIT Press.

Adams, M. (2001). Alphabetic anxiety and explicit, systematic phonics instruction: A cognitive-science perspective. In S. Neuman & D. Dickinson (Eds.), *Handbook of early literacy research* (pp. 66–80). New York: Guilford Press.

Alborough, J. (2001). *Duck in the truck*. New York: HarperCollins.

Allington, R. (1995). Literacy lessons in the elementary schools: Yesterday, today, and tomorrow. In R. Allington & S. Walmsley (Eds.), *No quick fix: Rethinking literacy programs in America's elementary schools* (pp. 1–15). New York: Teachers College Press.

August, D., & Hakuta, K. (Eds.). (1997). *Improving schooling for language-minority children: A research agenda*. National Research Council and Institute of Medicine. Washington, DC: National Academy Press.

Baghban, M. (1984). *Our daughter learns to read and write: A case study from birth to three*. Newark, DE: International Reading Association.

Ballenger, C. (1999). *Teaching other people's children: Literacy and learning in a bilingual classroom*. New York: Teachers College Press.

Barone, D. (1999). *Resilient children: Stories of poverty, drug exposure, and literacy development*. Newark, DE: International Reading Association.

Barrera, R., Ligouri, O., & Salas, L. (1992). Ideas literature can grow on: Key insights for enriching and expanding children's literature about the Mexican-American experience. In B. Harris (Ed.), *Teaching multicultural literature in grades K–8* (pp. 203–241). Norwood, MA: Christopher-Gordon.

Barton, B. (1990). *Building a house*. New York: Mulberry Books.

Bear, D. R., Invernizzi, M., Templeton, S., & Johnston, F. (2000). *Words their way: Word study for phonics, vocabulary, and spelling instruction*. Columbus, OH: Merrill.

Bear, D., Invernizzi, M., Templeton, S., & Johnston, F. (2008). *Words their way: Word study for phonics, vocabulary, and spelling instruction* (4th ed.). Columbus, OH: Pearson Prentice Hall.

Beck, I., McKeown, M., & Kucan, L. (2013). *Bringing words to life: Robust vocabulary instruction* (2nd ed.). New York: Guilford Press.

Bergen, R. (2008). *Teaching writing in kindergarten: A structured approach to daily writing that helps every child become a confident, capable writer*. New York: Scholastic.

Biemiller, A., & Boote, C. (2006). An effective method for building meaning vocabulary in primary grades. *Journal of Educational Psychology, 98*, 44–62.

Bissex, G. (1980). *GYNS AT WRK: A child learns to write and read.* Cambridge, MA: Harvard University Press.

Blachman, B., Ball, E., Black, R., & Tangel, D. (2000). *Road to the code: A phonological awareness program for young children.* Baltimore: Brookes.

Bloodgood, J. W. (1999). What's in a name? Children's name writing and literacy acquisition. *Reading Research Quarterly, 34,* 342–367.

Bodrova, E., & Leong, D. (2005). Uniquely preschool. *Educational Leadership, 63(1),* 44–47.

Both-de Vries, A. C., & Bus, A.G. (2008). Name writing: A first step to phonetic writing? Does the name have a special role in understanding the symbolic function of writing? *Literacy Teaching and Learning, 12(2),* 37–55.

Branscombe, A. (1991). "But it ain't real!": Pretense in children's play and literacy development. In J. F. Christie (Ed.), *Play and early literacy development* (pp. 91–115). Albany: State University of New York Press.

Briggs, R. (1970). *Jim and the beanstalk.* New York: Coward-McCann.

Brown, M. (1942). *The runaway bunny.* New York: Harper & Row.

Brown, M. (1947). *Goodnight moon.* New York: Harper & Row.

Burningham, J. (1993). *Mr. Gumpy's motor car.* New York: Crowell.

Byrne, B., & Fielding-Barnsley, R. (1991). Evaluation of a program to teach phonemic awareness to young children. *Journal of Educational Psychology, 83,* 451–455.

Campbell, F., Ramey, C., Pungello, E., Sparling, J., & Miller-Johnson, S. (2002). Early childhood education: Young adult outcomes from the Abecedarian project. *Applied Developmental Science, 6,* 42–57.

Carle, E. (1996). *The grouchy ladybug.* New York: HarperTrophy.

Casbergue, R., McGee, L., & Bedford, A. (2008). Characteristics of classroom environments associated with accelerated literacy development. In L. M. Justice & C. Vukelich (Eds.), *Achieving excellence in preschool literacy instruction* (pp. 167–181). New York: Guilford Press.

Christie, J. F. (1991). Psychological research on play: Connections with early literacy development. In J. F. Christie (Ed.), *Play and early literacy development* (pp. 27–43). Albany: State University of New York Press.

Clay, M. M. (1998). *By different paths to common outcomes.* York, ME: Stenhouse.

Clay, M. M. (2002). *An observation survey of early literacy achievement.* Portsmouth, NH: Heinemann.

Clay, M. M. (2007). *Concepts about print: What have children learned about the way we print language?* Portsmouth, NH: Heinemann.

Cochran-Smith, M. (1984). *The making of a reader.* Norwood, NJ: Ablex.

Collins, A., Brown, J. S., & Newman, S. (1989). Cognitive apprenticeships: Teaching the crafts of reading, writing and mathematics. In L.R. Resnick (Ed.), *Knowing, learning and instruction* (pp. 453–491). Hillsdale, NJ: Erlbaum.

Comber, B. (2000). What *really* counts in early literacy lessons. *Language Arts, 78,* 39–49.

Connelly, L. (1988). *Bears, bears, everywhere* (N. C. Koeller, Ill.). Cypress, CA: Creative Teaching Press.

Cornell, E. H., Senechal, M., & Brodo, L. S. (1988). Recall of picture books by 3–year-old children: Testing and repetition effects in joint reading activities. *Journal of Educational Psychology, 80,* 537–542.

Cowley, J. (1989). *Yuck soup.* Bothell, WA: Wright Group.

Craig, S. (2006). The effects of an adapted interactive writing intervention on kindergarten children's phonological awareness, spelling, and early reading development: A contextualized approach to instruction. *Journal of Educational Psychology, 98(4),* 714–731.

Cunningham, P. (2000). *Phonics they use: Words for reading and writing.* New York: Longman.

dePaola, T. (1996). *Bill and Pete.* New York: Putnam.

Diamond, B. J., & Moore, M. A. (1995). *Multicultural literacy: Mirroring the reality of the classroom.* White Plains, NY: Longman.

Dickinson, D. K., & Smith, M. W. (1994). Long-term effects of preschool teachers' book readings on low-income children's vocabulary and story comprehension. *Reading Research Quarterly, 29,*104–122.

Dickinson, D. K., & Tabors, P. O. (Eds.). (2001). *Beginning literacy with language: Young children learning at home and school.* Baltimore: Brookes.

Diller, D. (2003). *Literacy work stations: Making centers work.* Portland, Me: Stenhouse

Duke, N. K. (2000). Print environments and experiences offered to first-grade students in very low- and very high-SES school districts. *Reading Research Quarterly, 37,* 456–477.

Duke, N. K., & Kays, J. (1998). "Can I say 'once upon a time'?": Kindergarten children developing knowledge of information book language. *Early Childhood Research Quarterly, 13,* 295–318.

Durkin, D. (1974–1975). A six year study of children who learned to read in school at the age of four. *Reading Research Quarterly, 10,* 9–61.

Edwards, P. A., & Danridge, J. C. (2001). Developing collaboration with culturally diverse parents. In V. J. Risko & K. Bromley (Eds.), *Collaboration for diverse learners: Viewpoints and practices* (pp. 251–272). Newark, DE: International Reading Association.

Entwisle, D. R., Alexander, K. L., & Olson, I. S. (1997). *Children, schools and inequality.* Boulder, CO: Westview Press.

Feldgus, E., & Cardonick, I. (1999). *Kid writing: A systematic approach to phonics, journals, and writing workshop.* Bothell, WA: Wright Group.

Fitzgerald, J. (1989). Research on stories: Implications for teachers. In K. D. Muth (Ed.), *Children's comprehension of text: Research into practice* (pp. 2–36). Newark, DE: International Reading Association.

Fontanel, B. (1989). *The penguin: A funny bird.* Watertown, MA: Charlesbridge.

Fountas, I., & Pinnell, G. (1996). *Guided reading: Good first teaching for all children.* Portsmouth, NH: Heinemann.

Fractor, J., Woodruff, M., Martinez, M., & Teale, W. (1993). Let's not miss opportunities to promote voluntary reading: Classroom libraries in elementary school. *The Reading Teacher, 46,* 476–484.

Fuchs, D., & Fuchs, L. S. (2005). Peer-assisted learning strategies: Promoting word recognition, fluency, and reading comprehension in young children. *Journal of Special Education, 39*(1), 34–44.

Gibbons, F. (1999). *Mama and me and the Model T.* New York: Morrow.

Gibson, J. T. (1999). *Developing strategies and practices for culturally diverse classrooms.* Norwood, MA: Christopher-Gordon.

Goldenberg, C., & Gallimore, R. (1991). Local knowledge, research knowledge, and educational change: A case study of early Spanish reading improvement. *Educational Researcher, 20,* 2–14.

Goldenberg, C., & Gallimore, R. (1995). Immigrant Latino parents' values and beliefs about their children's education: Continuities and discontinuities across cultures and generations. In P. Pintrich & M. Maehr (Eds.), *Advances in motivation and achievement: Culture, ethnicity, and motivation* (Vol. 9, pp. 183–228). Greenwich, CT: JAI Press.

Good, R., & Kaminski, R. (2005). *Dynamic Indicators of Basic Early Literacy Skills* (6th ed.). Eugene, OR: Institute for Development of Educational Achievement.

Good, R., Simmons, D., Kame'enui, E., Kaminski, R., & Wallin, J. (2002). *Summary of decision rules for intensive, strategic, and benchmark instructional recommendations in kindergarten through third grade* (Technical Report No. 11). Eugene: University of Oregon.

Greenwood, C., Carta, J., Baggett, K., Buzhardt, J., Walker, D., & Terry, B. (2008). Best practices in integrating progress monitoring and response-to-intervention concepts into early childhood systems. In A. Thomas & J. Grimes (Eds.), *Best practices in school psychology V* (pp. 535–548). Washington, DC: National Association of School Psychologists.

Gregory, A., & Cahill, M. (2010). Kindergartners can do it, too! Comprehension strategies for early readers. *The Reading Teacher, 63,* 515–520.

Gormley, W., Gayer, T., Phillips, D., & Dawson, B. (2005). The effects of universal Pre-k on cognitive development. *Developmental Psychology, 41*(6), 872–884.

Hanson, R. A., & Farrell, D. (1995). The long-term effects on high school seniors of learning to read in kindergarten. *Reading Research Quarterly, 30*(4), 908–933.

Hargrave, A. C., & Senechal, M. (2000). A book reading intervention with preschool children who have limited vocabularies: The benefits of regular reading and dialogic reading. *Early Childhood Research Quarterly, 15,* 75–90.

Harlan, J., & Rivkin, M. (2000). *Science experiences for the early childhood years: An integrated approach* (7th ed.). Columbus, OH: Merrill.

Harste, J., Burke, C., & Woodward, V. (1983). *The young child as a writer-reader and informant.* Bloomington: Indiana University Press.

Hart, B., & Risely, T. (1995). *Meaningful differences in the everyday experiences of young American children.* Baltimore, MD: Brookes.

Hart, B., & Risely, T. (2003). The early catastrophe: The 30 million word gap by age 3. *American Educator, 27,* 4–9.

Heisey, N., & Kucan, L. (2010). Introducing science concepts to primary students through read-alouds: Interactions and multiple texts make the difference. *The Reading Teacher, 63,* 666–676.

Helburn, S. (1995). *Cost, quality and child outcomes in child care centers.* Denver: Department of Economics, Center for Research in Economics and Social Policy, University of Colorado at Denver.

Helm, J., & Katz, L. (2001). *Young investigators: The project approach in the early years.* New York: Teachers College Press.

Hiebert, E., & Taylor, B. (2000). Beginning reading instruction: Research on early interventions. In M. Kamil, P. Mosenthal, P. Pearson, & R. Barr (Eds.), *Handbook of reading research* (Vol. 3, pp 455–482). Mahwah, NJ: Erlbaum.

Hildreth, G. (1936). Developmental sequences in name writing. *Child Development, 7,* 291–303.

Hindley, J. (2002). *Do like a duck does!* Cambridge, MA: Candlewick Press.

Hoff, S. (1958). *Danny and the dinosaur.* New York: Harper & Row.

Hutchins, P. (1968). *Rosie's walk.* New York: Macmillan.

Individuals with Disabilities Education Improvement Act. (2004). P.L. 108-466.

International Reading Association and the National Association for the Education of Young Children. (1998). Learning to read and write: Developmentally appropriate practices for young children. *The Reading Teacher, 52,* 193–216.

Intrater, R. (1995). *Two eyes, a nose, and a mouth.* New York: Scholastic.

Invernizzi, M., Justice, L., Landrum, T., & Booker, K. (2004–2005). Early literacy screening in kindergarten: Widespread implementation in Virginia. *Journal of Literacy Research, 36*(4), 479–500.

Isbell, R. T. (1995). *The complete learning center book.* Beltsville, MD: Gryphon House.

Isbell, R. T., & Exelby, B. (2001). *Early learning environments that work.* Beltsville, MD: Gryphon House.

Johnston, R. S., Anderson, M., & Holligan, C. (1996). Knowledge of the alphabet and explicit awareness of phonemes in pre-readers: The nature of the relationship. *Reading and Writing: An Interdisciplinary Journal, 8*, 217–234.

Justice, L. M., Pence, K., Bowles, R. B., & Wiggins, A. (2006). An investigation of four hypotheses concerning the order by which 4-year-old children learn the alphabet letters. *Early Childhood Research Quarterly, 21*(3), 374–389.

Kellogg, R. (1969). *Analyzing children's art.* Palo Alto, CA: National Press Books.

King, K. (2012). Writing workshop in preschool: Acknowledging children as writers. *The Reading Teacher, 65*(6), 392–401.

Klenk, L., & Kibby, M. (2000). Re-mediating reading difficulties: Appraising the past, reconciling the present, constructing the future. In M. Kamil, P. Mosenthal, P. Pearson, & R. Barr (Eds.), *Handbook of reading research* (Vol. 3, pp. 667–690). Mahwah, NJ: Erlbaum.

Krashen, S. (1982). *Principles and practices in second language acquisition.* Oxford, UK: Pergamon.

Ladson-Billings, G. (1994). *The dreamkeepers: Successful teachers of African American children.* San Francisco: Jossey-Bass.

Leonhardt, D. (2010). The case for $320,000 kindergarten teachers. Retrieved July 7, 2013, from *www.nytimes.com/2010/07/28/business/economy/28leonhardt.html.*

Lesman, P., & deJong, P. (1998). Home literacy: Opportunity, instruction, cooperation and social-emotional quality predicting early reading achievement. *Reading Research Quarterly, 33*, 294–318.

Lester, H. (1998). *Tacky in trouble.* New York: Scholastic.

Lifter, K., Mason, E., & Barton, E. (2011). Children's play: Where we have been and where we could go. *Journal of Early Intervention, 33*(4), 281–297.

Lonigan, C. J., Allan, N., & Lerner, M. (2011). Assessment of preschool early literacy skills: Linking children's educational needs with empirically supported instructional activities. *Pschology in the Schools, 49*(5), 488–501.

Lonigan, C. J., Burgess, S. R., Anthony, J. L., & Baker, T. (1998). Development of phonological sensitivity in 2- to 5-year-old children. *Journal of Educational Psychology, 90*, 294–311.

Lonigan, C. J., & Wilson, S. B. (2008). *Report on the revised Get Ready to Read! Screening Tool: Psychometrics and normative information* (Technical Report). New York: National Center for Learning Disabilities.

Maclean, M., Bryant, P., & Bradley, L. (1987). Rhymes, nursery rhymes, and reading in early childhood. *Merrill–Palmer Quarterly, 33*, 255–281.

Manning-Kratcoski, A., & Bobkoff-Katz, K. (1998). Conversing with young language learners in the classroom. *Young Children, 53*, 30–33.

Manyak, P. (2008). Phonemes in use: Multiple activities for a critical process. *The Reading Teacher, 61*(8), 659–662.

McCarthy, P. (2008). Using sound boxes systematically to develop phonemic awareness. *The Reading Teacher, 62*(4), 346–349.

McConnell, R. (2002). *Individual growth and development indicators.* Minneapolis: University of Minnesota.

McGee, L. (2007). *Transforming literacy practices in preschool: Research-based practices that give all children the opportunity to reach their potential as learners.* New York: Scholastic.

McGee, L. (2013). Read me a story: Reaping the benefits of reading for young children. In R. Reutzel (Ed.), *Handbook of research-based practice in early education* (pp. 364–379). New York: Guilford Press.

McGee, L., & Dail, A. R. (2010). Phonemic awareness instruction in preschool: Research implications and lessons learned from Early Reading First. In M. McKenna, S. Walpole, & K. Conradi (Eds.), *Promoting early reading: Research, resources, and best practices* (pp. 59–77). New York: Guilford Press.

McGee, L. M. (2003). Book acting: Storytelling and drama in the early childhood classroom. In D. M. Barone & L. M. Morrow (Eds.), Literacy and young children: Research-based practices (pp. 157-172). New York: Guilford Press.

McGee, L. M., & Richgels, D. J. (1989). "K is Kristen's": Learning the alphabet from a child's perspective. *The Reading Teacher, 43*, 216–225.

McGee, L. M., & Richgels, D. J. (2000). *Literacy's beginnings: Supporting young readers and writers* (3rd ed.). Boston: Allyn & Bacon.

McGee, L. M., & Richgels, D. J. (2012). *Literacy's beginnings: Supporting young readers and writers* (6th ed.). Needham, MA: Allyn & Bacon.

McGee, L., & Schickedanz, J. (2007). Repeated interactive read-alouds in preschool and kindergarten. *The Reading Teacher, 60*, 742–751.

McGee, L. M., & Tompkins, G. (1981). The videotape answer to independent reading comprehension activities. *The Reading Teacher, 34*, 430–431.

McGee, L., & Ukrainetz, T. (2009). Using scaffolding to teach phonemic awareness in preschool and kindergarten. *The Reading Teacher, 62*, 599–603.

McGill-Franzen, A. (2006). *Kindergarten literacy: Matching assessment and instruction in kindergarten*. New York: Scholastic.

McGill-Franzen, A., Allington, R., Yokoi, L., & Brooks, G. (1999). Putting books in the room is necessary but not sufficient. *Journal of Educational Research, 93*(2) 67–74.

McGinty, A., & Justice, L. (2010). Language facilitation in the preschool classroom. In M. McKenna, S. Walpole, & K. Conradi (Eds.), *Promoting early reading: Research, resources, and best practices*. New York: Guilford Press.

McKissack, P. (1988). *Mirandy and Brother Wind*. New York: Knopf.

McMillon, G., & Edwards, P. (2000). Why does Joshua "hate" school . . . but love Sunday school? *Language Arts, 78*, 111–120.

Meier, D. R. (2000). *Scribble scrabble, learning to reading and write: Success with diverse teachers, children, and families*. New York: Teachers College Press.

Middendorf, C. (2008). *Differentiating instruction in kindergarten*. New York: Scholastic.

Miller, E., & Almon, J. (2009). *Crisis in the kindergarten: Why children need to play in school*. College Park, MD: Alliance for Childhood.

Milteer, R., Ginsburg, K., & Mulligan, D. (2012). The importance of play in promoting healthy child development and maintaining strong parent-child bond: Focus on children in poverty. *Pediatrics, 129*(1), e204–e213.

Mol., S., Bus, A., & De Jong, M. (2009). Interactive book reading in early education: A tool to Stimulate print knowledge as well as oral language. *Review of Educational Research, 79*, 979–1007.

Morris, D. (1983). Concept of word and phoneme awareness in the beginning reader. *Research in the Teaching of English, 17*(4), 359–373.

Morrow, L. M., & Rand, M. (1991). Preparing the classroom environment to promote literacy during play. In J. F. Christie (Ed.), *Play and early literacy development* (pp. 141–165). Albany: State University of New York Press.

Murphy, S. J. (2000). *Beep beep, vroom vroom!* New York: HarperCollins.

Murray, B. A., Stahl, S. A., & Ivey, M. G. (1996). Developing phoneme awareness through alphabet books. *Reading and Writing: An Interdisciplinary Journal, 8*, 306–322.

Myers, P. (2005). The Princess storyteller, Clara Clarifier, Quincy Questioner, and the Wizard: Reciprocal teaching adapted for kindergarten students. *The Reading Teacher, 59*(4), 314–324.

National Center for Children in Poverty. (1998). Child poverty rates remain high despite booming U.S. economy. *News and Issues, 8*, 1.

National Center for Education Statistics. (1996). *NAEP 1994 reading report card for the nation and states*. Washington, DC: U.S. Department of Education, Office of Educational Research and Improvement.

National Center for Education Statistics. (1999). *Literacy in the labor force: Results from the National Adult Literacy Survey*. Washington, DC: U.S. Department of Education.

National Center for Education Statistics. (2000). *America's kindergartners*. Washington, DC: U.S. Department of Education.

National Early Literacy Panel. (2008). *Developing early literacy: Report of the National Early Literacy Panel*. Washington, DC: National Institute for Literacy. Available at *http://lines.ed.gov/publications/pdf/NELPreport09.pdf*.

National Governors Association Center for Best Practices & Council of Chief State School Officers. (2010). *Common Core State Standards for English language arts and literacy in history/social studies, science, and technical subjects*. Retrieved December 4, 2012, from *www.corestandards.org/ELA-literacy*.

National Reading Panel & National Institute of Child Health and Human Development. (2000). *Report of the National Reading Panel: Teaching children to read: An evidence-based assessment of the scientific research literature on reading and its implications for reading instruction*. Washington, DC: National Institute of Child Health and Human Development, National Institutes of Health.

Neuman, S. B. (2006). N is for nonsensical. *Educational Leadership, 64*(2), 28–31.

Neuman, S. B. (2009). *Changing the odds for children at risk: Seven essential principles of educational programs that break the cycle of poverty*. New York: Teachers College.

Neuman, S. B., Bredekamp, S., & Copple, C. (2000). *Learning to read and write: Developmentally appropriate practice*. Washington, DC: National Association for the Education of Young Children.

Neuman, S. B., & Celano, D. (2001). Access to print in low-income and middle-income communities: An ecological study of four neighborhoods. *Reading Research Quarterly, 36*, 8–26.

Neuman, S. B., & Dwyer, J. (2010). Developing vocabulary and conceptual knowledge for low-income preschoolers: A design experiment. *Journal of Literacy Research, 43*, 103–129.

Neuman, S. B., & Kamil, M. L. (2010). *Preparing teachers for the early childhood classroom: Proven models and key principles*. Baltimore, MD: Brookes.

Neuman, S. B., Newman, E., & Dwyer, J. (2011). Educational effects of a vocabulary intervention on preschoolers' word knowledge and conceptual development: A cluster-randomized trial. *Reading Research Quarterly, 46*, 249–272.

Neuman, S. B., & Roskos, K. (1993). Access to print for children of poverty: Differential effects of adult mediation and literacy-enriched play settings on environmental and functional print tasks. *American Educational Research Journal, 30*, 95–122.

Neuman, S. B., & Roskos, K. (1997). Literacy knowledge in practice: Contexts of participation for young writers and readers. *Reading Research Quarterly, 32*, 10–32.

Neuman, S. B., & Roskos, K. (2012). Helping children become more knowledgeable through text. *The Reading Teacher, 66*(3), 207–210.

Newkirk, T. (1989). *More than stories: The range of children's writing*. Portsmouth, NH: Heinemann.

Oppenheim. (1996). *Have you seen bugs?* New York: Scholastic.

Ouellette, G., & Senechal, M. (2008). Pathways to literacy: A study of invented spelling and its role in learning to read. *Child Development, 79*(4), 899–913.

Paley, V. G. (1990). *The boy who would be a helicopter*. Cambridge, MA: Harvard University Press.

Pappas, C. (1993). Is narrative "primary"? Some insights from kindergartners' pretend readings of stories and information books. *Journal of Reading Behavior, 25*, 97–129.

Payne, C., & Schulman, M. (1998). *Getting the most out of morning message and other shared writing lessons.* New York: Scholastic.

Pellegrini, A. D., & Galda, L. (1982). The effects of thematic-fantasy play training on the development of children's story comprehension. *American Educational Research Journal, 19,* 443–452.

Pentimonti, J., Zucker, T., Justice, L., & Kaderavek, J. (2010). Informational text use in preschool classroom read-alouds. *The Reading Teacher, 63*(8), 656–665.

Piasta, S., Petscher, Y., & Justice, L. (2012). How many letters should preschoolers in public programs know? The diagnostic efficiency of various preschool letter-naming benchmarks for predicting first-grade literacy achievement. *Journal of Educational Psychology, 104*(4), 945–958.

Pienkowski, J. (1980). *Dinnertime.* Los Angeles: Price/Stern/Sloan.

Plourde, L. (1997). *Pigs in the mud in the middle of the rud.* New York: Blue Sky Press.

Polacco, P. (1990). *Thunder cake.* New York: Philomel.

Potter, B. (1902). *The tale of Peter Rabbit.* London: Frederick Warne.

Price, L., Van Kleeck, A., & Huberty, C. (2009). Talk during book sharing between parents and preschool children: A comparison between storybook and expository book conditions. *Reading Research Quarterly, 44,* 171–194.

Purcell-Gates, V. (1988). Lexical and syntactic knowledge of written narrative held by well-read-to kindergartners and second graders. *Research in the Teaching of English, 22,* 128–160.

Purcell-Gates, V. (1996). Stories, coupons, and the *TV Guide*: Relationships between home literacy experiences and emergent literacy knowledge. *Reading Research Quarterly, 31,* 406–428.

Purcell-Gates, V., & Dahl, K. (1991). Low-SES children's success and failure at early literacy learning in skills-based classrooms. *Journal of Reading Behavior, 23,* 1–34.

Purcell-Gates, V., McIntyre, E., & Freppon, P. A. (1995). Learning written storybook language in school: A comparison of low-SES children in skills-based and whole language classrooms. *American Educational Research Journal, 32,* 659–685.

Ray, K., & Glover, M. (2008). *Already ready: Nurturing writers in preschool and kindergarten.* Portsmouth, NH: Heinemann.

Rhodes, L., & Nathenson-Mejia, S. (1992). Anecdotal records: A powerful tool for ongoing literacy assessment. *The Reading Teacher, 45,* 502–509.

Richgels, D. J. (2002). Informational texts in kindergarten. *The Reading Teacher, 55,* 586–595.

Richgels, D. J. (2003). *Going to kindergarten: A year with an outstanding teacher.* Lanham, MD: Scarecrow Press.

Richgels, D. J. (2013). Talk, write, and read: A method for sampling emergent literacy skills. *The Reading Teacher, 66*(5), 380–389.

Richgels, D. J., Poremba, K. J., & McGee, L. M. (1996). Kindergartners talk about print: Phonemic awareness in meaningful contexts. *The Reading Teacher, 49,* 632–642.

Rieben, L., Ntamakiliro, L., Gonthier, B., & Fayol, M. (2005). Effects of various early writing practices on reading and spelling. *Scientific Studies of Reading, 9*(2), 145–166.

Roberts, T. (2008). Home storybook reading in primary or second language with preschool children: Evidence of equal effectiveness for second-language vocabulary acquisition. *Reading Research Quarterly, 43,* 103–130.

Roskos, K., & Neuman, S. B. (2001). Environment and its influences for early literacy teaching and learning. In S. B. Neuman & D. K. Dickinson (Eds.), *Handbook of early literacy research* (pp. 281–292). New York: Guilford Press.

Rowe, D. (1998). The literate potentials of book-related dramatic play. *Reading Research Quarterly, 33,* 10–35.

Santoro, L., Chard, D., Howard, L., & Baker, S. (2008). Making the *very* most of classroom read-alouds to promote comprehension and vocabulary. *The Reading Teacher, 61*, 396–408.

Scarborough, H. (1991). Early syntactic development of dyslexic children. *Annals of Dyslexia, 41*, 207–220.

Scanlon, D., Anderson, K., & Sweeney, J. (2010). *Early intervention for reading difficulties: The interactive strategies approach*. New York: Guilford Press.

Schickedanz, J. (1998). What is developmentally appropriate practice in early literacy?: Considering the alphabet. In S. Neuman & K. Roskos (Eds.), *Children achieving: Best practices in early literacy* (pp. 20–35). Newark, DE: International Reading Association.

Schickedanz, J. A., & Collins, M. F. (2013). *So much more than the ABCs: The early phases of reading and writing*. Washington, DC: National Association for the Education of Young Children.

Schulman, M., & Payne, C. (2000). *Guided reading: Making it work*. New York: Scholastic.

Schweinhart, L., Montie, J., Xiang, Z., Barnett, W., Belfield, C., & Nores, M. (2005). *Lifetime effects: The High/Scope Perry preschool study through age 40*. Ypsilanti, MI: High/Scope Press.

Sendak, M. (1963). *Where the wild things are*. New York: HarperCollins.

Seuss, Dr. (1957). *Cat in the hat*. New York: Random House.

Sipe, L. (2008). *Storytime: Young children's literary understanding in the classroom*. New York: Teachers College Press.

Smith, E., Pellin, B., & Arguso, S. (2003). *Bright beginnings: An effective literacy-focused PreK program for educationally disadvantaged four-year-old children*. Arlington, VA: Educational Research Service.

Smith, S. S., & Dixon, R. G. (1995). Literacy concepts of low- and middle-class four-year-olds entering preschool. *Journal of Educational Research, 88*, 243–253.

Smolkin, L. B., & Donovan, C. A. (2002). "Oh excellent, excellent question!": Developmental differences and comprehension acquisition. In C. Block & M. Pressley (Eds.), *Comprehension instruction: Research-based best practices* (pp. 140–157). New York: Guilford Press.

Snow, C. E., Burns, M. S., & Griffin, P. (Eds.). (1998). *Preventing reading difficulties in young children*. Washington, DC: National Academy Press.

Stahl, S. A., & Murray, B. A. (1994). Defining phonological awareness and its relationship to early reading. *Journal of Educational Psychology, 86*, 221–234.

Stein, N. L., & Glenn, C. G. (1979). An analysis of story comprehension in elementary school children. In R. O. Freedle (Ed.), *Advances in discourse processes: Vol. 2. New directions in discourse processing* (pp. 53–120). Norwood, NJ: Ablex.

Stevens, R., Van Meter, P., & Warcholak, N. (2010). The effects of explicitly teaching story structure to primary grade children. *Journal of Literacy Research, 42*, 159–198.

Storch, S. A., & Whitehurst, G. J. (2002). Oral language and code-related precursors to reading: Evidence from a longitudinal structural model. *Developmental Psychology, 38*(6), 934–947.

Strickland, D. S. (1994). Educating African American learners at risk: Finding a better way. *Language Arts, 71*, 328–336.

Sturges, P. (1999). *The little red hen (makes a pizza)*. New York: Dutton Children's Books.

Taylor, D., & Dorsey-Gaines, C. (1988). *Growing up literate: Learning from inner-city families*. Portsmouth, NH: Heinemann.

Tilly, W. (2008). The evolution of school psychology to a science-based practice: Problem solving and the three-tiered model. In A. Thomas & J. Grimes (Eds.), *Best practices in school psychology V* (Vol. 1, pp. 17–36). Washington, DC: National Association of School Psychologists.

Tompkins, G., & McGee, L. M. (1989). Teaching repetition as a story structure. In K. D. Muth (Ed.), *Children's comprehension of text: Research into practice* (pp. 59–78). Newark, DE: International Reading Association.

Ukrainetz, T. A., Cooney, M. H., Dyer, S. K., Kysar, A. J., & Harris, T. J. (2000). An investigation into teaching phonemic awareness through shared reading and writing. *Early Childhood Research Quarterly, 15*, 331–355.

Van den Broek, P. (2001). *The role of television viewing in the development of reading comprehension.* Washington, DC: U.S. Department of Education.

van Kleeck, A., Vander Woude, J., & Hammett, I. (2006). Fostering literal and inferential language skills in head start children with language impairment using scripted book-sharing discussions. *American Journal of Speech-Language Pathology, 15*, 85–95.

Villaume, S. K., & Wilson, L. C. (1989). Preschool children's explorations of letters in their own names. *Applied Psycholinguistics, 10*, 283–300.

Vygotsky, L. S. (1978). *Mind in society: The development of higher psychological processes.* Cambridge, MA: Harvard University Press.

Wadsworth, O. (1992). *Over in the meadow: An old counting rhyme.* New York: Scholastic.

Walker, D., Greenwood, C., Hart, B., & Carta, J. (1994). Prediction of school outcomes based on socioeconomic status and early language production. *Child Development, 65*, 600–621.

Weisch, J. (2008). Playing with and beyond the story: Enhancing book-related pretend play. *The Reading Teacher, 62*, 138–148.

Wells, G. (1986). *The meaning makers.* Portsmouth, NH: Heinemann.

Wells, R. (1981). *Timothy goes to school.* New York: Puffin.

Wenner, M. (2009). The serious need for play. *Scientific American Mind*, 22–29.

Wertheimer, R. F., Moore, K. A., Hair, E. C., & Croan, T. (2003). *Attending kindergarten and already behind: A statistical portrait of vulnerable young children.* Washington, DC: Child Trends.

Whitehurst, G. J., & Lonigan, C. J. (2001). Emergent literacy: Development from prereaders to readers. In S. B. Neuman & D. K. Dickinson (Eds.), *Handbook of early literacy research* (pp. 11–29). New York: Guilford Press.

Whitehurst, G., & Lonigan, C. (2002). *Get Ready to Read! Screening Tool.* New York: National Center for Learning Disabilities.

Willems, M. (2004). *Knuffle Bunny: A cautionary tale.* New York: Hyperion.

Wood, A. (1999). *Silly Sally.* New York: Harcourt.

Wright, T., & Neuman, S. (2009). Purposeful, playful pre-K: Building on children's natural proclivity to learn through language, literacy, mathematics, and science. *American Educator*, 33–39.

Wu, L. (2009). Children's graphical representations and emergent writing: Evidence form children's drawings. *Early Child Development and Care, 179*(1), 69–79.

Yaden, D., Smolkin, L., & Conlon, A. (1989). Preschoolers' questions about pictures, print convention, and story text during reading aloud at home. *Reading Research Quarterly, 24*, 188–214.

Yolen, J. (1987). *Owl moon.* New York: Putnam.

Ziolkowski, R., & Goldstein, H. (2008). Effects of an embedded phonological awareness intervention during repeated book reading on preschool children with language delays. *Journal of Early Intervention, 31*(1), 67–90.

Zucker, T., Justice, L., Piasta, S., & Kaderavek, J. (2010). Preschool teachers' literal and inferential questions and children's responses during whole-class shared reading. *Early Childhood Research Quarterly, 25*, 65–83.

Zucker, T., Ward, A., & Justice, L. (2009). Print referencing during read-alouds: A technique for increasing emergent readers' print knowledge. *The Reading Teacher, 63*(1), 62–72.

Index